A HISTORY OF SPAIN

Published

Iberia in Prehistory*
María Cruz Fernández Castro

The Romans in Spain[†]
John S. Richardson

Visigothic Spain 409–711
Roger Collins

The Arab Conquest of Spain, 710–797
Roger Collins

The Contest of Christian and Muslim Spain, 1031–1157[†]
Bernard F. Reilly

Spain's Centuries of Crisis: 1300–1474
Teofilo F. Ruiz

The Spain of the Catholic Monarchs 1474–1520
John Edwards

Spain 1516–1598: From Nation State to World Empire*
John Lynch

The Hispanic World in Crisis and Change, 1598–1700*
John Lynch

Bourbon Spain, 1700–1808*
John Lynch

Spain in the Liberal Age: From Constitution to Civil War, 1808–1939
Charles J. Esdaile

Spain: From Dictatorship to Democracy, 1939 to the Present
Javier Tusell

Forthcoming

Caliphs and Kings 798–1033
Roger Collins

Spain 1157–1300: A Partible Inheritance
Peter Linehan

* Out of print
[†] Print on demand

Spain's Centuries of Crisis
1300–1474

Teofilo F. Ruiz

A John Wiley & Sons, Ltd., Publication

This paperback edition first published 2011
© 2011 Teofilo F. Ruiz

Edition history: Blackwell Publishing Ltd (hardback, 2007)

Blackwell Publishing was acquired by John Wiley & Sons in February 2007.
Blackwell's publishing program has been merged with Wiley's global Scientific,
Technical, and Medical business to form Wiley-Blackwell.

Registered Office
John Wiley & Sons Ltd, The Atrium, Southern Gate, Chichester, West Sussex,
PO19 8SQ, United Kingdom

Editorial Offices
350 Main Street, Malden, MA 02148-5020, USA
9600 Garsington Road, Oxford, OX4 2DQ, UK
The Atrium, Southern Gate, Chichester, West Sussex, PO19 8SQ, UK

For details of our global editorial offices, for customer services, and for information
about how to apply for permission to reuse the copyright material in this book please
see our website at www.wiley.com/wiley-blackwell.

The right of Teofilo F. Ruiz to be identified as the author of this work has been
asserted in accordance with the UK Copyright, Designs and Patents Act 1988.

Library of Congress Cataloging-in-Publication Data
Ruiz, Teofilo F., 1943–
  Spain's centuries of crisis : 1300–1474 / Teofilo F. Ruiz.
    p. cm. – (History of Spain)
  Includes bibliographical references and index.
    ISBN-13: 978-1-4051-2789-9 (hardcover : alk. paper) ISBN: 978-1-4443-3973-4
(paperback : alk. paper)   1. Spain–History–711-1516.   I. Title.
  DP99.R85 2007
  9462.02–dc22

                                                                    2007003775

A catalogue record for this book is available from the British Library.

This book is published in the following electronic formats:
Wiley Online Library [ISBN 9780470690956]

Set in 10.5/12.5pt Minion by Graphicraft Limited, Hong Kong
Printed in Malaysia by Ho Printing (M) Sdn Bhd

1   2011

To Sofía Rose

Contents

Preface and Acknowledgments   viii
Map 1: Spain in the Late Fifteenth Century   xi
Map 2: The Crown of Aragon and the Western Mediterranean
    in the Late Middle Ages   xii

1 At the Dawn of a New Century: The Spains around 1300   1

2 Medieval Spain in the Late Middle Ages: Society and
   Economy   28

3 The Answers of Politics: Spain, 1300–1350   51

4 Toward Trastámara Spain, 1350–1412   72

5 Spain in the Fifteenth Century: Toward the Rule of
   the Catholic Monarchs, 1412–1469   86

6 The Sinews of Power: Administration, Politics, and Display   110

7 Muslims, Jews, and Christians in a Century of Crisis   139

8 Culture and Society in an Age of Crisis   164

9 Epilogue   196

Notes   202
Bibliographical Essay   217
Index   228

Preface and Acknowledgments

Writing the history of Spain in the late Middle Ages, as I will reiterate in the first chapter, is not an easy task. The diversity of political players and entities, the endless conflicts between noble factions, urban oligarchies, and the Crown, the numerous and violent challenges to royal authority, and severe social and economic crises stood in sharp contrast to vigorous and innovative cultural transformations, linguistic changes, and signal administrative reforms. All of these components paved the way for Spain's later primacy of place among western European powers in the early modern period.

In attempting to reconstruct the history of the two most important realms in the peninsula – the kingdom of Castile (Castile-León) and the Crown of Aragon – from around 1300 to the marriage of Ferdinand and Isabella in 1469 and Isabella's ascent to the throne in 1474, I have placed that troubled history and the general evolution of political, administrative, and cultural life within the context of the long-term crises that plagued most of the West from the late thirteenth century to the end of the Middle Ages. By emphasizing crises and the demands they placed on Spanish women and men, I have also sought to see administrative, political, religious, and cultural innovations as responses to, as well as shaped by, the general late medieval crises. These developments had also their counterparts in growing antagonism against religious minorities and the end of religious pluralism in the peninsula. They were also paralleled and influenced by vigorous and novel cultural production.

Chapter 1 provides a general view of the Spanish realms in 1300 and seeks to place the events of that year and the next century and a half within the long sweep of Spanish medieval history. A brief foray into the geographical features of the peninsula and the links between topography and political life leads us to chapter 2. In that chapter I describe the different aspects of Spain's social, economic, political, and structural crises from the late thirteenth century into the late fifteenth, with emphasis on the impact of the crises on political institutions and practice.

Chapters 3 to 5 offer a chronological narrative of Spanish political life, highlighting the ebb and flow of peninsular conflicts and territorial expansion and contrasting the different paths followed by Castile and Aragon. In chapter 6 I turn to those administrative, fiscal, and institutional changes that, while the crises raged, set the foundations for either stronger royal authority in Castile or formal "constitutional" arrangements in the Crown of Aragon. True "sinews" of power, these institutional innovations provided the framework for new ways of articulating power. Chapter 7 focuses on the intertwined histories of Muslims, Jews, and Christians. I would argue that the clear deterioration of these relations in the period after 1300 reflected, to a large extent, the shifting context in which different religious groups interacted. The crises of late medieval society had, on the whole, nefarious consequences for Jews and Muslims, and the Christians' (or at least some Christians) growing hostility towards them was also a complex and perverse response to the general crises affecting the peninsular realms. Finally, the last chapter examines cultural production – mostly literary culture, festivals, and other cultural artifacts – as paralleling and emerging from the troubled climate of the age.

***

Were I to list all those to whom I owe a debt of gratitude, the list would be so extensive as to duplicate the length of this book. The sparse notes and the more extensive bibliographical essay do not begin to reflect the large number of scholars and students whose works and comments have informed these pages. Angus Mackay, a historian of rare understanding and insightfulness, and a generous friend, was to have written this volume originally. The reader, I fear, will be short-changed. No matter how very hard I have tried, this book would never match that which Angus Mackay would have written. That this particular volume is preceded by Peter Linehan's book, *Spain, 1157–1312*, in Blackwell's History of Spain series and is followed by John Edwards' *The Spain of the Catholic Monarchs* honors me greatly. I could not think of more distinguished company, and their contributions to Blackwell's History of Spain have been a very strong incentive to attempt to make a contribution worthy of their distinction as scholars. I have known Peter Linehan for many years and have greatly benefited from his insightful comments and exceedingly generous friendship. John Edwards' work has also been an enduring source of inspiration and a model for my own.

At UCLA, Lynn Hunt, Margaret Jacob, Ron Mellor, David Myers, David Sabean, Arch Getty, Patrick Geary, Muriel McClendon, Steve Aron, Kevin Terraciano, and Geoffrey Symcox have provided the scholarly community in which it has always been a pleasure to do research and writing. Graduate and undergraduate students have provided me with vigorous critiques and helpful comments. I have learned much from the work of Gregory Milton, Claudia Mineo, Jenny Jordan, and Bryan Givens. In the United States Paul Freedman, David Nirenberg, William C. Jordan, Olivia R. Constable, and Daniel Smail have always given their unreserved support.

Abroad, as always, Jacques Le Goff, John H. Elliott, Jacques Revel, Adeline Rucquoi, Manuel González Jiménez, Hilario Casado, Judith Herrin, Denis Menjot, and others have encouraged my work and taught me by example. At Blackwell, Tessa Harvey, Gillian Kane, Angela Cohen, Rebecca du Plessis, and Janet Moth have been extremely generous with their help and understanding. John Lynch, the general editor of the series, has been equally supportive and encouraging. To them I owe a great debt of gratitude. Scarlett Freund, my friend and wife, is, as I have written many times before, the enduring reason for which I live and write. But this book is dedicated to my granddaughter Sofía Rose Ruiz. Born on December 11, 2005, she, my first grandchild, has brought me joys and feelings I did not know existed. And this book is dedicated to her in the hope that – not unlike those fifteenth-century Castilian poets who wrote in search of remembrance – many years from now, when she reads this, she knows that I was lovingly thinking of her.

Map 1 Spain in the late Fifteenth Century
Source: based on Edwards, J. *The Monarchies of Ferdinand and Isabella* (Historical Association pamphlet), p. 4

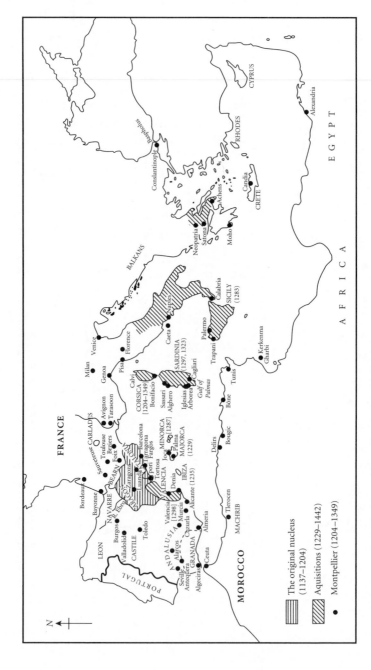

Map 2 The Crown of Aragon and the Western Mediterranean in the late Middle Ages
Source: Bisson, T. *The Medieval Crown of Aragon: A Short History* (Oxford, 1986), p. 91

Chapter 1

At the Dawn of a New Century
The Spains around 1300

The dawn of a new century in 1300 was marked in Rome, and elsewhere throughout the medieval West, with lavish celebrations. The Great Jubilee drew thousands of pilgrims to the capital of Western Christianity, and Dante, writing the first lines of his *Divine Comedy* two years later, chose Good Friday 1300 as the date for his fictional encounter with Virgil and the date for the wrenching journey through Hell, Purgatory, and Paradise, and to his final vision of the Godhead. On November 15, 1300, Ferdinand (Fernando) IV, king of Castile, León, Asturias, Galicia, Toledo, and of the wide collection of other kingdoms and territories that constituted the realm of Castile in the Middle Ages, exempted Don Esteban and his wife, Doña Inés, both citizens of Burgos, from all taxes, except for *moneda forera* (a tax paid to the Crown for maintaining the stability of the coinage), as a reward for Esteban's efforts as a surgeon.[1] That same year, under the authority of the regents, Ferdinand's mother, María de Molina, and his uncle, the Infante Don Henry (Enrique) – for the king was still a minor – the young king granted similar privileges and exemptions to men and women throughout the realm, issued charters to municipalities, made donations to monasteries, and other such examples of royal largesse and power.

In 1300 other extant documents in Castile, the Crown of Aragon, Navarre, and even the Muslim kingdom of Granada reveal mostly the normal and mundane affairs of everyday life. Property transactions, donations, wills, monastic protests against noble encroachment and abuses, and royal attempts – more often than not failed attempts or ignored by a restless nobility – to restore order are similar in many respects to those of preceding and succeeding decades. In the Iberian peninsula, 1300 was not the dramatic watershed that the arrival of the new century marked for other parts of Europe. Yet, though not charged with the symbolic weight that it had in other realms throughout the medieval West, many Castilians, Aragonese,

Catalans, and other people living in Spain had a keen awareness of events transpiring elsewhere. Spaniards, as did many other western Europeans, flocked to Rome in search of indulgences or of the many pleasures (and pains) of medieval tourism in 1300.

For those living in what we know today as Spain, the excitement about the new century must have been a bit disconcerting and a further reminder, despite the great strides made to integrate the peninsula into European affairs from the late eleventh century onwards, of a disconnect with the rest of the medieval West. Throughout medieval Spain the year was identified in the documentation as *era de* (the era of) 1338. The Spanish 1300 had, in fact, occurred in what, for most of the rest of Europe, was still 1262. The real 1300, if we can call calendrical conventions real, thus passed without too many momentous events or without many of those signal watersheds around which traditional historiography has been built. Nonetheless, dramatic transformations were already in the making, and the diverse Spanish realms faced harder and more troubling times in the decades ahead. For one, Castilians, Aragonese, Catalans, and Valencians, though still dating their documents by the old formula that placed the beginning of the Christian era 38 years before Jesus' birth, were increasingly aware of being chronologically out of step with the rest of Europe. Some documents after 1300 noted both the ancient traditional forms of dating and the dating norms in use in other European kingdoms. By the late fourteenth century, all the Spanish realms had abandoned the old style of dating and embraced the rest of Europe, choosing Christ's birth as the appropriate chronological marker.

Regardless of the confusing chronological situation and the absence of dramatic events to mark the year, the Spanish realms, as they faced the dawning of a new century in 1300, did so with the accumulated experiences, institutional developments, and social strife of centuries of political evolution. Before focusing on Spain's historical development in the late Middle Ages, it may be useful to probe the context in which the Spanish realms evolved in the fourteenth and early fifteenth centuries.

A Plurality of Spains

Defining what Spain was in the Middle Ages, beyond a geographical concept, is as difficult as it may be today in the age of autonomous regions and recent calls for regional secession or wider autonomy. In 1300 the Iberian peninsula was fragmented into a diversity of realms and political entities. They contrasted with each other in terms of political organization, language, social and economic structures, topography, and history. The peninsula's political fragmentation reflected the historical developments of an earlier period and the slow emergence of distinct kingdoms after the Muslim invasion. What, then, were the different political entities comprising medieval Spain in 1300?

Castile

The largest in terms of territory and population was the kingdom of Castile. It extended over most of the central and northwestern areas of the peninsula, with borders on the Bay of Biscay in the north, the Atlantic and the Mediterranean in its southern frontier, Portugal in the west, and Aragon, Navarre, and Granada in the east, north, and south respectively. The kingdom of Castile was itself a composite of numerous other kingdoms and territories added either by conquests or familial alliances over the course of the Reconquest, that is, over a period running effectively from the early tenth century to the fourteenth. Its rulers were never described simply as kings of Castile, but their long and often repeated titles articulated the sense of an amalgam of what had once been independent realms, now brought together under the power of one king (or queen). Asturias, León, Galicia, Castile, Toledo, Córdoba, Seville, Murcia, the lordship of Molina, and the Basque homeland were among some of the most important holdings constituting the late medieval kingdom of Castile-León. And the diversity of these realms was great indeed. From their geographical and climatic differences to their peculiar historical developments, patterns of cultivation and rural life, rights of the peasantry, and the role of regional nobilities in the running of the realm, the kingdoms and territories that formed Castile were, in many respects, as distinct from each other as Castile was from other Iberian realms. And matters could become even more complicated when we consider religious plurality and antagonisms that flourished in Castile, as they did elsewhere in the peninsula, during the late Middle Ages.

The Crown of Aragon

If Castile was a complicated polity, the Crown of Aragon was infinitely more so. At least most of the Castilian realm enjoyed some linguistic unity – with the exception of parts of the Basque country and Galicia, where significant parts of the population remained faithful to their original regional languages. The Crown of Aragon was also a collection of realms, but unlike its powerful Castilian neighbor, each of its main components or political units – the kingdom of Aragon, Catalonia (in its many different incarnations as the county of Barcelona or Principality, but never a kingdom), and the kingdom of Valencia (conquered by James [Jaume] I in 1238) – retained its political autonomy, representative assemblies, and distinct linguistic and cultural identity. The Crown of Aragon was, in fact, a federation of realms, and the unfortunate kings of these polities had to deal with each of them individually and, one should add, carefully. As will be seen in greater detail in later chapters, the social, economic, and political structures of Aragon, Catalonia, and Valencia were quite different from each other and, often, to the chagrin of their collective master, at odds with each other. In the best of circumstances, the Crown of Aragon foreshadowed the European Union. In the worst of circumstances, it was a contentious arrangement, with each of the units jealously defending its rights and privileges. Ruling the Crown of Aragon was an art, and a very difficult art at that.

An expansive realm in spite of its political fragmentation, in 1282 the king of the Crown of Aragon gained control of Sicily. In the early four-teenth century, a dependent kingdom, that of Majorca (with its capital in Perpignan in southern France and enjoying control of the Balearic Islands), came into being. Aragonese and Catalan outposts prospered in the former lands of the Byzantine empire in the east. Thus, throughout the period under study, a great deal of the political and commercial history of the Crown of Aragon was defined by the relation of its original and permanent core (Aragon, Catalonia, and Valencia) to its outlying regions and kingdoms – southern France, the Balearic Islands, Sardinia, Sicily, and Naples. And by the end of the fifteenth century, these long historical ties drew Spain inexorably into Italy.

Navarre

Perched on both sides of the Pyrenees, the ancient kingdom of Navarre had been the hegemonic political power in the peninsula in the late tenth and early eleventh centuries and the progenitor of a series of Iberian realms (Aragon, Castile). Culturally and linguistically diverse (because of the large Basque presence in some regions of Navarre), the kingdom wavered uncertainly between French and Iberian ruling houses, and its identity, as either French or Spanish, was not fully defined until the early sixteenth century. Ironically, if the kings of the Spains in the eleventh century were the children or descendants of Sancho the Great (1000–35) of Navarre, Juan Carlos, the present ruler of Spain, is the descendant of Henry of Navarre (Bourbon) who became king of France in 1589 and kept his claims to his ancestral lands alive in the face of the Spanish annexation of the kingdom in the early sixteenth century.

Granada

After the great Christian conquests of most of southern Spain in the early thirteenth century, the kingdom of Granada, one of the kingdoms of *taifas* that had emerged from the demise of the Cordoban Caliphate in the 1030s, became the last outpost of Islam in the peninsula. From 1300 until its final surrender in 1492, Granada remained the touchstone defining Castile's, and to a much lesser extent other Christian realms', political actions in the peninsula. Although a tributary kingdom, paying large sums to the kings of Castile throughout most of this period, Granada was a prosperous realm and an important center for learning and the arts in the fourteenth and fifteenth centuries. Through its great maritime outlet at Málaga (southwest of the city of Granada itself), Granada and its hinterland maintained important commercial and cultural links to North Africa and to the vast commercial networks of Dar-al-Islam (the lands of Islam). Blessed with a hard-working and thrifty population, Granada exported silk cloth and other luxury items. Islamic foreign travelers, such as Ibn Batutah and Abd al-Bäsit, commented on the economic and cultural vigor of the region in the fourteenth and fifteenth centuries. Granada's Nasrid rulers could engage in great architectural projects, such as the incomparable Alhambra, even while paying heavy tribute to the Castilian kings. When the end came in the late fifteenth century, Granada withstood the Christian onslaught for more than a decade before its surrender.

Portugal

Though not part of the story told in this book, Portugal was the other peninsular realm. Emerging as an independent kingdom only in the late eleventh and early twelfth century, the Portuguese chose very different paths from those followed by their Iberian neighbors. The Portuguese advance into Muslim territory in the peninsula came to a close in the mid-thirteenth century. By 1300, the Portuguese were already poised for their great and successful gambit in the Atlantic and southward along the coast of Africa, but though they looked outward for their expansion, Portugal's history remained inextricably bound up with that of other Iberian realms, above all, Castile.[2]

Geography, Climate, and Languages

Iberian political fragmentation mirrored its geographical, climatic, and linguistic diversity. Although geography does not entirely dictate historical developments, one cannot deny the enduring impact which the rough topography and climate (in specific parts of the peninsula) had in the making of Spain. Historians, John H. Elliott and Fernand Braudel most notable among them, have long emphasized the role which poor and thin soils, scant rain, high mountains, and meager rivers have had on the evolution of Spain as a political entity and on the transportation networks necessary for the economic well-being of the peninsula.[3] Large sections of Spain provided little return for the peasants' endless toil. The land yielded its fruits only by intense and exhausting work, and late winter storms, of which there were too many for comfort, could swiftly wipe out all the year's labor.

Politically, the Spains fractured along the spines of mountain ranges crisscrossing the peninsula. After all, there are few places, with perhaps the central Castilian plain (which itself rises to a very high altitude) as an exception, in which mountains do not loom on the horizon. If topography dictated the emergence of particular political entities, climate also shaped different types of agriculture and organization of the soil. The abundant rain falling on most of northern Spain led to specific types of agriculture, village organization, and relations between villagers and their royal, ecclesiastical, or secular lords. The plains of Old and New Castile – the dominant geographical feature of the peninsula – generated other patterns of organizing rural spaces and peculiar ties between town and countryside, between free peasants and their lords. Iberia's southern region, with its different ecology, irrigation patterns, and the influence of an ancient Islamic heritage and husbandry, yielded yet another type or types of social, economic, and political organization.

One must be cautious, however, about reducing Spain to a series of neatly stacked geographical areas. The reality and impact of Spanish geography and climate on political communities were far more complex than the heuristic categories deployed in travel guides or general books such as this. Regions overlapped. Small ecological niches – where social and economic structures and development over time did not follow well-laid-out patterns – can be found in abundance. Human agency, millennia old, was always at work, transforming the topographical and climatological realities of the peninsula.

The Diverse Geographies of Spain

Green Spain

In this rough and brief sketch of Spain's geography and climate, one could easily posit a series of distinct Spains, following not the artificial boundaries resulting from historical circumstances but the unalterable dictates of topography. First, in a broad band running throughout most of northern Spain – from the Atlantic coast in the west to the Mediterranean in the east – lies Green Spain, a region of abundant rain, moderate summers and winters (except in the eastern parts close to the Pyrenees), high mountains and small villages dotted across the countryside. The economy of the region emphasized fruit trees, dairy farming, livestock raising, fishing (on the Basque, Cantabrian, and Asturian coasts), and other agricultural and maritime activities associated with mountain regions and the sea. The Pyrenees and their offshoots constituted the dominant feature of the region. Rising majestically, from the Bay of Biscay in the west to the Costa Brava (the Mediterranean shore of Catalonia) in the east, the Pyrenees served as a natural border with France, though mountain passes all along the range provided easy access for pilgrims, merchants, and armies. Liminal regions – the val de Aran, Andorra, and Navarre itself – shifted political loyalties, depending on the course of events and the relative strength of realms on either side of the mountain range. The spurs of the Pyrenees (among them the impressive Picos de Europa range in Cantabria) dug deep into the northern areas of Aragon, Catalonia, the Basque country, Cantabria, and Asturias. Traveling from Andorra to La Seo d'Urgell (in northern Catalonia) and from La Seo toward the Mediterranean shore, one is struck by the ruggedness of the territory and the difficulties in negotiating even today, with modern roads and tunnels, an easy transit from one region to another.

Green Spain did not of course constitute a single geographical unit, nor did it develop into a single political entity. In the northwest, the mountains of Galicia, though they did not rise as high as mountains did east of Villafranca del Bierzo (the natural gateway into the region), marked a natural frontier with Asturias and León. By 1300, land tenancy in Galicia had been spectacularly fragmented. It was a region of predatory and unruly lordships, and peasant grievances against lordly abuses would explode in open rebellion in the late fifteenth century in the rebellion of the Hermandiños.[4] With temperate climate and abundant rain well suited to livestock and some forms of agriculture, Galicia, with an extensive shoreline on the Atlantic and magnificent and well-protected harbors (rías), also developed a strong maritime tradition – fishing, trading, and seafaring. From La Coruña and other estuary (ría) harbors, Galician merchants and seafarers maintained steady relations with English and Flemish ports. In the countryside, its ancestral language, Galician, remained alive, as did a poetical tradition which had flourished in the twelfth century, that of the cantigas, though this was beginning to wane under the impact of Castilian in the fourteenth century.

Further east, the regions of Asturias, Cantabria, and the Basque coast also enjoyed a temperate climate and high rainfall. Through the Asturian ports of Gijón and Llanes, the Cantabrian coastal towns of San Vicente de la Barquera, Santander, Castro Urdiales, and Laredo, and their Basque counterparts, Bermeo, Fuenterrabía, San Sebastián, and Bilbao, the region offered many entry points for a robust traffic with England, Flanders, and southern France from the mid-thirteenth century onwards. From there, goods were carried south to the great mercantile distribution center of Burgos on the northern Castilian plains, or to Victoria and Logroño, gateways to Navarre and further east to Aragon. Green and humid, the peasants of this sub-region of northern Spain held their lands on long-term or life-lease contracts or owned them outright. Villages in the region had long gained substantial concessions from their lords and the Crown.

Tetzel, a German traveling through the region in the sixteenth century, describes it pejoratively as a land where one finds "few hens, eggs, cheese, and milk (because there are no cows) . . . people ate little meat, feeding themselves only on fruits."[5] Tetzel's account, typical of foreign travelers in the late Middle Ages and the early modern period, echoes the negative assessments of the Basque and Cantabrian lands and of their people found in the famous twelfth-century pilgrimage guide to Compostela (the *Liber Sanct Jacobi*),[6] but it stands in sharp contrast to the praise of Spain and, in particular, to the idealization of the mountain region, just a few kilometers south of Cantabria and the Basque homeland, found in the *Primera crónica general* and the *Poema de Fernán González* (both dating to the mid-thirteenth century). The *Primera crónica general* engaged in a general praise of Spain (not just the mountains), drawn from the older panegyric of Spain found in St. Isidore's work. The anonymous *Poema de Fernán González* zeroed on a small region of northern Castile which ecologically and topographically resembled Green Spain far more than it did the meseta of northern Castile. In exalted tones, the mountains are seen as paradisiacal lands of abundant pasture and livestock, of mild winters and temperate summers.[7] The truth, as always, lies somewhere between Tetzel's indictment and Castilian medieval authors' effusive praise of the land. The land was rich only in some specific areas, surrounded often by waste lands (the *páramos*) and infertile ground. It was not rich enough to support a large population or to generate large surpluses.

Moving eastward, the Pyrenees mountains blocked the benign influence of the sea, rendering the contrasts in temperatures in northern Aragon and northwestern Catalonia far sharper than in Cantabria or the Basque country. The region is far more rugged, less easily open to the rest of the world. Even today, as pointed out earlier, the roads from France to Andorra (an area under the jurisdiction of the bishop of Urgell in the Middle Ages) and from La Seo d'Urgell, an ancient and important bishopric in northwestern Catalonia (Andorra is around 20 km from La Seo), to Figueras (close to the Mediterranean coast) are difficult and trying ones. Further, if the mountains toward the west were, as Fernand Braudel has argued not always correctly, places of freedom, that is, that peasants were fairly free from lordly abuse, northern Catalonia witnessed the harshest and most enduring form of serfdom in western Europe in the fourteenth and fifteenth centuries.[8] Westward from Catalonia into the large county of Ribagorza (in northern Aragon), the preconditions for predatory and violent lordship and for systemic civil war in the sixteenth century were already in place. Thus, although geography and climate were somewhat similar along the broad band of Green Spain, social structures, types of village organization, and relations between peasants and lords varied from west to east. Such diversity was even greater in the high plains that dominated the center of the peninsula.

The Spains of the high plains

The high plains that dominate most of the center of the peninsula constitute Spain's salient topographical feature. The origins of the expansionist kingdom of Castile lay there. It was the great reservoir of soldiers, and, after 1300, it dominated, politically and culturally, most of Spain's history. Cutting a great swath from the Portuguese border in the west – where the high plains began to slope to the ocean – to Catalonia in the east, and from Green Spain in the north to Andalusia in the south, the mesetas of Old and New Castile, as well as the arid plains around Zaragoza in the kingdom of Aragon, rose to impressive average altitudes. In Old Castile and León, the plain rose between 1,800 to 3,000 feet in 66.5 percent of the surface. 31.4 percent reached even higher average altitude, between 3,000 and 6,000 feet, while in the regions of Avila and León more than 50 percent of the territory was over 3,000 feet. Further east in the region of Soria, an area close to the Aragonese border, 70 percent of the land was over 3,000 feet in altitude. These impressive heights dictated the climate and agricultural destiny of the region.

Winters are long and harsh, summers hot and short. Rain and running water were always in short supply during the Middle Ages. The soil is often thin and poor, except for river banks and small ecological niches. In Castile and northern Aragon's stark and emotionally moving landscapes, villages rose next to small rivers, often at a great distance from each other. Foreign travelers or modern poets, Antonio Machado above all, have lyrically described a countryside often denuded of trees, of villages, and of human habitation. Its proud people – pride is a continual charge in the harsh descriptions of Spaniards in early modern travel literature – worked very hard with meager results. But these seemingly negative impressions need to be modified and corrected by the many exceptions and successes found in Castile and Aragon in spite of its geographical and economic disadvantages. Along the banks of the Ebro river on the outskirts of Zaragoza, thriving large village communities – inhabited often by Mudejars and then by Moriscos – tended the fertile floodplains. The prosperity of these villages, Gelsa, Codo, Pina, and others, stood in sharp contrast with the arid plains which one can still see from the road between Barcelona and Zaragoza, and from the rugged spurs of the Pyrenees, easily visible north of the road.

New Castile, the lower region of the high plains south of Madrid, was a land of transhumance and vineyards and different in every respect from the northern plain. The northern Rioja region, celebrated without dissent by foreign travelers, was a rich area, producing superior-quality wine and benefiting from fertile, cereal-growing lands. If the land did not always yield great profit, the transhumance did. It was mostly Old Castile taxes, paid by hard-working and suffering peasants and by the transhumance, that provided the resources for the great enterprises of Castile in the fifteenth century and the even more ambitious projects of the early modern Spanish monarchy. Complexity and diversity, and the distinct habitats found abundantly throughout the region, undermine any effort to present a monochrome picture of Spanish topography and resources.

Above all the topography and climate of the high plains of Castile and Aragon fostered the cultivation of cereals and the tending of transhumant livestock. Although in the fourteenth and fifteenth centuries villagers still sought to grow as wide a variety of crops as possible – thus we find cereal growing in Green Spain and viticulture everywhere – lack of rain and poor soil conditions determined a great deal of the predominant economic activities. What was grown and how it was grown helped shape social and political life, as it did patterns of population throughout the land. Far more significant, one must always remember that the sharp contrast between Green Spain and the central plains, a contrast that is vividly evident to anyone crossing the mountain passes between northern and central Spain or between central Spain and Andalusia today, placed significant stress on Spanish men and women. Everything changed as you moved from one region to another. How one would work the land, organize the village community, use agricultural tools, or plow the land changed as one crossed geographical boundaries. The types of crops were different. Different cultures and even languages stood as continual challenges to the peripatetic Castilians,

Aragonese, Catalans, and others in the peninsula. And these contrasts were even more pronounced as one crossed into southern Spain.

Southern Spain: the ancient lands of al-Andalus

Deeply imprinted by its Roman and Muslim past, southern Spain, running from the Algarve and the Atlantic coast in the west to the region of Valencia and the Mediterranean in the east, also included a diversity of habitats and a variety of ecological and climatic systems. Within southern Spain one must distinguish between mountains and flood plains, between coastal and interior regions. In western Andalusia, the Sierra Morena divides the sloping plains of New Castile and La Mancha from the fertile areas on the banks of the Guadalquivir and lower Guadiana rivers. Access to the fertile western Andalusian lands could be easily gained through the ancient Roman road, the Silver Road or *camino de la plata*, running from Salamanca through the Extremaduran towns of Cáceres, Badajoz, and finally Mérida, and then by other east–west roads that led from Mérida or Cáceres to Seville and/or Córdoba. This was the road followed by a large group of Navarrese merchants and their servants, traveling from Estella in Navarre to Seville in 1351. Their long and well-documented journey tells us a great deal about communications within the peninsula, about food and road conditions. Their experiences belie the often repeated assertion about the difficulties of traveling across Spain.[9]

Further east from the Silver Road, the mountain pass of Despeñaperros provided a well-traveled gateway from New Castile into the south. Important battles, Las Navas de Tolosa in 1212 and Bailén during the Napoleonic Wars in the early nineteenth century, were fought in the region. Control of the region was crucial because Despeñaperros and the road going to Jaén and, further southeast, to Granada were in many respects important geographic keys to Andalusia. South of the Sierra Morena in western Andalusia lay a land of irrigation. Its agricultural patterns were distinct from those of the north, with olive trees, vineyards, and produce balancing cereal production. Toward Extremadura and throughout western Andalusia abundant pasture lands became the final destination of ever larger flocks of sheep and other livestock engaged in the great transhumance or Mesta (the seasonal movement of livestock from summer to winter grazing lands) from the mid-thirteenth century onwards.

A land dominated by latifundia, western Andalusia was a region of landless peasants, large villages, and a growing exporter of its staples: wine to England and elsewhere in the peninsula and eventually to the New World, olive oil to the northern parts of the Spanish realms and to trans-Pyrenean markets, leather goods, fruit, and other regional commodities. Whitewashed villages, distinct patterns of agriculture, and the ever-increasing lure of the Atlantic defined, and still define, western Andalusia as distinct from the rest of the Spains. By the late fourteenth century and the first half of the fifteenth, Andalusian seafarers sailed into the Atlantic from the coastal towns of Puerto de Santa María, San Lucas de Barrameda, Palos de Moguer, and the great bay of Cádiz. These sites, long associated with the enterprise of the Indies, were already, more than a century before the encounter with the New World, the launching point for Castile's conquest and settlement of the Canary Islands and the establishment of a significant Spanish outpost on the Atlantic Ocean.

Moving eastward, Andalusia changes dramatically. As we approach the city of Granada or its great maritime outlet to the south, Málaga, the terrain grows more abrupt and hard to negotiate. Fabled Granada, Islam's last outpost in the peninsula, is girded by a circle of mountains, the Sierra Nevada, the Sierra Morena, and the Alpujarras mountain range. Colder at high altitudes than western Andalusia – snow can be seen from the Alhambra gardens into the spring – central Andalusia yielded, nonetheless, some of the same products: olive groves in the Jaén area and on the hills sloping to the Mediterranean, the ubiquitous vineyards, some cereal production, but also, in the valleys of the Alpujarras and elsewhere, mulberry trees and silkworms, feeding into a very profitable silk-weaving trade.

In the late fourteenth and early fifteenth centuries, Granada and Málaga were prosperous cities, benefiting immensely from their trade with North Africa and its Muslim Mediterranean connections, and as mediator between Christian consumers and the goods produced in Dar-al-Islam. Throughout Granada and its vast hinterland, Arabic was spoken. Granada's successes, in spite of its military inferiority and political dependence on Castile, compare quite positively with Christian Murcia, its neighbor to the east, where agriculture had collapsed after the Christian conquests of the mid-thirteenth century, and almost matched the prosperity of Valencia in the mid-fifteenth century. Both Murcia and Valencia, the first part of the Castilian realms and the second a separate kingdom within the federation of the Crown of Aragon, were fully Mediterranean lands, sharing with other regions in the Mediterranean basin topographical and climatic characteristics. With hot summers and temperate winters (though it can get really cold in winter months), these were also lands of irrigation (above all Valencia), though, as noted, the Christian occupation of Murcia had ruined the irrigation works there in the second half of the thirteenth century. Valencia enjoyed vast areas of fertile soils which made it one of the most productive agricultural regions in the peninsula. Worked mostly by Arabic-speaking Mudejars

(Muslims living under Christian rule), people who had a long history of careful and enlightened husbandry, the *huerta* (garden) of Valencia served as the engine for the growing prosperity of the city and served as the foundation for Valencia's successful rivalry with Barcelona for a share of the western Mediterranean trade.[10]

Geographical, Topographical, Climatic, and Linguistic Diversity Revisited

This rough and impressionistic sketch of Spain's geographical and cultural pluralism glosses only superficially over transitional areas. Although political borders, when borders began to emerge slowly in the late Middle Ages, more or less followed the contours of mountains and rivers, throughout Spain small regions straddled different realms. Small ecological variants make any attempt at imposing a unified vision of Spain's geography and climate a misguided enterprise. The Rioja, as pointed out earlier, was such a region. It stood in the liminal space between Castile and Navarre. Its trade moved as much northward to the Basque ports as it did westward to the great commercial distribution centers on the plain, Burgos above all, along the always busy Road to Compostela, or eastward to Estella and Pamplona, the quintessential Navarrese cities.

Spain has an abundance of such regions. Extremadura, lying between Portugal and western Andalusia; the Bierzo, serving as a gateway to Galicia; Ribagorza or Urgell in northern Aragon and Catalonia respectively, both of them very different in many respects from Mediterranean Catalonia. If I emphasize this, it is to highlight the perils of easy generalizations. Plurality, diversity, and exceptionalism are the abiding terms when dealing with Spanish history, and they applied equally to religious filiation, political organization, or linguistic communities.

Toward 1300

The history of Spain does not begin *in medias res*, in 1300, as Dante's personal journey did. As we have seen above, 1300 did not signal a sea-change in either the social, economic, political, or cultural structures of the Spanish realms. No "great event," no *grande journée* in the style of traditional French historiography is identifiable. For Spaniards, as we have seen, it was not even 1300 but 1338. The story that is to be told in the following chapters, that is, that of Spain from 1300 to the marriage of Isabella and Ferdinand in 1469 and the consolidation of their rule in 1474, was shaped by a series of events taking place in the preceding centuries. Clearly, it is not my purpose here to summarize the entire history of Spain from Roman times to 1300 as a prelude to this volume. Earlier books in this series already do so superbly. Nonetheless, it may prove useful to lay out some of the most salient patterns of development without which the fourteenth and fifteenth centuries and their legacy of enduring crises would be incomprehensible.

It is a traditional paradigm in Spanish medieval history that the interplay and overlapping of three distinct themes – reconquest (crusade), pilgrimage, and repopulation – lie at the heart of medieval Spanish history. It may be useful to spell out what each of these three developments meant for contemporaries and what they mean for historians today.

Reconquest

Broadly defined, the Reconquest was both the physical act of conquering lands held by the Muslims and its ideological concomitant: the argument by clerics and other learned supporters of conquest that there was a historic link between Visigothic Spain and the Christian kingdoms of the late Middle Ages. One can think of three crucial stages in this process: (a) from the Arab conquest in 711 to the demise of the Caliphate in the 1030s; (b) from the emergence of the fragmented Muslim kingdoms of *taifas* (the different small kingdoms emerging from the wreckage of the Caliphate in the 1030s) to the battle of Las Navas de Tolosa in 1212 and the crushing defeat inflicted on the Almohads by an international Christian coalition; (c) from 1212 to the fall of Granada in 1492.

During the first stage, it is hardly possible to speak of a Reconquest ideology. Although there were serious attempts to link the Asturian–Leonese monarchy with the Visigothic heritage – the so-called Visigothic or neo-Gothic revival under Alfonso III and his descendants – the small Christian kingdoms were too weak or divided to mount any serious military challenge to Córdoba's power. As late as the end of the tenth century, Muslim armies could strike deep into Christian territory – as al Mansur did in 999 when he raided Compostela – with total impunity. Christians allied with Muslims against other Christians. Christian kings came to Córdoba to pay obeisance to their Muslim masters, to be granted the boon of marrying some lesser member of the Caliph's court, or to receive the benefits of the Muslims' superior medical knowledge. There was a slow reoccupation of the soil, that is, the settlement of Christians in empty or semi-empty areas in the north (see below) but no fully formulated ideology of Reconquest, even though there was a growing sense among the clerical elite and royal courts of the antagonism and differences between Christians and Muslims.[11]

After the demise of the Caliphate, Christian and Muslims entered an uneasy period in which signal Christian victories such as Alfonso VI's conquest of Toledo in 1085 or Ruy Díaz de Vivar's (the Cid) short-lived conquest of Valencia in 1094 were met by Muslim counter-offensives that either checked or reversed Christian advances. Pressed hard by the Christians in the north, Muslim Spain remained free from Christian conquest because waves of invaders from North Africa – first the Almoravids in the eleventh century and then the Almohads in the mid-twelfth century – effectively checked Christian advances. They brought with them, besides their military prowess, a more strict observance of Islam and a more aggressive attitude toward Christians and Christianity. These shifts to a harsher attitude had their counterpart and precedent in Christian society. From the early eleventh century onwards and originating north of the Pyrenees, a religious reform movement swept western Christendom. By the last decades of the century, Cluniac houses had risen throughout Spain, and Cluniac monks became important advisers to Spanish kings or began to monopolize some of the most important ecclesiastical offices in the land. Bernard, a Cluniac monk, became the first archbishop of reconquered Toledo and adviser to King Alfonso VI (1065–1109). The Roman ritual was imposed on the Castilian Church, replacing – not without some stiff opposition – the ancient Mozarabic rite in 1080. In Aragon, the kings became papal vassals and accepted their crowns from the Pope. With Cluny and French clergymen also came the idea of the crusade (even though crusading ideals were also in the making in Iberia before the First Crusade) and the conflation of territorial struggles with sectarian warfare. The Reconquest had now completed its development as a form of religious ideology.[12]

After the crushing Christian victory at Las Navas de Tolosa in 1212, the Christians gained the upper hand once and for all. In a series of swift campaigns between the 1230s and 1260s, the realms of Castile and the Crown of Aragon conquered most of southern Spain (Córdoba 1236, Valencia 1238, Seville 1248). Granada alone remained unconquered and the last Muslim outpost in the peninsula. Why did it take almost 300 more years, between 1212 and 1492, to reap fully the gains of Las Navas de Tolosa? The answer is found in the years following the Christian victory of 1212, above all, in the critical span of the fourteenth and early fifteenth centuries. A period of intense crises, these upheavals partially forced the Christian realms to turn their attention inward and to face other critical and far more pressing issues festering in their midst. The nature of these crises and the manner in which the different realms coped with them is the actual topic of this book and will be described in greater detail in later chapters.

Pilgrimage

One of the crucial components in the making of Spain (above all Castile) was the popularity of the pilgrimage to Compostela and its social, cultural, and economic impact on Spanish society. Beginning in the early tenth century and reaching its highest point in the twelfth, pilgrims poured, though a series of well-defined routes, across the Pyrenees to the tomb of St. James at Compostela. With the pilgrims came Cluniac monks and new monasteries – we have just seen what a significant role they played in fostering crusading ideals and grafting them on to the secular struggles against Islam. With pilgrims also came settlers, new towns, commercial links to northern Europe, the development of the bourgeoisie in the towns along the pilgrimage route, and the insertion of the peninsula into wider European mercantile and cultural networks. These, the rise of the bourgeoisie and of a monetary economy, are complex processes to be explored in greater detail below, but they transformed Spanish medieval society, propelling significant changes in mentality.

Repopulation

If the pilgrimage to Compostela transformed large regions of Spain (parts of northern Aragon, northern Castile, León, and Galicia) and had enduring consequences for the religious and cultural life of Christian Iberia, the royal, lordly, and ecclesiastical efforts to populate newly conquered lands with Christians led to a dramatic shift in population from north to south, with concomitant social and economic consequences. Attracted by liberal new *fueros* (charters) and by the distribution of newly conquered territories, Christian settlers poured into the south, sometimes altering, as the case of Murcia shows, ancient patterns of cultivation, or driving the Muslims into exile, as was the case in western Andalusia in the 1260s, or turning them into a semi-servile labor force, as happened in the region of Valencia in the late 1230s. Conquest and redistribution of population brought advantages and profits, but they also had an extremely negative impact on every aspect of Spanish society. In many ways, these overlapping themes, Reconquest, pilgrimage, and repopulation, came to dramatic resolutions in the first half of the thirteenth century, laying the groundwork – not always for the better – for later historical developments.

A Sense of the New Around 1200

In a recent book, *From Heaven to Earth: The Reordering of Castilian Society, 1150–1350,* I have glossed extensively Julio González' (a noted Spanish medievalist) formulation of the early thirteenth century as a period with a "taste for novelty." New young kings, Ferdinand III (1217–52) in Castile, James (Jaume) I (1213–76) in the Crown of Aragon, and Afonso II (1211–23) in Portugal, led their respective realms in bold new directions. More than that, they ushered into the peninsula the sea-change transformations sweeping Europe at the end of the twelfth century and the beginning of the thirteenth. In the first half of the thirteenth century, new forms of spirituality came into being in the wake of the broad reforms undertaken at the Fourth Lateran Council (1215). New liturgical forms and stricter enforcement of religious practices entered Spain shortly after 1215. With them also came restrictive measures against lepers, Jews, and Muslims and willful attempts to segregate them from Christian society. Deeper and more enduring changes, however, had been in the making throughout Spain since the last decades of the twelfth century.

Structural Changes

The period running roughly from the death of Alfonso VII, the last Castilian king to claim the title of emperor in 1156, to the starting point of our inquiry in 1300 witnessed dramatic transformations in the social, economic, cultural, and institutional structures of the Iberian realms. It is time now to spell out what these changes were, for they shaped Spanish history in the late Middle Ages. These transformations, most of them very visible to contemporaries and reflected poignantly in chronicles and literary works, led to the emergence of new values and new ways of thinking and dealing with the material world, the afterlife, and religious difference. By 1300 Spain had been transformed in ways which differed radically from the world of the mid-twelfth century. These changes took place within specific contexts, that is, social and economic developments underpinned the broad transformation of values and the dramatic increase in cultural production and education.

Trade, money, and urban life

These developments were not evenly distributed throughout the peninsula. Around 1200 Barcelona was already, and had been for a while, an important mercantile hub and urban center. As such, Barcelona presided over an extensive commercial network extending into the western Mediterranean and its productive hinterland. Seville, still under its Muslim king of *taifas*, had already gained the commercial importance that catapulted the city to prominence in the peninsula in later centuries. Drawing agricultural goods from its rich surrounding countryside, the Aljarafe, and keeping important trade connections with North Africa and eastern Mediterranean markets, Seville was a prosperous commercial entity, attracting northern Christian merchants into its wide commercial networks. Other parts of medieval Spain, however, were waking up to the complexities of mercantile affairs, to the lure of a true money economy and urban life.

In late twelfth-century Iberia, trade flowed mostly in two directions. One was the already mentioned flow of goods in and around Barcelona. It was trade with southern France and the western Mediterranean. The other pattern of trade was that linking the Christian north with the Muslim south. It was a trade dominated by Muslim luxury goods, spices, silk, iron works, leather, and other products, and resulting from Muslim mastery of some of these trades. The Christian north, the kingdoms of Castile and León, sent agricultural goods, livestock, and raw materials south, while it continued the long process of extracting surpluses from al Andalus through raids and tribute. By the late twelfth century, Castilian trade had begun its century long reorientation toward northern markets. Textiles (mostly from Flanders) and other finished goods began to flood the Castilian and Leonese markets. From the recently resettled or newly founded maritime towns on the Bay of Biscay, hides, tallow, and iron were exported to England, Flanders, and France. After 1300, large quantities of high-quality wool also began to make their way by sea to the great textile-manufacturing centers in the Low Countries. Trade with northern Europe served also as a conduit for new ideas and for the importation of northern European social structures and values.

Together with the new commercial patterns and material exchanges, the late twelfth and early thirteenth centuries witnessed the heyday of the pilgrimage route to Compostela. The throng of pilgrims making their way along the Milky Way, as the road was also called, was one of the most significant reasons for the development of urban centers in northern Castile. While Barcelona and Valencia (after 1238) had already developed an aggressive bourgeois society, in northern Castile, the period after 1150 witnessed the birth of mercantile elites and the flourishing of craft activities in many of the towns on the pilgrimage road. Some of these towns, as was the case with Burgos, became important distribution centers for foreign trade and presided over impressive mercantile networks, its merchants traveling to England and Flanders from the thirteenth century onwards. Thus, together with new patterns of trade in the peninsula, a monetary economy also developed as coins began to circulate in greater quantities throughout the Spanish realms. As a result a new bourgeois culture came into being in many parts of Spain with distinct new values.

Among some of these new values were, besides a different perception of property as spatial, new ways of thinking about salvation and the afterlife. Partly because of the spread among Christians in western Europe of the belief in Purgatory – which Jacques Le Goff, a noted French medieval historian, traces to the late twelfth century – or partly because of the new sensibilities of the rising mercantile groups and their fear that their activities may lead to eternal damnation, new ways of relating to the sacred came into being. What do I mean by that? In Christian society, the accumulation of wealth, the lending of money at interest, and other such activities that demanded a close involvement with the material world had always raised deep suspicion and fear of eternal damnation. The injunction of the Gospels rang with alarming clarity: A camel will go through the eye of a needle before a rich man enters the Kingdom of Heaven. By the late twelfth century, such ideals came into direct conflict with the growing accumulation of capital and with a society – in Spain and elsewhere – where mercantile and artisanal groups were mostly concerned with making money. Christianity offered two options: a life of goodness and the selfless renunciation of one's wealth will be rewarded in heaven; a life of wickedness and greed will be punished eternally in hell. By the twelfth century, this harsh choice was no longer tenable, and the Church bent to the new spiritual needs of the bourgeoisie. Purgatory came into being (as a spatial place in the same sense in which property was also now thought of as spatial) as an alternative. It allowed those with wealth and dubious occupations to enter into a bargain for salvation. Through their wills and through donations, merchants and other members of the urban elites entered into frantic business transactions to secure their salvation.

By purchasing masses and candles, building chapels, and other pious activities, those who lived outside the feudal structures sought to reduce their time in Purgatory and to gain eternal salvation. These new attitudes toward the sacred allowed merchants to deploy their wealth in the pursuit of grace. They allowed them to effectively put their material gains to the service of a program of salvation. This was most obvious in their acts of charity, which now became highly ritualized and symbolic and which came to fulfill a dual purpose. On the one hand, charity to a specific few, a hand-picked and symbolic number of the poor, was one of the deeds aimed at reducing time in Purgatory; on the other hand, charity to the poor served to reiterate the social standing of the donor and served as a constant reminder of the distance between those who had and those who did not within Spanish urban society. This included such highly symbolic acts as having bread given to 12 or 24 poor men and women over one's grave on the day of burial, or handpicking the poor from those in one's neighborhood, dressing them in burlap or sackcloth, and requiring them to march behind the body of the donor in the funeral procession.

At the same time, measures against the poor in the form of legislation restricting their mobility, or pejorative literary representations of them, began to circulate throughout Spain. The poor were thrown out of Barcelona in the late thirteenth century. Beggars were forced to require royal licenses to beg in early fourteenth-century Castile. The *Siete partidas*, the great law code composed in the 1250s and 1260s, created categories of the poor, indicating who should be helped (the very old, children, women, and the infirm) and who should be forced to work (the able-bodied, young men, those capable of work) and denied charity. What all these measures pointed to was the rapid rise in the number of poor people. New towns were centers for mercantile exchanges and new values; they were also breeding grounds for a new type of poverty in the Spanish realms and elsewhere in western medieval Europe.

Money and Land

Other changes began in the late twelfth century but their impact was cumulative over the centuries that followed. The rise of urban elites throughout the peninsula and their newly found economic power found an outlet in investment in the land market. Merchants and well-to-do artisans began, from the 1200s onwards, to purchase lands in villages around the city. These were the territories which lay under the jurisdiction of the city (lands and small villages which belonged to the territory of the city, *alfoz* in Castilian). Some of these urban hinterlands were expansive indeed, challenging the jurisdiction and authority of lords and monasteries. By the thirteenth century, urban dwellers had obtained a firm grip on the countryside surrounding Spain's urban centers. Merchants, craftsmen, and other members of the urban elites bought land from peasants. In turn, some of these peasants became journeymen, that is, they remained on the land as daily workers, landless peasants. Outside buyers and some well-to-do peasants were at the vanguard of the movement to consolidate property in the village, and this also signaled a very early erosion of the commons. What I mean by this is that, as peasants sold their property and a few men began to monopolize or control entire villages, they also gained control of the common lands – pasture lands and other property held in common by all the citizens of the village. By the late thirteenth and early fourteenth centuries, property transactions show the buying and selling of rights to the commons.[13]

In parts of Old Catalonia, the region north and west of Barcelona, lords were successful in imposing harsher conditions on their servile peasants. This is a development which, as noted earlier, has been carefully studied by Paul Freedman in his book, *The Origins of Peasant Servitude in Medieval Catalonia*. It is a remarkable story indeed. As serfdom began to wane throughout most of the medieval West, lords in some areas of northeastern Spain were able to reimpose restrictive controls over their peasants. The story of the *remenças* (the peasants who had to pay a fee to purchase their freedom) is a remarkable one and will be told in some detail in a later chapter. For more than a century and a half, they struggled to gain their freedom and finally achieved it in 1486, the only successful peasant uprising in the medieval West.

Language

Another development during this period before 1300 was the extraordinary growth of the vernacular. This phenomenon occurred in two distinct ways. In Castile, the vernacular (the Castilian language) began to make serious inroads into the local documentation by the late twelfth and early thirteenth centuries. This coincided with the birth of new vernacular literature, most notably the *Poem of the Cid* (ca. 1206), and the poetry of Gonzalo de Berceo around the middle of the thirteenth century. From the preferred language of material transactions at the turn of the century, Castilian became the official language of royal business by the late 1240s and 1250s. This shift from Latin to the vernacular took place in under 50 years and preceded such linguistic shifts throughout western Europe by more than two centuries. It was clear that by the late twelfth century, Latin documents already included vernacular words or syntax closer to the vernacular than to formal Latin. By the 1220s many areas of Old Castile (northern Castile) had already shifted completely to the vernacular, and by the 1240s and 1250s royal scribes were changing from Latin to Castilian within the same year and, in some cases, within the same day.

This spectacular transformation had a great impact on Castilian life and values. It meant that all the business of government was to be transacted in Castilian. The ordinances of the Cortes or representative parliaments, the legal system, royal charters, and correspondence were all written in the vernacular. At one level, this meant the partial removal of ecclesiastics, who had long enjoyed a monopoly of Latin, from royal government and bureaucracy. At another level, wills and donations composed until them in a formulaic Latin came to be under the direct control of lay donors and testators. It is not surprising that, after the 1220s, coinciding with the slow acceptance of the idea of Purgatory, most pious donations in wills consisted of assignments of rents but not of the actual property. From thenceforth, property was to be kept within the family and whatever was given to the Church was to be carefully monitored by the will's lay executors. This meant the slow economic collapse of the Castilian Church and the growing laicization (secularization) of the royal and municipal bureaucracies and of everyday practices. Far more significant, chronicles and histories, written in Latin by ecclesiastics until the beginning of the thirteenth century, were, by the 1250s, composed exclusively in Castilian. The royal chronicles, written in the vernacular by laymen under the king's patronage, began to advance the interest of the monarchy and served as a form of ideological propaganda tool for the new and growing sense of a Castilian identity distinct from that of other Iberian realms or from that of religious minorities in their midst.

The reasons for this linguistic change were complex indeed, but one obvious reason was that, in contrast to the Crown of Aragon, there was no full formal notarial culture in Castile. Notaries, who had gained a monopoly of a formulaic Latin for material transactions, wills, and other such legal instruments in Mediterranean medieval Europe, did not make inroads into Castile's daily life, with some exceptions such as Seville, until much later. By then, the vernacular had already triumphed and there was no moving back to the old linguistic patterns. What is most peculiar is that while Castile was undergoing such extensive changes, the Crown of Aragon, in spite of a vigorous vernacular literature, retained Latin, at least partially, as the language of royal affairs until much later.[14]

This swift linguistic shift was an exclusive Castilian phenomenon. In the Crown of Aragon, above all in Catalonia, while there was, as noted above, a significant literary movement in the vernacular, there was no official change of language. The northern regions of the Crown of Aragon, above all Old Catalonia, were part of an older civilization, that of Occitania. From the late eleventh century, troubadour poetry, romances, and historiography had been produced in Provençal, the language of southern France. The cultural ties binding Catalonia with the area around Toulouse, Perpignan, Carcassonne, and other southern urban centers made for a very dynamic and original cultural production. Catalan was the language of the people, of chronicles and histories, such as those written by Muntaner, and for pious works and romances, such as those written by Ramón Llull, so that in many respects the Catalan language was far more widespread as a language of culture than Castilian was in the early thirteenth century. Yet, for material transactions and the affairs of everyday life, the power of notaries and their formulaic Latin was still too great to be overthrown.

The Conquest of the South and Structural Transformations: Castile and the Crown of Aragon

During the first half of the thirteenth century, Castile, Portugal, the kingdom of Asturias–León, and the Crown of Aragon (Aragon and Catalonia) made impressive gains in al-Andalus. Ferdinand III's conquest of Córdoba in 1236 and of Seville in 1248 transformed the structure of Castilian society. With the settlement of Christians in the region of the Guadalquivir, there were no immediate technological gains in the exploitation of the land, nor was there an increase in the production of food. On the contrary, the conquest and the rebellion of the Mudejars in the early 1260s, and their subsequent expulsion from the land, disrupted the normal pattern of irrigation, cultivation, and harvest. Galloping inflation and unsuccessful efforts by Alfonso X in 1252, 1258, and 1268 to deal with inflation through price controls and sumptuary laws were clear signs of the deteriorating Castilian economy. In addition, petitions for remission of taxes by impoverished municipalities, demographic dislocations, the rise of anti-Semitic legislation (most of it economic in nature), localized famines, lawlessness in the countryside, civil war, and debasement of the coinage were clear manifestations or examples of some of the evils plaguing Castilian society after the mid-thirteenth century. In fact, Castile knew little stability in the 200 years that followed what seemed to contemporaries the greatest victories and territorial gains in the realm's history.

Inflation, resulting from the sudden availability of new wealth from the conquest, and food scarcity, due to the collapse of agriculture in north and south, were major problems until the mid-fourteenth century and the onslaught of the Black Death. Although other parts of western Europe suffered only a mild inflationary rise until the late thirteenth century, in Castile prices began to rise rapidly as early as the 1250s. The fourteenth century did not bring any improvements.

Economic underdevelopment

As early as the twelfth century the kingdoms of Castile and León exported raw materials and imported finished goods, and this helped shape Spain's economic structure in the following centuries. Fine cloth from Flanders accounted for a staggering cash outflow, and imports were not limited to luxury items but included a whole range of basic manufactured goods. Castile's main exports were iron, wool, hides, and livestock (especially horses, when not banned by royal decree), grain, cordovan, wine, cumin, and almonds. These changes in trade patterns should be placed within the peculiar demographic and territorial transformations of the mid-thirteenth century. By 1250, Castile had almost doubled its territory as a result of the conquest of Seville without any significant increase in its population, above all after the expulsion of the Muslims (or Mudejars) from the land after 1264. What took place was a redistribution of the population of Castile. Attracted by the new lands and by the houses, lands, and servants that Ferdinand III and Alfonso X distributed to the conquering armies, a considerable number of people migrated from the northern plains to Andalusia.

Although the migration included people from all levels of society, after a failed royal attempt to replicate the social and economic patterns of northern Castile by settling small and independent farmers on the land, the magnates, the military orders, and the Church received the lion's share of the land and income of the newly gained territories. With these great lords came many field hands attracted by the higher wages, the climate, and the expansion of the system of transhumance to the grazing lands of the south. The cereal-producing areas of the north were affected by out-ward migration, and production decreased, causing food shortages and even local famines. The south was not oriented toward cereal production, but toward a wine, olive, and livestock economy. Together with the worsening climatic conditions of the early fourteenth century and the growth of wool exports and the Mesta (the guild of sheep herders granted royal protection in 1276), the decline of northern agriculture dealt a severe blow to the traditional economy of Castile.

An additional problem was changes in land tenure. Although large estates had been formed in northern Castile long before 1248, a good number of free peasants with smallholdings retained ownership of their lands. The conquest of Seville marked the end of this way of life for many of them. After the late 1250s, land in Andalusia was concentrated in the hands of a few *ricos hombres* (rich men or magnates), the military orders, and religious corporations. As a result of the acquisition of these rich new lands, there was a dramatic increase in the wealth of these sectors of society without a parallel increase in the Crown's income. This brought about a political and economic shift in the relationship between king and nobility.

Moreover, as a result of the conquests of Córdoba and Seville, the tribute money paid to Castile by the kings of Andalusia (the *parias*) was drastically reduced. Alfonso X's income from the tribute decreased by around 58 percent from that of his father, Ferdinand III, with most of the lost income finding its way to the coffers of the *ricos hombres*. The magnates' new wealth was not used solely to the detriment of the Crown, but increased wealth augmented their political power. The history of the century after the conquest of Seville turns, therefore, around this conflict between the Crown and the high nobility, with the non-noble urban knights (*caballeros villanos*) as the third side of the political triangle. Pressed by the magnates' new political influence, Alfonso took two key actions: sumptuary laws against the high nobility's unrestricted displays and the granting of tax exemption to the non-noble knights.

In 1255 and 1256 Alfonso X granted new privileges to the non-noble knights of most of the Castilian and Leonese cities, exempting from most taxes those citizens who owned houses within the city walls and who also had horses and arms fit for warfare. As a social category, the non-noble urban knights (there were also rural non-urban knights, that is, well-to-do farmers who maintained horse and weapons, were liable for military service, and received some forms of tax exemption for their services) began to play a leading role in the affairs of the kingdom. Although the non-noble knights dated from earlier centuries and had played significant roles in the military affairs of the Reconquest, the royal privileges of the mid-thirteenth century marked a turning point in the social, political, and economic history of Castile. In less than 50 years the non-noble knights monopolized municipal offices in most Castilian cities, bought most of the land around the cities, and gained control, as they did in Burgos and Avila, of the most important ecclesiastical benefices. In return the king hoped for, and often received, their military support against the magnates and access to the cities' fiscal resources. Moreover, as the non-noble knights gained control of their respective cities, they came into conflict with those below them. Pressured from below by the disfranchised petite bourgeoisie, the non-noble knights welcomed royal interference in the affairs of the cities and, by the 1340s, the takeover of municipal administration by royal officials (the *regimiento*) became a political reality. For a brief period, royal control of the urban centers became one of the most significant gains of the Castilian monarchy, but then the disorders of the late fourteenth century weakened royal control anew.[15]

Territorial expansion in the east took on a different face and yielded a very different outcome. The kings of Aragon and counts of Barcelona had participated actively in the work of the Reconquest. Peter (Pere) II fought with great distinction at the battle of Las Navas de Tolosa, and the Aragonese–Catalan realm was guaranteed a sphere of influence and expansion in eastern Mediterranean Iberia. In 1238 James I conquered the very rich and prosperous Muslim kingdom of Valencia. In contrast to the pattern followed by the Castilian kings, James allowed Valencia to emerge as an independent kingdom and to be federated with the other two older realms: Aragon and Catalonia. After 1238 the Crown of Aragon was composed of the three entities, and James became the king of Valencia, a distinctive realm with its own parliament, laws, and, eventually, language (a form of Catalan).

Moreover, the conquered Muslim population was not expelled from either the cities of the Valencian kingdom or from its countryside. Most of the Mudejar population remained on the land, carrying on the same jobs as they had done before. The Crown of Aragon thus avoided the deep structural and economic crises affecting Castile. The agricultural productivity of the Valencian hinterland did not diminish radically, nor were the patterns of cultivation and basic fiscal models of exploitation altered. Unlike in the western parts of the peninsula, agricultural production remained at a high level, and the Mudejars preserved a profitable culture of irrigation and husbandry until the final expulsion of the Moriscos (nominally Muslims converted to Christianity) in the early seventeenth century. This does not mean at all that Aragonese and Catalans (who provided the bulk of he Christian settlers) were more understanding and tolerant than Castilians. It means simply that they chose different, and often more efficacious, ways of dealing with conquered people.

The conquest of Valencia, however, marked the end of Aragonese–Catalan expansion in the peninsula. The kings of the Crown of Aragon relinquished their rights to expansion into Murcia, and for all practical purposes looked elsewhere for territorial gains. Aragonese and Catalan expansion to the Balearic Islands, into Sicily (by the early 1280s), and even into the eastern Mediterranean can only be understood in the context of a closing of the Crown of Aragon's frontier with Islam. Indeed, there were Aragonese and Catalan raids upon Granada and frontier conflicts with Castile in the region of Murcia, but these activities paled when compared to the vigor with which the Crown of Aragon moved into other Mediterranean lands.

Valencia's autonomy and prosperity also had unintended consequences. One must trace to this period the slow and inexorable decline of Barcelona. This ancient city remained a populous and important center for Mediterranean trade, but its fortunes began to be slowly eclipsed by Valencia's rising star. In many respects, the Crown of Aragon's conquest of the south had a number of consequences that were diametrically different from those affecting Castile. They can be summarized in a few words. First and foremost, by partially withdrawing from peninsular affairs and seeking areas for expansion in the Mediterranean and Italy, the Crown of Aragon projected itself into the wider European scene and gained access to the impressive cultural revival under way in Italy. But in doing so it ceded to Castile's hegemony in the peninsula. Castile was the stronger of the two realms in terms of population and resources, but in the thirteenth century it was not altogether clear that it could eventually become the core of a developing Spanish nation.

Second, by turning Valencia into an independent realm within the federation of kingdoms comprising the Crown of Aragon, the kings of the Crown of Aragon strengthened the autonomy of the individual realms and probably made impossible any centralization of power in the future. Castile became supreme in the peninsula because it could, as the Catholic Monarchs did, centralize its administration; the Crown of Aragon could not and did not wish to do so. Again and again, the rulers of Aragon, Catalonia, and Valencia gave way to local and regional interests to the detriment of royal power. Finally, the vitality of Valencia, its vast agricultural region, its strategic geographical location, and its easy access to North African markets and Mediterranean ports led to its growing importance within the economy of the Crown of Aragon. This meant the slow decline of Barcelona, growing political strife in that city, and growing resistance to royal authority. Barcelona could no longer serve as the economic engine for the entire region. A whole series of other important social and political developments followed from that decline: from the growing enserfment of peasants and the rise of political factions to growing mistrust of royal authority. All of these factors deeply affected the subsequent history of the Spanish eastern kingdoms and played an important role in the story that must be told in the following chapters.

Chapter 2

Medieval Spain in the Late Middle Ages

Society and Economy

Years of Crises

A series of disasters befell all of the medieval European kingdoms during the fourteenth and fifteenth centuries. Climatic changes led to shorter and wetter summers and colder winters – the so-called mini-Ice Age – which compounded the problems created by structural crises, excessive taxation, the high cost of endemic warfare, overpopulation (in some areas of Europe), peasant and urban rebellions, and plague. Local and regional contexts, however, often shaped the course of each of these individual crises. The plague, to give just one example, was the same illness everywhere, but how individuals and authorities reacted to its onslaught differed from place to place. The Black Death's long-term consequences also depended on a whole host of circumstances. We know, for example, that in Siena the population of the city was renewed within a short period of time by intense migration from the countryside. In England and Castile, many of the villages wiped out by the plague and by other factors such as famine or violence were never repopulated, and these "lost villages" disappeared from history.

The Spanish Realms

The story or stories to be told throughout this book always unfolded within the context of long-term structural crises – in the plural because it was the conjunction of different types of crises that made the period so difficult – and against the backdrop of dramatic and cataclysmic events sweeping the peninsula from the mid-thirteenth century to the reforms of the Catholic Monarchs. One may, of course, question the term crisis to describe such a long period of time. Critical events became so deeply intertwined with daily life that contemporaries were aware only of the high points of despair, illness, and violence, and not always able to see the underlying threads that connected one catastrophe to another. How did different peninsular social groups change, adapt, and relate to each other in this period? How did the economy develop or crash? How did the Crown's response to crisis shape its institutional and political development in this period? The success of the Catholic Monarchs in reshaping Castile in the waning decades of the fifteenth century could not have happened without the many royal attempts, though often failed and incomplete, to bring some order to the chaos sweeping Spain and to chart new social, economic, and political agendas. Remarkably and in spite of the crises, the kingdoms of Castile, the Crown of Aragon, Navarre, and even Granada developed new and vigorous forms of political life, new religious practices, and a dazzling cultural output.

These achievements will be explored later, but for now it might not be improper to invoke Johannes Huizinga's *The Autumn of the Middle Ages* and to see Spanish history in the late Middle Ages through Huizinga's explanatory scheme: a society plagued by endemic and horrific violence and by a morbid pursuit of fame and remembrance, yet capable of generating artistic works of rare beauty. In this world, through romance, festivals, and knight-errantry, the upper groups in society constructed the life beautiful: one in which life imitated art and vice versa; one in which aesthetic pursuits stood as a bulwark against the unbearable transformations of medieval life and institutions. But it was not only about beauty and the aestheticized life. It was also about power, and strife over who would, in the end, wield authority.

Population

We should face first the thorny but important issue of population and of the impact of population in the shaping of the late medieval crisis in Spain. One of the traditional explanations for the onset of the late medieval crisis (and I use the singular to conform to traditional ways of looking at this period) has been to see the problems of population and production in Malthusian terms (from Thomas Malthus' influential work, *The Essay on Population*, 1798). In this view a rise in population throughout the medieval West from 1000 onwards created substantial population pressure on the land. By the late thirteenth century this led to the cultivation of marginal lands to feed the growing number of people. Cultivation of marginal lands dramatically lowered the crops' yield ratio, bringing shortages of food and localized famines. Together with other factors (adverse climate, widespread warfare, inflation, and other such critical events), these developments sent most European societies into a downward spiral and opened the door for far more devastating blows: the great famines of 1315–21, popular rebellions, endemic war, and the plague.

The Malthusian explanation, however, cannot be accepted for Spain. In the Iberian peninsula, though some local demographic pressure can be documented, population pressure was never the problem. Paradoxically, the feebleness of Spain's demographic growth and the decline in the number of inhabitants from the late thirteenth century onwards created stresses which, although different from those affecting other Western medieval realms, led to similar outcomes. I have already discussed in detail the causes and consequences of the late medieval crisis in Castile, and there is no need to explain these points in great detail once again, though further explanations are required for the lands of the Crown of Aragon.[1] Clearly, the population shift from north to south in Castile and, to a lesser extent, in the Crown of Aragon from Aragon and Catalonia to Valencia affected agricultural production adversely. Catalonia, for example, was severely disrupted by outward migration into the 1350s.[2] New crops in the south, the expulsion of the Mudejars (Muslims living under Christian rule) from western Andalusia in the mid-1260s, and the semi-enserfment of Mudejars in Valencia altered, as has been noted in the previous chapter, social relations, the nature of agricultural production, and patterns of trade. The rapid rise in salaries in western Andalusia after the Castilian conquest reflected to a degree the dearth of population and the limited availability of labor in the region. The harsh reimposition of serfdom in Old Catalonia is yet another telling sign of lordly desire to secure a labor force in the rearguard of territorial expansion in the south and the lure of better wages and what seemed at the time to be better working conditions. As we now know, this proved to be illusory and the final outcome for peasants in southern Spain was a rather miserable existence as landless journeymen.

From the 1250s onwards, monasteries and other ecclesiastical establishments gave their lands to peasants in long-term or perpetual leases in growing numbers. These long-term leases were given under considerably better terms than in previous centuries and seem to have been the only effective means for ecclesiastical institutions to keep their holdings under cultivation. In the early fourteenth century the ordinances of the Castilian Cortes were a sobering reflection of the rapid decline of population and the erosion of the tax base. Procurators attending the frequent meetings of the Cortes requested from the Crown a reduction in taxes because of the ills plaguing the realm (the violence of nobles, failed crops, excessive taxation, and the like) and the obvious decline in population.

A few examples from Castile will suffice to illustrate my point. In 1304 Ferdinand IV, king of Castile, reduced the taxes paid by the town of Silos – in this case the tax paid by the town (the *fonsadera*) in lieu of military service. Ferdinand IV's grant amounted to a 25 percent reduction in one particular tax. Medieval rulers, often facing spiraling expenses, were seldom willing to give up or reduce their fiscal rights. Ferdinand agreed to this reduction because the lands of Silos were "very diminished" and "very depopulated." Alfonso XI confirmed the tax reduction in 1329, when obviously conditions in the region of Silos had not improved at all. In Covarrubias, the tax rolls were reduced to 54 tax payers in 1311 and the number ratified by Alfonso XI's regents in 1314. Covarrubias, an important town in the region of Burgos, had only 54 recognized taxpayers contributing to the royal fisc because of its municipal council's insistent claims of poverty and population decline. Further reductions in the number of contributors were granted by Alfonso XI's regents in 1315. Though taxpayers always tend to exaggerate hardship and resist paying more, royal inquests yielded the same evidence and led the Crown to accept, albeit reluctantly, the new demographic realities and diminishing tax base.[3]

In the harsh and violent political and economic climate of the 1320s and 1330s, villages were abandoned, the land went uncultivated and turned to waste, and the Crown accepted a reduction in the number of taxpayers when faced with the grim reality that Castile's population was vanishing. Although the Crown held on to its prerogatives as long as it could, the realities on the ground were otherwise. In 1326, royal agents set the number of taxpayers in Ventosa, a small village in northern Castile, at 10, but by then the village was actually deserted; its inhabitants had fled to Navarre. What kind of conditions could there have been at the local level when peasants, usually bound to their villages and to the soil, found the situation so intolerable that they left their houses and lands behind and moved elsewhere? And these were not isolated or peculiar cases. The examples are alarmingly numerous.[4]

In the harsh years between 1310 and 1330 royal inquests into the rate of taxation and the number of taxpayers still yielded roughly the same result: an acknowledgment that there were fewer people to tax and, consequently, the need to reduce taxes. The numerous examples found in the extant documentation point to the link between a diminishing population and the pressure to raise funds for the ever-increasing cost of administering the kingdom and fighting wars. The question of course remains: how many

Table 2.1   Population Comparison (1300–1480)

	ca. 1300	ca. 1480
Catalonia	550,000	260,000
Aragon	200,000	250,000
Valencia	200,000	250,000
Mallorca	50,000	55,000
Navarre	100,000	100,000
Castile-León	4,500,000	4,500,000

Source: J. A. García de Cortázar, Historia de España Alfaguara II: La época medieval (Madrid, 1973), 391.

people lived in the Spanish kingdoms by 1300? Were there real population losses during the more than a century and a half covered by this book?

Although it is almost impossible to provide reliable demographic information before the early modern period, García de Cortázar estimated that Castile had around 4,500,000 inhabitants at the end of the thirteenth century, while the Crown of Aragon had over 1,000,000 inhabitants among its three composite kingdoms. Catalonia led with over half a million, with Aragon proper and newly conquered Valencia with over 200,000 each, while around 80,000 lived in Majorca.[5] Bisson, on the other hand, has argued that population estimates for the Crown of Aragon have tended to be low, projecting a population of as many as 1,200,000 for the eastern kingdoms and as many as 6,000,000 for Castile. Whatever figure we accept (I tend toward the lower figure), the population of the largest two Spanish realms (neither Navarre, with around 100,000, nor Granada is included in these calculations) pales in comparison with neighboring France, with an estimated population of 20,000,000 or more.

By the end of the fifteenth century, estimates place the population of Spain at a lower level than it had been almost 200 years before. García de Cortazar's stunning comparison of estimated population figures from around 1300 and 1480 are revealing indeed.

Demographic Changes Reconsidered

These figures, a very rough estimate and representative of the tenuous reality of medieval demography, show exceedingly modest increases in population for Aragon, Valencia, and Majorca in almost two centuries, no gains for Castile, and catastrophic losses for Catalonia. In spite of the robust economic and demographic recovery under way in 1480, the population of the Spains was still lower than it had been in 1300. Barcelona, severely hit by plague and by Valencia's fierce competition, may have had a population of around 50,000 inhabitants in 1340, making it the largest city in the peninsula, and only 20,000 in 1477, easily overtaken by booming Valencia, Seville, and, perhaps, Toledo.[6] Demographic stagnation underpins the troubled social and political landscape of the Spanish realms and, as imprecise as these calculations are, they speak volumes as to the harsh conditions of the period. This does not mean at all, however, that demographic decline was universal. Some areas – Seville and Valencia are the best examples – drained population from the north to the south. Seville became the largest city in Iberia, reaching almost 100,000 inhabitants *before* the discovery of the New World. There were opportunities for growth but not everywhere. But if Seville and Valencia were growing at a very fast rate, and the population as a whole was declining, what was happening elsewhere in the peninsula?

The evidence can be dramatic. In the *Libro becerro de las behetrías*, a large (but partial) survey of royal, noble, and ecclesiastical fiscal rights undertaken in northern Castile in 1351 in the wake of the Black Death, the data provides stunning evidence for the deterioration of northern Castile's economy and population. The evidence is horrifying. By the mid-fourteenth century, between one-quarter and one-fifth of all the villages in northern Castile listed in the census had been deserted (see table 2.2). In those villages that still remained in existence, the criteria for taxation and seigneurial rights had often been reduced from the level of the early thirteenth century, reaffirming the area's loss of population and economic decline.[7] Clearly, the table indicates different patterns of desertion. Villages on the plain, where violence and plague could move swiftly from one location to another, suffered a higher rate of depopulation than fairly isolated and difficult-to-reach mountain hamlets.

In 1349 Peter the Ceremonious, king of the Crown of Aragon, imposed restrictions on wages and prices throughout his motley lands. Two years afterwards, in 1351, the Cortes of Castile followed suit by imposing similar limitations on wages and prices, a reflection of the dearth of labor and the desire by those on top to control the job market. At the same time, in what was quite a radical attempt, considering Castile's long history of a free peasantry, the *Fuero viejo* of Castile, reissued around the 1350s, sought unsuccessfully to bind peasants to the soil in an attempt to secure labor for seigneurial lands.[8] Although these noble attempts to impose harsh restrictions on the peasantry and, if at all possible, to bind them to the land (replicated throughout the medieval West) failed in Castile, they were successful

Table 2.2   Deserted Villages in the Becerro

Merindad	Location	No. of villages	No. of deserted villages
Cerrato	Plain	112	56
Infantazgo de Valladolid	Plain	98	35
Monzón	Plain	97	22
Campos	Plain	71	21
Carrión	Plain	119	41
Villadiego	Plain	107	21
Aguilar	Plain and mountain	262	40
Liébana	Mountain and plain	131	15
Saldaña	Plain	195	42
Asturias de Santillana	Mountain	207	12
Castrojeriz	Plain	121	30
Candemuño	Mountain	79	18
Burgos-Ubierna	Mountain	121	22
Castilla la Vieja	Mountain	534	87
St. Domingo de Silos (partial)	Plain	148	26
Total		2,402	488

Source: Ruiz, *Crisis and Continuity*, 321.

in parts of the Crown of Aragon, where the Old Catalonian peasantry was bound to the soil in even harsher conditions, and Mudejars in the Ebro river basin (Aragon) and in Valencia's hinterland became further bound to their masters and to the land.

Inflation, Declining Revenues, and Violence

Population losses were deeply imbricated with other structural problems that dominated Spanish history throughout the fourteenth and fifteenth centuries. The first challenge to Spaniards was the rapid increase in prices from the mid-thirteenth century onwards. Inflation delivered yet another blow to the well-being of the Spanish realms. Attempts to impose some controls on prices and wages appeared regularly from the 1260s into the fourteenth century. At the 1268 *ayuntamiento* of Jerez (a meeting of the king with Castile's urban and mercantile representatives) a strong effort was made to control the rate of inflation, but without success. Through the next century and a half, the ordinances of the Cortes sought to lower the cost of credit and to ensure the availability of capital, but the repetitive nature of these measures attests to their ineffectiveness. That attempts at fiscal reforms and control of prices and wages often ended up being inexorably linked to attacks against the Jews only added to the social unrest generated by deteriorating economic conditions, rising prices, and diminishing fiscal resources.[9]

At the same time, while kings and parliaments (the Cortes of Castile and the individual Cortes or Corts of the Crown of Aragon) sought to control inflation and to reform the economy, the kings of Castile and of the Crown of Aragon, faced with deteriorating economic conditions and the rising cost of warfare and governance, continued to debase their coinage. In doing so frequently and arbitrarily, they inflicted great harm on the economy and on their people. In many respects, the history of the Spanish realms can also be read as the progressive debasement of their respective coinages, which, while producing short-term benefits for individual rulers, had a cumulative deleterious impact on the Spanish economy.[10]

Inflation, weaker coinage, and the disruption of foreign markets because of the general western European economic downturn led to a severe decrease in royal, as well as in noble, income. Medieval monarchies had become quite sophisticated by the end of the thirteenth century. The new demands of warfare and of expanding bureaucracies, combined with the growing expenses of the court, forced kings throughout Europe to scramble for additional sources of income. The best example of this frantic search for money and for untapped revenue sources is Philip IV of France (1285–1314) who, in rapid succession, savaged Jews, Lombard bankers, the Templars, and anyone else he could get his hands on to raise badly needed cash. And all, in the end, to no avail.[11]

In the Spanish realms, the kings of Castile and the Crown of Aragon, besides profiting from the abolition of the Templars at the Council of Vienne (1312), launched multi-pronged programs to raise funds. These efforts were most obvious in the kings' frequent requests to their Cortes for extraordinary subsidies, for taxes to prevent the devaluation of the coinage (which they immediately proceeded to devalue), for the introduction of new taxes, for the extortion of funds from those unable to withstand relentless royal pressure – Jews, Muslims, and the Church (which under the prodding of royal claims to launch crusades against the Muslims in the south was often drained of its resources) – and for the outright violent appropriation of new sources of income.

Operating within the established parameters set by the law, the Castilian kings requested relief from the urban representatives to the Cortes almost on an annual basis, arguing that those funds were necessary to address the realm's needs. Granting the right to farm taxes or working deals with urban representatives – who collected the taxes but who were also exempted from them – the Castilian kings gave up some of the additional income they may have collected by strong-arm tactics for the assurance of the urban elites' cooperation and urban agreement to royal fiscal demands and military needs. It was not only in the setting of the Cortes that the kings sought to work out political deals that had, over the long run, important consequences. In the mid-1340s Alfonso XI, in policies to be explored in greater detail later, gained control of urban centers throughout Castile and sought to bring peace – by interjecting royal power into urban conflicts – by reducing the social antagonism between urban elites and those below. Although Alfonso XI's measure – the imposition of the *regimiento* (officials to administer the towns) – was a rather complex process, it also allowed the Crown, as it did the Catholic Monarchs 200 years later, to gain access to urban fiscal resources.

At a time when the Castilian Crown faced a great deal of noble opposition and a renewed Muslim threat in the south – the Merinid invasion of strategic southern ports – it needed more money. One solution was new permanent forms of taxation. A tax of Muslim provenance, the *alcabala*, instituted as a temporary measure to finance Alfonso XI's siege of Algeciras in 1342, became, after the Cortes' successive extension of the original grant, a permanent tax and an important source of income for the Crown.[12] As such, the *alcabala* came about as a response to a fiscal and political crisis. Other royal attempts to meet the challenges of eroding income will be explored in greater detail in later chapters, but, as will be seen, the experiences of the Crown of Aragon were not intrinsically different.

The Crown of Aragon

Unlike the kings of Castile, the kings of the Crown of Aragon had three very distinct realms and troublesome representative assemblies to face in trying to make some sense of changing social and economic conditions. As was the case in Castile, the Crown of Aragon also suffered from sparse population (in relation to its vast territories) and unproductive lands, with the notable exception of the fertile Ebro river bank near Zaragoza, the fabled *huerta* (gardens) of Valencia, and some areas of Catalonia and elsewhere throughout the Aragonese realms. When one consider that the entire population of Aragon proper probably, despite the estimates given above, did not reach 200,000 inhabitants and that Valencia, though far richer and more attractive, had a similar population, then one can imagine the difficulties faced by the rulers of the Crown of Aragon in addressing the impeding crises. Large numbers of Mudejars in Aragon and Valencia, most of them closely dependent on the nobility, and a substantial number of Jews in Catalonia contributed to a heterogeneous social landscape which made raising money – who paid what and to whom? – rather difficult.

Attempts to regulate prices and wages in 1349 and 1350 had the same limited and negative impact that these measures had in Castile. More significantly, the diverse and often contradictory political exigencies of the three realms forced the kings into endless compromises and concessions, and made their ability to carry out reforms or bold economic and/or political initiatives quite difficult. And since the Aragonese, Catalan, and Valencian nobility commanded such lofty status and enjoyed such far-ranging privileges, the kings did not have an easy time dealing with them either. They did try, however, to do the best they could. In 1346 Peter IV ordered the minting of new gold coins, seeking to place the Catalan–Aragonese–Valencian economy on a solid footing. He did not count on the havoc and economic disruption brought by the plague a mere two years afterwards, and the gold florin of Barcelona underwent frequent devaluations to 75 percent of its value by 1365.[13] Remarkably, in spite of a decreasing population, plague, social unrest, and other ills, the mercantile economy of the Crown of Aragon's urban centers remained fairly vital, providing some much-needed solace from the wide-ranging crises.

Violence

The royal chronicles, those of Ferdinand IV's and Alfonso XI's minority in particular, are an endless tale of noble violence and disorder on the one hand and of nobles murdered by the king's orders on the other. Violence did not come about solely because of the deeper crises affecting the realms, above all demographic losses and the erosion of the tax base and noble income. After all, a great deal of the violence resulted from an increase in political conflict within Iberia, civil war, and the growing complexity of warfare in the fourteenth and fifteenth centuries. One could easily argue that political instability and its concomitant, wars between the different Spanish realms, was an intrinsic part of the larger crises of medieval society.

In considering the issue of violence and of its impact on late medieval Spain, one cannot help but evoke Huizinga's famous description of the violent tenor of society. Medieval men and women lived perpetually under the shadow of endemic violence. In the Spanish realms, the procurators to the Cortes protested again and again against widespread violence and bemoaned the royal inability to protect the people at the bottom from noble excess. This was yet another indication of the failure of medieval rulers to preserve order. But violence had different faces. Between 1300 and 1469, the Iberian kingdoms engaged in frequent armed conflicts. Peace was, more often than not, a short interlude between frontier skirmishes between Christian kingdoms, raids against Muslim lands (or defenses against Muslim counter-raids, and occasionally full-fledged military engagements). Invasions from Morocco and Christian attempts to repel them complete this chaotic picture (see chapters 3 and 4 below). Beyond the violence promoted and carried out by rulers, the Iberian realms suffered the great scourge of civil wars and of the spilling over into Iberia of the conflict between France and England – the Hundred Years War. For the moment, it will suffice to note that, in the decade following the devastation of the plague, Castile sank into a bloody and disruptive civil war. French and English troops – Edward, Prince of Wales (the famous Black Prince) and the French constable Bertram Du Guesclin led military campaigns in Spain – roamed through the peninsula, though mostly in the western areas and in Castile, inflicting a heavy toll on the social, economic, and political well-being of the realms.

Although conflicts between Iberian kingdoms led to large financial costs and imposed great burdens on the faltering Spanish economies, these wars mostly affected border areas. Most of the battles and raids took place in those liminal and fluid spaces between kingdoms. In many respects these conflicts were attempts to define and redefine emerging territorial frontiers. They were costly affairs, but they were not necessarily punishing to the general population in the rearguard of the border wars. And even in the affected areas the local population had long learned to get out of the way and to profit from these recurring events. At times, as for example in the raids against Granada, there was great profit to be made in terms of ransom, tribute, and slaves.

Civil war was another matter. Civil war in the Middle Ages did not mean of course what it does today, involving whole populations in bloody strife and animated by regional, ethnic, and/or religious conflicts. By civil war – the more appropriate term may be dynastic disputes or factional conflicts – I mean the pitting of one or several members of the royal family against the ruler, or groups of magnates competing against each other for control of a regency or a weak king. Such were the cases of the minorities of Ferdinand IV, Alfonso XI, and Henry III, or the strife during the reigns of John II and Henry IV respectively. These conflicts were in reality familial conflicts, involving large, extended families in deathly contests for power and prestige. If these encounters had been limited to the narrow circles at the top they would not have been so destructive. Instead they drew vast circles of noble retainers, servants, and bourgeois allies, creating a permanent state of violence. Affecting the quality of daily life, the armed conflicts of the magnates and royal families drew, into their widening maelstrom, almost everyone in the realm.

These struggles could be kingdom-wide or localized. The perennial strife in Barcelona between the Biga (nobles and landlords) and the Busca (merchants, artisans, and laborers) often spilled into, and was influenced by, the wider politics of Catalonia and the Crown of Aragon (see below). The feudal violence in Ribagorza, where a noble family terrorized the countryside into the late sixteenth century, is yet another indication of the enduring nature of these problems. Most of them date from before 1300, and they continued to plague parts of Spain long after the end of the Middle Ages. Within this category of factional strife and as part of wider social conflicts one may also include attacks against religious minorities (and sometimes even by religious minorities against Christians).

The real burden of violence, especially as it impacted peasants, the most numerous and vulnerable segment of the population, was random noble violence. Freed from constraints or fear of reprisal by the Crown's weakness, driven by the need for more income in the face of declining revenues and dependent peasants, many member of the nobility engaged in wanton and predatory acts of violence. The period between 1300 and 1469 witnessed the worst of it, and one can only understand the awe and devotion that Ferdinand and Isabella elicited throughout their reign and in the Golden Age if one acknowledges the disorder and pervasive violence of the century and a half before their reforms and restoration of order. This violence ranged from noblemen scorching peaceful villages in the area of the Rioja in the first half of the fourteenth century – leading to the peasants having to flee their ancestral homes and abandon their fields – to urban noble factions attacking the constable of Castile, Don Miguel Lucas de Iranzo, in the 1460s under the cover of anti-converso riots, to the endemic strife in urban centers between urban elites and disfranchised citizens. The latter was most vivid in Barcelona in the already mentioned conflict between the Biga and the Busca, but the contours of social upheaval in Barcelona were replicated throughout Spain in the internecine violence between nobles, citizens, and those below, and the even more appalling attacks by nobles against defenseless peasants. In Segovia some of these disgruntled groups burned one of the towers of the town's cathedral in the 1320s. Alfonso XI responded in kind, as will be seen in the next chapter, by torturing and executing those responsible for these acts. It would require more than a single book to illustrate in sufficient detail the heightened sense of uncertainty and the expectation of violence. One example will suffice.

The case of Ribafrecha, a small village under the jurisdiction of the monastery of Santa María de Nájera, is instructive. The village was attacked and sacked by a rebellious nobleman, John Ferrández de Bezla, in either 1315 or 1316, during the troubled years of Alfonso XI's minority. The village's crops were burned, its gardens looted, and the remains of its defenses – for the situation had become so dire as to force small villages to build walls – taken over and turned into a stronghold from which Ferrández de Bezla could scourge the surrounding countryside. When dislodged from his ill-gotten gains by a combination of noble forces – those of John Alfonso de Haro, a great territorial lord in the region – and the urban militias of nearby Logroño, Ribafrecha's unfortunate peasants had no place to go, migrating to another location and founding a new village named Oriemo.[14] John Alfonso de Haro became a serious troublemaker later in Alfonso XI's reign and was murdered by order of the king.

The ordinances of the Cortes present a vivid portrait of realms burdened by the weight of violence and the excesses of the high nobility and, quite often, royal agents. From direct acts of violence – the usual attacks on villages, noble-sponsored banditry, disruption of commerce – to the illegal exaction of taxes, those at the bottom of society or religious minorities bore the results of a deteriorating economy, the breakdown of order, and civil strife. At the Cortes of Burgos in 1301, Ferdinand IV, king of Castile, agreed to the procurators' demands that powerful men (*omes poderosos*) cease to buy or to grab municipal property. In addition, castles and fortresses, used as the base for *malfetrías* (evil deeds) should be torn down. The same year at Zamora, the king's response to the urban procurators retold the grim tale of nobles keeping gangs of *malfechores* who had robbed, destroyed, and burned villages. Added to these complaints one finds descriptions of the usual illegal appropriation of lands by nobles and military orders. No petition to the Crown, however, could be as revealing as the one in which the procurators to the Cortes asked the king to forbid nobles, fighting to avenge the death of one of their men, "to kill peasants, rob them, cut their trees and vineyards, burn [their farms], and steal their cattle."[15]

During the troubled first quarter of the fourteenth century, these complaints are repeated almost verbatim in successive meetings of the Cortes: "the *malfechores* who go around the land, killing and stealing and doing great evil in the villages and in the countryside [*defuera dellas*] and [do so] under the protection [*se acogen*] of Infantes, *ricos omes*, and other powerful men."[16] These petitions portray a countryside bereft of order where powerful nobles sponsored terror and crime. Feudal lords, firmly entrenched in castles and strongholds, engaged in predatory behavior toward their dependent peasant population, or, more likely, against the peasants of their enemies, ecclesiastic institutions, and municipal councils. The peasants' complaints, those presented at the Cortes or those of the rebellious Hermandiños in the late fifteenth century, have an eerie similarity to the anguished cries of two centuries earlier illustrated in Bisson's *Tormented Voices*.[17] At the end it was not even about freedom, for at least the Castilian peasants were free; it was about surviving in the endless disturbances plaguing the Spanish realms from the late thirteenth century onwards.

In an important book written more than two decades ago, Salustiano Moreta Velayos explores the relentless activities of those he called, in the book's title, *malhechores feudales* (feudal evildoers). The word *malfechor* or *malhechor*, a term used frequently by medieval writers, was intimately linked to the description of noble criminal activity in the ordinances of the Cortes and other contemporary sources (*malfetría*). As damning as the word is, it does not reach the level of bitterness achieved by the literary metaphors found in the satirical and critical poetry of the next century and a half. Written by court poets, many of them members of the high nobility, these poems, bemoaning and unmasking the endemic violence of those on top against those below, represent a critique from within, that is, a keen awareness by some members of the ruling groups of what the violence was doing to the kingdom.

In Ruy Páez de Ribera's poem dedicated to Queen Catalina (Catherine of Lancaster), one of the regents during John II's tumultuous minority (extending from 1406 to 1419), the author decries the high nobility's disdain of honor and praise for the sake of wealth. After scorning some high-born families as worthless – the Castros and the Laras most of all – and eulogizing the family of López Dávalos, Ruy Páez de Ribera proceeds to paint a tragic portrait of nobles who failed to protect peasants (their duty according to the *Siete partidas* and the concept of medieval society as divided into three orders). The peasants had reached such dire straits that they were forced to sell their clothes to satisfy moneylenders and rent collectors.[18] The same sentiments are echoed in the *Coplas de la panadera* which tell the story of the battle of Olmedo (1445) and contrast the fatuousness and cowardice of the high nobility and the peasants – in this reading peasants are vile and cowards as well – who, caught in the middle of battle, flee the violence. Far more damning is Iñigo de Mendoza's satirical *Coplas de Mingo Revulgo* where, in a much-quoted line, the nobility are compared to wolves and the peasants to lambs. And, as is the case in the real world, wolves love nothing better than to eat lambs.[19]

In spite of these protests, literary representations of the peasantry and even of urban dwellers could also reach very hostile levels. The Infante Don Juan Manuel (1282–1348), one of those aspiring to the regency during Alfonso XI's minority and among the greatest troublemakers in 1320s and 1330s Castile, relegated peasants and merchants to a very lowly status in the medieval tripartite hierarchy of society. Even though Don Juan Manuel had himself been defeated by urban militias on several occasions, in his social formulation he could neither see the fluidity of medieval Spanish society nor the worth and military prowess of those beneath his social rank.[20]

Of greater virulence were the arguments advanced by many in Catalonia to justify the peasants' enserfment. As Paul Freedman has brilliantly shown, the "legend of the cowardly peasants," that is, those who refused to fight against the Islamic invasion or to join the Christians in fighting Muslim lords, served to legitimize the harsh dues and the limitations on freedom and mobility imposed on peasants throughout Old Catalonia. Bondage was, according to this formulation, the rightful punishment for the peasants' lack of courage and loyalty to their faith. This legitimation of oppression had its counterpart in numerous pejorative representations of the peasantry. Though these representations appear as a trope for all of the medieval West (though perhaps less pronounced in Castile) and could at times be ambiguous, they do, nonetheless, point to the troubled relationship between those on top and those below in the context of Christianity and the fellow-ship of all men in Christ.[21] The consequences were disastrous for the Spanish realms and, in particular, for the peasantry. And even worse was in store.

Famine, War, Plague, and Rebellion

It has long been a commonplace to depict the late medieval crisis as resulting from the combined impact of four major disasters or series of disasters. These so-called "four horsemen of the apocalypse," to borrow an eschatological metaphor from the biblical book of Revelation and the title of many textbook sections on the late Middle Ages, have always been identified as hunger (famine), war, plague, and revolution. In terms of the general medieval West, hunger meant the devastating famine or famines that affected most of Europe (but not Spain) between 1315 and 1321 and killed a large percentage of the population. By war, most late medieval chroniclers meant the Hundred Years War which, beginning roughly in 1337, lasted into the second half of the fifteenth century and consumed most of France, England, and neighboring realms in its wake. Rebellions or revolutions described the peasant and urban upheavals that disrupted most of Europe throughout the late Middle Ages – among them the Karls in 1320s Flanders, the Pastoreaux in France and northern parts of Aragon in the same decade, and the better-known peasant risings in France (the Jacquerie in the late 1350s) and England (in 1381), and the bitter urban rising of the Ciompi in Florence in 1378. Social upheavals continued throughout the fifteenth and sixteenth centuries, as Europe adjusted to the social and economic transformations marking the transition to the early modern period. As for the plague or Black Death, it struck most of Europe between 1348 and 1351, killing, depending on the location, between 25 percent and 60 percent of the population. And the plague returned every generation into the seventeenth century.

The Spanish realms: famine

When we turn to the different Spanish kingdoms, the picture is altogether different from that in northern Europe. For one, the great famines of 1315–21, induced mainly by climatic changes and Malthusian pressures, did not affect Mediterranean lands or most parts of southern Europe. As a consequence, in 1315, a year marked by great scarcity of corn in northern Europe, Castile exported some of its grain surplus to England. If the Spanish realms were spared the general famine of 1315–21 this did not mean that it completely escaped famine. But, unlike most parts of northern Europe, these famines were either local occurrences or of short duration. Such was the case reported in the chronicle of Ferdinand IV in 1301. The description is a stark one and reveals how contemporaries reacted to widespread hunger:

> And this year there was throughout the land a very great hunger; and men died of hunger in the squares and streets, and there was such great mortality that . . . maybe one-quarter of all the people in the land died; and the hunger [famine] was so great that people ate grass bread, and there never was a time [in the history of the] world that witnessed such a great famine [hunger] and such widespread mortality.[22]

Even if we allow for the typical exaggeration and literary flair of medieval chroniclers, the presence of acute hunger among the population elicited a response. In the far more somber ordinances of the Cortes, one finds references to widespread famines in northern Castile in the 1340s and other such shortages triggered by regional bad weather, violence, or demographic decline.[23] Famine, accompanied by social agitation, became endemic in Barcelona and its hinterland after 1325 and until the plague which, by killing many, solved some of the problems created by food scarcity. Yet in 1358, to give an example, locusts destroyed most crops in Catalonia, creating local food shortages, demographic losses, and social unrest. Escaping the more widespread famines was indeed fortunate for the Spanish realms, but it did not prevent them from suffering the perennial cycle of famines so prevalent in the Middle Ages. The relationship between food production and population remained a precarious one in most parts of Europe until the eighteenth century and the spread of the agricultural revolution. Spain was no exception in that respect.

War

As noted above, the more than century and a half covered by this book was a period of unremitting warfare. Although Spain was spared some of the most bloody conflicts of the Hundred Years War, long and destructive campaigns were fought in the peninsula as part of that conflict, and also as part of the Castilian civil war of the 1360s. The Castilian fleet also saw frequent action in the English Channel, fighting, depending whether it was under Peter I or the Trastámara usurper, on either side of the war. Both the Black Prince (Edward, Prince of Wales) and the French constable Bertram Du Guesclin, undertook long campaigns in Iberia, taking sides in the conflict between Peter I, the Cruel, and his half-brother Henry of Trastámara (see chapter 4).

In the south, Alfonso XI had to meet the threat of the Merinids and died himself of the plague – the only king in Europe to do so – while besieging Gibraltar in 1350. Most of the 1340s was spent by the Castilian monarchs resisting a Muslim invasion in western Andalusia. The kings of the Crown of Aragon, besides dealing with internal conflicts, fought the kingdom of Castile, and Castile fought Aragon, so many times in the period under study as to make anyone dizzy in trying to reconstruct the details of each particular conflict. The count-kings (a term used to identify the rulers of Aragon, Catalonia, and Valencia) faced frequent military campaigns in the Mediterranean, from a long and protracted insurrection in Sardinia to military incursions in the Levant. Granada remained a point of constant armed hostility. Wars with other Iberian kingdoms were frequent (Castile's wars against Portugal seem to have been as much of a recurring act as Castile's armed struggles against Aragon). One needs to emphasize that, although the Spanish kingdoms did not know the full misery that was visited on France at Crecy, Poitiers, and Agincourt (the great battles of the Hundred Years War, all won by England), Castile and Aragon faced misery and expense enough.

Plague

Far more damning to all the Spanish kingdoms was the plague. The Black Death, a named derived from the dark boils or bulbous growths that appeared on the victims' bodies, made its way from the East and entered western Europe in merchant ships arriving in Sicily. Transmitted by flea bites or airborne by coughing and sneezing, the plague, in its most virulent form, was almost always fatal. The bubonic plague swept most of Europe between 1347 and 1351, though its greatest impact and virulence was felt between 1348 and 1350. Historians have estimated that between one-third and as much as one-half of the entire population of western Europe died as a consequence of the plague, but these percentages do not reflect the grim realities brought about by pestilence. While some localities escaped unscathed others suffered greatly or were completely wiped out.

For the Spanish realms, one must assume that the plague reached the peninsula through eastern or southern ports, spreading inland from the coastal areas. When this happened or how plague was carried to specific areas is, however, not known. In Castile, the ordinances of the Cortes, the *Libro becerro de las behetrías*, and the chronicles of Alfonso XI (1312–50) and Peter I (1350–66) mention in passing the *grand mortandad* (the large number of people killed by the plague). We do not have for any of the Spanish realms the dramatic descriptions that are extant for Florence, Siena, or France: the first-hand accounts of Boccaccio, Agnolo di Tura, and others. We do not know precisely how many people actually died, or what were the long-term consequences of the plague, though historians have long argued about the short- and long-term effects of the sickness. We do, however, have enough tangential, and sometimes even explicit, information to begin to comprehend the Black Death's devastating impact. First, as noted earlier, the only ruler to die from the plague in all of Europe was Alfonso XI, king of Castile, who died of the sickness in 1350 while at the siege of Gibraltar. Alfonso's death was a terrible blow to Castile and opened a period of civil disturbances. As for the campaigns against the Merinids, the siege had to be lifted as the plague spread among the combatants, making military operations impossible for a year or so.

We also know that in both the Crown of Aragon and in Castile the documentation for the period between 1350 and 1360 is sparse. It seems, as one looks into the archives or in published collections, as if life had stopped. The cathedral of Burgos, to give just a single example, had one of the most active scriptoria in all of Castile, with records kept of all the grants the church received and the chapter's management of its benefices. Although the number of documents extant in the cathedral archives seems to have been

Table 2.3   Number of Documents Extant in Northern Castile, 1350–1369 (partial)

Place	1330–9	1340–9	1350–9	1360–9
Burgos cathedral	76	68	41	34
Mons. San Juan	9	7	1	2
Santo Domingo de la Calzada	13	4	9	8
Albelda and Logroño	15	27	19	17

Source: Ruiz, *Crisis and Continuity*, 320.

declining from the 1320s onwards – perhaps as a reflection of the crises – for the 15 years between 1350 and 1365 the number drops dramatically. Table 2.3, reflecting extant holdings in cathedral and monastic archives throughout the region, may help us understand how the plague slowed down the pace of life in northern Castile. At the cathedral of Burgos there are no extant documents for the period between October 2, 1349 and March 9, 1350, reflecting perhaps the height of the plague's impact on the city. The table also shows the uneven reaction to the spread of the pestilence, even in areas which, as is the case on the institutions mentioned in the table, were close to each other and all connected by the pilgrimage road.

Material transactions – selling and buying of lands, land leases, and other economic exchanges – declined precipitously. The few such transactions extant for the period point to a world in which, at least in some localities, it was hard to find labor. There are extant agreements in which a landowner would give half of his property away to someone in return for five years of labor on his remaining half. The rents which the cathedral of Burgos collected from farms and mills dropped by almost half, and in the case of mills, where extant sources allow us to trace the movements of rents over decades, not only did the cost of renting a mill fall by 50 percent or more, but the cathedral chapter was unable to find clients for some of its mills. The attempts to set prices and introduce wage controls at the meeting of the Castilian Cortes in 1351 also reflected the dearth of labor and the need to secure workers at a reasonable price. In Castile, as has been noted, there were also failed attempts to impose harsh work obligations on agricultural labor and to tie peasants to the soil. The latter was an unprecedented move in a land, such as Castile, without a history of bondage.

Spanish historians have long argued that the population levels existing in Spain before the Black Death were not restored until the end of the fifteenth century and the beginning of the sixteenth. That is, it took almost a century and a half to return to the pre-plague level. Whether because of the plague or because of deteriorating economic conditions that had plagued the region from the 1250s onwards, in the great *Libro becerro de las behetrías*, a great survey of peasants' fiscal obligations to their ecclesiastical, noble, and royal lords undertaken in 1351, more than one-fifth of all the villages in northern Castile were either deserted or had experienced drastic demographic decline. Many of these villages were never repopulated and remained only as slowly vanishing references to their previous existence in later documents (see table 2.2 above).

In the Crown of Aragon, especially in Barcelona and its hinterland, the information is far more precise. Local histories, such as that of Girona, point to rates of mortality fluctuating between 25 and 35 percent, but in the nearby plain of Vic and its eponymous diocesan center as many as two-thirds of the population may have been killed by the pestilence. Catalonia seems to have been particularly hard hit, the plague taking almost half of its population. There, more than anywhere else, the plague may have had a devastating and long-term impact. Recurrences of the illness, though not always with the same etiology or with anything approaching the same mortality rate, took a heavy toll on the lives and morale of people in Catalonia and elsewhere in Spain. In the case of Barcelona, and by extension Catalonia, the plague may have been the most important factor for the city's and the region's decline in the late Middle Ages.

Other social, cultural, and psychological consequences emerged from the plague years. Not different from other parts of Europe, the Black Death unleashed long-simmering anti-Jewish sentiments in many parts of Spain. Although violence against the Jews and, to a lesser extent, against the Muslims was not universal, blaming religious minorities for the catastrophes in Barcelona, Valencia, and other areas set the stage for even more widespread violence in 1391. Since these attacks, though triggered by the plague, are part of the much larger history of Christian, Jewish, and Muslim relations, they will be examined in greater detail in chapter 7. For now, one must remember what a tragic mix it was. As the plague struck down people indiscriminately (and Jews and Muslims in equal or larger ratios), one of the favorite responses to the pestilence's onslaught was to attack, rob, and kill Jews and Mudejars. The plague was not just about one getting sick and most probably dying. It was also about providing new openings for violence and social upheaval, and challenging the ability of medieval rulers to preserve order and protect their subjects.

The Black Death came also in the wake of demographic losses and dislocations, of violence by a rapacious nobility, of almost endemic internecine conflict. The plague encouraged selfishness and punished selflessness – those who fled usually lived, those who stayed and helped the sick usually died. The sickness must have had a deleterious impact on the people who lived through the horror. The morbidity of daily life, the vivid representations of death and dying in contemporary art, the new cults of suffering, and other such responses are all echoed in the *General Dance of Death* (written in the late fourteenth century), and in the pessimistic poetry of the period, such, as for example, Rabbi Sentob of Carrión's *Proverbios morales* (see chapter 8). These and other works, with their emphasis on death, gave a pessimistic and lugubrious patina to the age. The plague may have been after all just another one of the many problems besetting society, but its impact was swift and profound.

Rebellion

The history of social risings in the Spanish realms in the late Middle Ages is a complex and contradictory one. In most parts of western Europe either the failure of the nobility or the Crown's rapacity led to a complete break-down of the social order and to widespread and large regional uprisings. Remarkably, the Spanish realms witnessed such risings only on the periphery and never at the centre. Social conflicts were of course widespread throughout Spain. These ranged from vocal and violent encounters at the meetings of Castilian municipal councils, when disfranchised taxpayers came to protest the urban patriciate's social and political monopoly of urban institutions – as can be deduced from Alfonso XI's charter creating the *regimiento* (see chapter 6) – to peasant raids on each other's properties or their refusal to pay rents to their ecclesiastical lords. There was in Spain during the Middle Ages a permanent level of violence and resistance.[24] Along the same pattern, anti-Jewish and anti-Muslim violence or the urban disturbances at Alcaraz, chronicled in detail by Angus MacKay, can also be seen as part of an enduring legacy of violence against noble oppression or social inequality. Nonetheless, neither in Castile, Aragon, or Valencia do we find large uprisings. Large regional rebellions had to wait for the sixteenth century: the *comunero* revolt in Castile in 1521, the Valencian *Germanías* in the same year, and the risings in Aragon in 1592. And even these uprisings were very different from each other, with only the *Germanías* having a real popular flavor.

I have long been intrigued by the absence of large uprisings at the core of the medieval Spanish realms, especially considering how troubled social and economic conditions were. Only the year 1391, which witnessed widespread attacks against the Jews, approached the level of contemporary rebellions in the rest of Europe. My own attempts to answer these questions have so far been unsatisfactory and inconclusive, and only a multiperspectival explanation can be offered. The ebb and flow of the Reconquest and the constant conflict with the Moorish kingdoms provided a release for pent-up anger. Raids against Muslim lands in a society where most males, regardless of social filiation, were liable for military service was a form of escape from irreconcilable social tensions. The martial nature of the Castilian monarchy and its non-sacral character (see chapter 6) also eliminated some of the religious motivations for widespread resistance. In other words, there is no evidence of the kind of millenarian agitation found, for example, in the 1381 English risings or in the Hussite upheavals in fifteenth-century central Europe. The targeting of Jews, conversos, and, to a lesser extent, Muslims as victims of popular unrest also worked to fend off direct confrontations with the established order. It is true that anti-Jewish violence was partly an attack against those above, specifically the Crown and the nobility. Jews and conversos were clearly identified as being complicit with the Crown and the nobility as tax farmers, collectors, and administrators. In Morvedre, as Mark Meyerson has shown, Jews served as the town's *baillis* in the late thirteenth century to endless complaints by the Christian population.[25] For these reasons and other social and economic factors that are not easily perceptible as deterring rebellion – a large wool export economy in Castile after 1350 and the importance of the transhumance, tribute from Jews and Mudejars – neither of the two main kingdoms of Aragon and Castile witnessed widespread popular unrest.

But the Spanish realms did have a popular uprising which was peculiar in many respects. The revolt of the *remenças* (peasants bound to the soil who had to pay a fee, a *remença*, to obtain their freedom) in northern Catalonia lasted for more than two centuries, making it more of a long-term insurgency than an actual rebellion. The *remenças* uprising included alliances between the king of the Crown of Aragon and the peasants against elements of the high nobility and even commercial urban interests. As such the *remenças* were not typical of the fourteenth- and fifteenth-century uprisings elsewhere in Europe, which pitted those below against those on top. Their rebellion was instead part of a complex political process; the outcome was a political one as well. *Remença* representatives were so well organized and capable as to be able to travel to the Neapolitan court of Alfonso V, the ruler of the Realms of Aragon, sometime between 1450 and 1455 after the king had granted the peasants the right of association in 1448. Although they could negotiate directly with the Crown, the Old Catalonian peasants' rebellion was not, as Paul Freedman has pointed out, "the revolt of a confident, privileged segment of the peasantry, throwing aside a few vestigial and annoying rights. It was, rather, a hard-fought struggle over seigneurial power."[26] They had real grievances. Their status and the harsh conditions (*mals usos*) under which they labored and lived were completely out of step with conditions elsewhere in Europe and the rest of Iberia. The *remenças* were serfs and, as such, bound to the soil, toiling under heavy social and economic burdens, open to predatory lordly assaults on their women and daughters. One of their grievances was precisely the exploitation of their women, who were drafted as wet-nurses to the prejudice and ill health of their own children. And, finally, *remenças* were quite unique in that they were successful! At the Sentencia of Guadalupe (1486), Ferdinand II, king of the Crown of Aragon and consort to Isabella of Castile, granted the peasants the right to purchase their freedom. This they did, moving from bondage to freedom and from dismal conditions to relative prosperity by the end of the Middle Ages and the beginnings of the early modern period.

One is almost forced to ask, at the end of this litany of disasters and crises, how the Castilians, Aragonese, Catalans, and Valencians managed to endure. Endure they did. The crises themselves were not as monochrome or as continuous as depicted here. They endured because rulers and subjects strove doggedly against the troubles of the age. Long ago my teacher, Joseph R. Strayer, wrote about the promise of the fourteenth century and how, in the midst of great catastrophes, the institutions and cultural revival of the late fifteenth century were forged as a response to the evils of the time. It is to these responses and promises that we turn now.

Chapter 3

The Answers of Politics

Spain, 1300–1350

Faced with what seemed almost insurmountable challenges, Spanish rulers developed political strategies and programs, seeking to ameliorate the tide of plagues, bad weather, civil strife, and general violence. These responses were not always successful or even consciously undertaken. To begin with, many of the difficulties were, as has been seen, the outcome of the selfishness of the nobles or of the urban elites' political maneuvering on behalf of their own interests. More often than not, some measures, meant to alleviate specific problems, only worsened them. But slowly over the century and a half between 1300 and 1469, administrative, institutional, and cultural foundations were laid down that allowed for a restoration of central authority and for Spain's eventual ascendancy to the forefront of the European powers by the end of the Middle Ages.

Introduction

In examining the responses to crises, this chapter and the next three will provide brief chronological accounts of political developments in medieval Spain's two core polities: the kingdom of Castile and the Crown of Aragon. There is certainly a plethora of good political narratives for the period under study, and these three chapters make liberal use of them. But to tell what happened is not enough. Questions to be raised in these chapters, and to be reprised later on in chapter 6, are: How did kings in this period relate to the nobility, to the Cortes, and to the cities in their respective realms? What were the relations between Castile and the Crown of Aragon, and between the core realms and other kingdoms in Iberia and Europe? What sort of institutional reforms were implemented? How successfully? What was the nature of kingship in both areas?

These questions barely begin to tap the ebb and flow of social and political transformations that occurred in this period. Special attention must also be given in a separate chapter (chapter 7) to Christians' relations with the Jews and Muslims in their midst. The changing royal treatment of religious minorities was also a manifestation of and a response to the instability of the late Middle Ages. Similarly, culture in general, from changes in religious observance and extravagant festivals to the writing of romances and other literary creations, represented yet another response to the harsh realities of daily life in fourteenth- and fifteenth-century Spain (see chapter 8).

In describing political developments in the Iberian peninsula one is always faced with the unresolved question of chronological periodization. Kings in each of the realms did not rule precisely at the same time; nor do extraneous temporal landmarks – the plague or the violence against the Jews in 1391 – though peninsula-wide phenomena, provide proper chronological boundaries. For the sake of clarity, I have divided the description of political life into three periods. The first one begins shortly before 1300 and extends to 1350 for Castile and to the end of the reign of Peter IV, the Ceremonious, in 1387 for Aragon. For Castile, our terminus is a logical one, as 1350 coincided with the worst onslaught of the Black Death and with Alfonso XI's death. For Aragon, Peter IV's long and productive reign is almost a period unto itself. A second chronological set runs between 1350 in Castile and 1387 in Aragon to the Compromise of Caspe in 1412 when the regent of Castile, Ferdinand of Antequera, was elected king of the Crown of Aragon. From 1412 onwards one family, the Trastámaras, ruled Castile, the Crown of Aragon, and, by the early half of the fifteenth century, Navarre as well. Chapter 5, therefore, carries the story from 1412 to the marriage of Ferdinand of Aragon and Isabella of Castile in 1469 and to the early years of Isabella's reign in 1474, when Ferdinand succeeded to the Crown of Aragon. Close familial ties in this later period did often generate far more problems than encourage peaceful cooperation.

Castile, 1300–1350

Ferdinand IV (1295–1312)

Ferdinand IV's short – a mere 17 years, of which six were taken by his minority and a bitterly contested regency – and undistinguished reign came closer to the political fragmentation of the kingdom than at any other time during the fourteenth and fifteenth centuries. His rule saw a further increase in the high nobility's demands for a share in the political and economic administration of the Castilian realm and in their arrogance and wanton violence. The early fourteenth century also witnessed the selfish and disruptive behavior of the princes of the blood. It seems that in the late Middle Ages, above all in Castile, there were always far more younger members of the royal family than was necessary for the health of the kingdom or for an orderly royal succession. And, finally, balancing all these unwelcome developments, the weakness of the Crown prompted the urban elites and representative assemblies of Castile (Cortes) to take on new responsibilities and power.

In 1300 Ferdinand IV, born on December 6, 1285, ruled over the diverse kingdoms that comprised Castile-León. Having become king on the death of his father, he inherited not only the extensive political troubles left by Sancho IV, but also the contested claims to his rule. His parents' marriage had been declared an uncanonical union. His own father, Sancho IV, had illegally and against the wishes of his own father and king, Alfonso X, set aside his nephew Alfonso de la Cerda's rightful claims to the throne and wrested the Crown from him by force and rebellion. In reality, old Castilian custom gave Sancho the right to the throne, but Alfonso X's *Siete partidas* (not a legal code in force at that time) emphasized the right of primogeniture and Alfonso de la Cerda's (the son of Alfonso X's first deceased child) right to the throne. Thus Sancho IV came to the throne on the basis of flimsy claims, and his own father had cursed him on his deathbed and willed the throne elsewhere.[1] Sancho IV's reign is already described in great detail by Peter Linehan in an earlier volume in this series.[2] Sancho was not a fool or an incompetent ruler, though he was rather brutal in dealing with his enemies. He had, however, done something very right. His wife and queen, María de Molina, was a woman of extraordinary abilities, character, and resourcefulness. Becoming a regent for her son in 1295, she was able to balance and neutralize the princes of the blood, who wished for nothing better than to despoil the kingdom, or even capture the crown.

In spite of María's abilities, the six years between Ferdinand IV's ascent to the throne and his coming of age in 1301 were troubled years indeed. Though, as we have seen in chapter 2, serious economic problems were in the making in this period, for contemporaries the crisis was mostly about politics and power. C. González Mínguez, one of the few recent scholars who has studied Ferdinand IV's reign in detail, describes the period between 1295 and 1301 as the harshest in the enduring "civil war" besetting the country. The six-year regency, longer than usual, was dominated by the figure of the queen mother and by her efforts to restore order and to find support for her vulnerable son. An early tentative regency or governing council was organized in the wake of Sancho's death. It included Don

Gonzalo, the powerful archbishop of Toledo, the Infante Henry (Don Enrique, a younger brother of Alfonso X, uncle to Sancho IV, grand-uncle to Ferdinand IV, and a major troublemaker in the mid-1250s), and Don Nuño González de Lara, a representative of the high nobility. Cancelling an unpopular tax that had been levied by Sancho IV and that negatively affected commercial exchanges, the queen mother and her lukewarm and unreliable allies sought to secure urban support for the young king.

María de Molina's initial efforts were not particularly successful. The Infante John (Don Juan), taking a leaf from the book of the previous king, his brother Sancho IV, declared himself the rightful king in western Andalusia with the support of Muslim allies. At the other end of the kingdom, in eastern Castile, Don Diego López de Haro, brother to the recently murdered Don Lope Díaz de Haro, marched westward and reclaimed the lordship of Vizcaya, appropriated by the Crown after his brother's death in 1288. Betrayed by her allies, the Laras and the Infante Henry – each of them keenly eager to advance their own particular agenda – the queen mother turned to the municipal councils as the last bulwark for the preservation of royal authority and as the only defenders of the Crown against noble ambitions.

In a behavior pattern – specially in periods of troubled and contested minorities – repeated numberless times from the mid-thirteenth century to the rule of the Catholic Monarchs, most of the Castilian towns and most of the urban representatives to the Cortes rallied to the defense of the realm. This they did not do out of selfless love for the monarch and monarchy, though most of the main northern Castilian cities – Avila, Burgos, Segovia, Valladolid, and others – proved remarkably loyal to the Crown, but because the high nobility's anarchic actions were terrible for business and because the king was the ultimate source of urban privilege and tax exemption. At the Cortes of Valladolid (1295) María de Molina came close to complete defeat, her son's reign tilting in the balance. Her fellow co-regents betrayed her, pursuing their own alliances and seeking to gain as much from the process as possible. Initially the urban oligarchy of Valladolid had even refused her and her son entry into the city. Yet at the Cortes of Valladolid, while the queen mother granted the urban procurators the right to collect taxes and to control fortresses in their respective cities' hinterlands, she gained precious support for her son. The Cortes recognized Fernando IV as the rightful king. These actions thwarted other noble pretenders to the Crown and signaled the urban centers' commitment to the survival of the dynasty and to order.[3] This pattern, imitated in future minorities and during some of the most difficult stretches in Castilian history, did not always work or lead to similar outcomes, but it worked fairly well sufficient times to preserve royal authority. The great Isabella herself made her claims to the Crown legitimate because of similar circumstances and the towns and Cortes' support. That is, the threat of noble rebellion often drew the towns of Castile into action in support of the king. That meant substantial fiscal resources and formidable urban militias placed at the Crown's service.

In the case of María de Molina and her son, Ferdinand IV, the issues were quite complex. Gaining urban support meant substantial concessions to the towns and the recognition of extensive urban autonomy. In many respects the history of Castile and, after 1474, Spain, is the history of the Crown's sustained efforts to erode or roll back urban privileges that had been granted in times of need. In 1295, however, the civil war troubling Ferdinand IV's minority led to the growing political role of urban centers and of procurators attending the frequent meetings of the Cortes. In the early fourteenth century, the Crown could not endure without urban support, and out of that need arose the decision to reckon with the urban elite's place in the governing of the realm and the heavy price to be paid for an alliance with urban centers. To gain Ferdinand IV's recognition as the legitimate heir and king, the Crown had to bribe its noble, ecclesiastical, and urban allies with concessions which limited royal authority and diminished its fiscal and political control of the realm.

The political ebb and flow of the young king's first year are too complex and involved to detail here fully. The Infante John's claims to the throne with the support of the king of Granada and, initially, with that of the king of Portugal, turned the struggle for the regency into an international conflict. The Portuguese monarch's intrusion into the conflict over the regency and the near-anarchy of Castile's succession politics drew substantial territorial concessions from María de Molina and an offer of marriage between Ferdinand IV and a Portuguese princess. This diverted a full Portuguese invasion, but did not buy full Portuguese cooperation. In the east, James II (Jaume II), king of the Crown of Aragon, also entered the fray, pushing into Castilian territory (specially in the area of Murcia), while supporting the claims of Alfonso de la Cerda to the throne. In 1295–6 Castile had been invaded on every front. In the west, the Portuguese, after their fleeting alliance with María de Molina and her son, turned their backs on their promise and allied once again with the rebellious Infante John. In the south and the east, armies from Granada and Aragon entered Castile and occupied substantial territory. That year, two claimants to the throne – the Infante John, who had been crowned king in the ancient city of León, and Alfonso de la Cerda, who, according to primogeniture and Alfonso X's will, had the best claim to the throne – forcefully moved to establish their claims to the realm. In the case of Alfonso de la Cerda, besides the Aragonese support, his claims had been recognized by the king of France. As this was not enough, in the northeast the powerful noble clan of the Haros and other thuggish noblemen created havoc throughout the region.

Only by understanding this free for all can one also understand to what extent the Castilian structural crises had a grim counterpart in the political arena. Only by seeing how desperate the situation was in 1295–6 can one judge the achievements of María de Molina in ushering her son to his majority and to his inheritance. As we come to the close of the thirteenth century, Castile stood on the edge of a precipice. Only the queen mother's ceaseless toil and her cunning use of bribes and concessions permitted the survival of a united realm. One real possibility in 1295–6 would have been a reversal to the fragmented kingdoms of earlier centuries. León, Asturias, and Galicia may have re-emerged as distinct kingdoms. Most of Andalusia could have become a la Cerda-ruled new realm. The Castilian political quandaries around 1300 only point to the fragility of most medieval political constructions in this period in spite of the progress kings had made in establishing their authority in the twelfth and thirteenth centuries. They also reaffirm – and this is worth repeating – the tremendous achievements of María de Molina in keeping her son's inheritance fairly undiminished in the face of such opposition.[4]

Even after Ferdinand IV came of age in 1301, the troubles did not abate, nor did, for that matter, the queen mother's tireless efforts on behalf of Castile and her son. As Ferdinand approached his majority, a series of circumstances helped turn the tide somewhat. First and foremost, the nobles were, as would be the case throughout the next 150 years, unable to act together with a single purpose. Gains by one faction of the nobility or familial clan immediately provoked the mistrust and opposition of other noble groups. The high nobility (magnates, *ricos hombres*) remained a painful thorn on the side of the Crown, but they could seldom agree on a long-term agenda. At the same time, James II, ruler of the Realms of Aragon, faced mounting difficulties and challenges in his own kingdoms, thwarting his interference in Castile and his support for war there. Eventually he had to turn his attention to pressing internal matters in the Crown of Aragon, abandoning Alfonso de la Cerda's cause. And the Castilian economy seems to have improved slightly, in spite of the political disturbances and a ferocious famine (see chapter 2). This allowed María de Molina and her son to make further fiscal concessions in a renewed search for urban and noble support. Also important for the survival of Ferdinand IV's rule was the papal bull which legitimized Sancho IV and María de Molina's children in 1301. The papal decision removed the most useful excuse – that Ferdinand IV was illegitimate – from those seeking to overthrow the king. The manner in which the queen mother borrowed from the vast symbolic and festive resources available to medieval rulers is worth the telling. When rumors began to circulate that the papal bull was a forgery, she ordered a solemn mass at the cathedral of Burgos. After the mass concluded, she had the papal document read to the throngs of nobles and citizens of Burgos assembled in the cathedral.[5]

In spite of this papal affirmation of the king's legitimacy, intermittent warfare between the Spanish realms and between factions of the nobility and the Castilian Crown continued at a steady pace during the years after Ferdinand IV's assumption of the Crown as an adult in 1301. As late as 1304, Aragonese control over most of Murcia was still under arbitration. And although negotiations that year – coupled with the death of the scheming Infante Henry – led to Alfonso de la Cerda's renunciation of his claims to the Castilian throne and the return of most of Murcia to Castile, the Aragonese still kept some important territorial gains in the region, including the cities of Alicante and Orihuela and other strategic places.[6]

In the topsy-turvy world of Castilian politics, the fierce struggle between Castile and Aragon gave way in 1306 to an alliance against Granada and to a complex triangular relationship between the North African Merinids, Castile, and Aragon against Granada's ruler, Muhammad III (1302–9). So much for the Reconquest! Though the Merinids had been, and remained, a far greater threat to Castile than Granada, Ferdinand IV was willing to play the diplomatic game in the hope of gains on his southern frontier. The capture of Gibraltar in August 1309 was perhaps the most notable military success of his otherwise undistinguished rule, but even that victory proved ephemeral. A treaty with Portugal, including a marriage to a Portuguese royal Infanta, brought some semblance of peace to the western frontier and diminished Portuguese support for rebellious nobles there. Yet this limited success was paid for, as noted above, by significant territorial losses to the Crown of Aragon. At home, the endemic violence, greed, and arrogance of the high nobility and royal princes set the stage for further troubles in the near future. When, on September 7, 1312, Ferdinand IV, barely 27 years old, died of maladies the nature of which historians are not fully agreed on (probably a heart attack), his son, Alfonso XI, not yet 1 year old, inherited a troubled kingdom and a rebellious and troublesome nobility. And, once again, the aging María de Molina had to rush to the breach to try to save her grandson's throne, as she had done her son's.

Alfonso XI (1312–1350)

One of the most interesting rulers of medieval Castile, Alfonso XI's reign still awaits some enterprising historian to provide us with a political biography and full study. Many of the documents from his long reign have now been published, and together with the chronicle(s) detailing the many and varied events that took place during it, these sources provide a formidable window onto Castilian society in the first half of the fourteenth century.[7]

Alfonso XI's 38-year rule can be divided into two distinct periods. Having become king when he was barely a year old, during the first 13 years of his reign, from 1312 to 1325, Castile was ruled by a regency in which María de Molina played a significant role until her death in 1321. As in most periods of minority, despite María de Molina's resourcefulness, the prevalent mood was one of anarchy and factional struggles between the king's uncles and other relatives, the high nobility, and the urban elites. As already seen, the onset of the late medieval crisis hit Castile particularly hard in the 1310s and 1320s. Contemporary accounts, above all the chronicle of Alfonso XI, decried the waves of violence and the spoiling of the realm. Most of the regents – the regency was a veritable carousel which regents got on and off depending on political circumstances – took little or no action to address the violence sweeping the land. Either because of their incompetence or greed, or because inaction (or the wrong action) was the way to secure the support of some faction of the high nobility, most of the regents followed policies which ran counter to the interests of the young king or the realm.[8]

The regency drew some familiar faces from Ferdinand IV's minority 17 years earlier. María de Molina, Alfonso XI's grandmother, again took on the central responsibility for defending the Crown. Her son and Alfonso XI's uncle, the Infante Peter (Don Pedro), also played a central role. The Infante John, Alfonso XI's grand-uncle and Sancho IV's brother, became an important figure in the new regency as well. This was the same Infante John who rebelled against Ferdinand IV and attempted to wrest the crown from the minor king between 1295 and 1301. His presence, almost as co-equal to María de Molina, speaks volumes about the fluidity of Castile's political landscape and the unsavory alliances that political exigencies forced upon those who ruled. In early documents from Alfonso XI's reign (1313, 1314, and so on), the queen mother is described as "my grandmother and tutor with whom is now *la chancillería* [the administrative and judicial royal authority] [as well] as the Infante Don Juan my tutor."[9] It is significant to note that María de Molina had kept control of the chancery in her hands. In later documents, the Infante Peter (Don Pedro), the king's uncle, is also mentioned as tutor, completing the first cast of regents. Most of the documents issued by these three in Alfonso XI's name – except for traditional confirmations of privileges – attest to deteriorating economic conditions or to growing disorder throughout Castile. As seen in chapter 2, these charters usually granted specific localities a reduction in the number of taxpayers because of the poverty of the land, the loss of population, and the excesses of the magnates.[10] Some other documents include royal letters ordering inquests into the abuses of royal officials and nobles.

In the great privileges (the so called *documentos rodados*) issued by the royal chancery and confirmed by the princes of the blood, the high ecclesiastical dignitaries, great nobility, and important royal officials, one can see a list of the entire cast of characters involved in the political disturbances plaguing Alfonso XI's minority. And since they are listed in a strict hierarchical order, one can also assume their respective power in relation to the king and to the regency, and, one should also add, responsibility for the disorder of the age. In a 1315 royal confirmation, the names of these political actors appear in a descending column of witnesses to the document. First and foremost we have the names of the main tutors, the Infantes John and Peter, followed by another member of the royal family, the Infante Philip (Don Felipe), soon to claim a significant place in the affairs of the realm. They are followed by the archbishops of Toledo and Compostela, the great ecclesiastical lords in the realm, and then Don Juan Manuel (his name is preserved here in the Castilian form because of his literary fame), a noted writer and an ambitious and perennial troublemaker who, through his descent from the beloved Ferdinand III (1217–52), claimed a leading role in Castilian affairs, even pretending the throne. We will see him in open conflict with Alfonso XI for the next three decades. This cast of great men, gathered at Burgos in August 1315, also included the heads of the leading noble families: de Haro, Saldaña, Mendoza, and others.[11]

Significantly, a mere month earlier, same year, same city, and in the presence of Alfonso XI and his regents, urban procurators from towns and cities throughout the realm joined around 100 *fijosdalgo* (lower nobility, *hidalgos*) to create an *hermandad* (see chapter 6 below), a league to combat the abuses of the powerful and to protect the property and interests of citizens and lower-ranking nobility. From every corner of the kingdom representatives from 98 different locations (more than 200 procurators altogether) came to Burgos. We know all these representatives by name, and in many cases – certainly those of Burgos, Avila, and other urban centers – can trace them back to the local documentation and place them within the specific social world of merchants and the urban patriciate. Towns sending representatives included some of the important cities in the realm – Burgos, Soria, Osuna, Segovia, Avila, León, Salamanca (but not Valladolid, Toledo, or Seville), a large number of leading Galician towns (but not Compostela), Andalusi, and Extremaduran urban centers, and coastal towns on the Bay of Biscay.[12]

This impressive urban showing illustrates the unusual alliance of urban interests with the lower nobility. They stood together, though often their fiscal and social interests were at odds, as a bulwark against the anarchic activities of some of the regents and magnates, and their bands of "feudal malefactors." In many respects, many things had changed from the previous minority. In 1295, María de Molina had been able to assert his son's legitimacy and with that his line's claims to the throne. Although some sought to assail Alfonso XI's right to rule, those doing so now stood on shakier ground. There was no serious attempt in 1315 to partition the kingdom, as had been the case in the concluding years of the thirteenth century; nor did Castile face serious foreign interference. Alfonso XI was, after all, the son of a Portuguese princess. The kings of the Crown of Aragon were caught up in Mediterranean and North African campaigns (see the discussion of the Realms of Aragon below and chapter 5) and could be placated by marriage alliances. Granada was mired in civil war, and Navarre was seriously neglected by its French masters. Far more important, the urban procurators to the Cortes, who had already been granted their wish to share in the governance of the realm during the troubled minority of Ferdinand IV, now took more decisive steps to bind the future and the survival of the monarchy to the cities. Political circumstances as well as her own proclivities led María de Molina to forge strong ties with patrician elites in the late thirteenth century. This alliance between the king and urban centers had its origins in the twelfth century and proved beneficial to both parties. The cities needed the Crown as much as the Crown needed the cities. In 1315 that alliance was reinvigorated, giving María and her grandson some breathing space to weather the storm.

In 1319 the Infantes Peter and John, both dominant members of the regency, died in battle on the Granada frontier. Immediately other claimants for control of the young king emerged, opening a new round of conflict. Yet another Infante John, son to the Infante of the same name, appears as guardian of the king in 1322, a year after María de Molina's death, but the Infante Philip and the always contentious Don Juan Manuel made sure they obtained as much profit from the confusion as possible. The latter arranged for the marriage of his daughter to the still minor king, hoping to control the Crown as the king's prospective father-in-law. But Alfonso XI surprised them all.

A mere 14 years old, Alfonso XI came of age in 1325 and immediately claimed to be able to rule on his own. And this assumption of his duties as king was accompanied by swift and bold deeds. As soon as Alfonso took these steps, the Infante John rose in open defiance of the king. Lured to a parlay at the village of Toro, Alfonso had the Infante John and his retinue murdered, following this act with the immediate confiscation of John's lands and their absorption into the royal domain. Assassination of disruptive nobles and their followers continued apace throughout the next decades.[13] Having dealt with the most immediate threat, Alfonso traveled to Segovia, where urban strife had led to the burning of one of the cathedral's towers. There he dispensed harsh justice to the guilty, cutting off their feet and hands, breaking their backs on the wheel, beheading some, and burning others. In the meantime, Don Juan Manuel, learning about the young king's decisive actions, abandoned his post as *adelantado* (the official in charge of the frontier) on Granada's border and fled to his own estates in Murcia. The king responded swiftly by reneging on his promise to marry Don Juan Manuel's daughter and made plans instead to marry the daughter of Afonso IV, king of Portugal. Since the Aragonese king has his attention focused on his own affairs, Alfonso had now the freedom to address the internal upheavals plaguing the realm.

Rather than provide a detailed description of Alfonso's long reign, it may prove far more useful to summarize some of its high (and low) points. Alfonso undertook important matrimonial alliances to secure international recognition and stability. His marriage to the Portuguese Infanta María brought peace, at least for a while, to his western frontier. His own sister Doña Leonor's marriage to Alfonso IV, king of the Realms of Aragon, brought peace on the eastern frontier. Don Juan Manuel was forced to submit and to pledge allegiance to the king (if only temporarily before reverting to his old practices) in 1329. Two years afterwards, in 1331, Alfonso de la Cerda, whose claims to the throne had so endangered Ferdinand IV's reign, renounced, once and for all, his claims to the throne in return for a substantial bribe. In 1332 in a peculiar ceremony which will be glossed in some detail in chapter 6, the king was knighted by the mechanical arm of a statue of St. James on the main altar of the cathedral in Santiago de Compostela, anointed on the shoulder, and crowned himself at the great royal Cistercian monastery of Las Huelgas de Burgos amidst great popular festivities.

In the south the rulers of Granada had been emboldened by Castile's internal strife, carrying out daring raids in western Andalusia. In addition, the Merinid rulers of Morocco entered into an alliance with Granada, now beginning to be pressed by Alfonso XI's energetic military forays in the frontier. Gibraltar fell to the Merinids in 1333, a devastating blow to the prestige of Alfonso and a critical strategic loss for Mediterranean and Atlantic seafaring. In the peninsula's confusing (a term which I use frequently in these pages) political atmosphere, main characters and alliances shifted from year to year. Thus, in spite of his marriage ties to Portugal, Alfonso XI's neglect of his queen and his open devotion to his mistress Doña Leonor de Guzmán led to worsening relations with the Lusitanian kingdom. Aragon was always suspicious of Alfonso XI's claims, specially after 1333 when the Castilian king signed a temporary peace with Morocco and Granada. Granada was of course always troubled by North African advances into the peninsula and reluctant to embrace fully and permanently an anti-Castilian coalition. Moreover, the perennial struggle for power within Granada's ruling families also meant that a new ruler, emerging from fratricidal plots, might completely change his political allies.

Throughout Castile, as much as Alfonso XI strove to restore order, violence by the nobility continued in the area of the Rioja and elsewhere, and abuses by royal agents and the high nobility remained a disturbing reality in the realm. Don Juan Manuel, though he had pledged fealty to the king, remained an active promoter of disorder jointly with Don Juan Núñez, Don Juan Alfonso de Haro, and other high nobles. The king's main focus, however, remained the frontier. After the fall of Gibraltar and the pressing Merinid threat, the *ida contra los moros*, the raids against Muslim lands, became central to Alfonso XI's policies. Not only did they appeal to the young king's chivalrous nature and crusading spirit – he has just founded the knightly order of La Banda, along the lines of but chronologically preceding the foundations of the orders of the Garter in England and the order of the Star in France – but it was also good policy. Campaigns in the south siphoned a good number of restless nobles away from troublemaking at home to a search for gains and service to the Crown. The lure of the great profit to be made always served as a powerful incentive. War against Granada or Morocco made collecting taxes and subsidies much easier. The Cortes and, most of all, a very pliant Church, could never resist the appeal of yet another crusade against Islam.

Alfonso XI's personal rule was therefore divided into attempts to restore order in northern and central Castile and frequent campaigns in the south against the Merinid and Granada's threat. Indeed a new Moroccan invasion brought a temporary cessation to the hostilities between Castile, Aragon (after Peter IV's ascent to the throne), and Portugal. With strong Portuguese support, Alfonso XI routed the Moroccan army on the banks of the river Salado on October 30, 1340. The battle checked any further threat of a North African invasion for the foreseeable future and represented the high point of Alfonso XI's military enterprises and reign. The chronicles gave the victory a signal place in their narrative, reflecting the importance that contemporaries, after a long lull in the Reconquest, attributed to the battle. It was followed by the sieges of Algeciras (taken in 1344) and Gibraltar, where the king died of the plague in 1350. Alfonso's victories began to promote in earnest, though much delayed by internal problems, Castile's long-standing claims to North Africa.[14]

On the home front, Alfonso XI carried out an important legislative reform at the Cortes of Alcalá de Henares in 1348 and forcefully curtailed urban autonomy and strife by naming royal officials to municipal posts (see chapter 6). Thus, in spite of the different crises that plagued his reign – violence of the nobles, demographic decline, international strife, and localized famines – the king made great strides toward restoring order and setting the realm on the right course.

All these things, however, he undid by his marital practices. His obvious disdain for his wife, and his love for his mistress, Doña Leonor de Guzmán, sowed the seeds for endless trouble after his death. Alfonso XI's legitimate and only heir was Peter (Pedro) I, but with Leonor he had a large number of children, most of them sons. To them he gave large estates, important positions, and titles. These grants included the mastership of the order of Santiago with all the fiscal and military resources associated with the order. The king's bastards, known collectively as the Trastámaras (from one of the titles given to the oldest, Henry [Enrique] of Trastámara), became first in the land, to the great and justified resentment of the Queen María and the heir Peter. When Alfonso XI died, refusing to abandon the siege of Gibraltar because of the appearance of the plague, his body was escorted to Seville by his bastard children and Leonor de Guzmán's relatives. But before entering Seville, they abandoned the cortège for fear of Peter's reprisals. In the next two decades and for many years afterwards, there would be hell to pay for Alfonso's having made his mistress Leonor and their many children together his real family in terms of affection and gifts.

The Crown of Aragon, 1300–1387

The Crown of Aragon's political developments in the fourteenth and early fifteenth centuries were shaped by three significant events in the previous century. Although these developments are explained in careful detail in an earlier volume in this series, we should note, even if briefly, these landmark events. They were, first, the battle of Muret (1213), in which Peter II (1196–1213), king of Aragon and count of Barcelona, died defending Catalonian rights in southern France and, ironically for a king known as "the Catholic," the heretical Albigensians from northern crusaders. Peter's defeat had important consequences for the Aragonese–Catalan realms. Although the Crown of Aragon remained a player north of the Pyrenees, for all practical purposes Catalonian hopes for hegemony in ancient Occitania were now at an end. This new political reality was ratified at the treaty of Corbeil (1258), in which James I gave up Aragonese–Catalan claims throughout most of Occitania.

Second, these losses may have become palatable because in 1238, James I, one of the greatest kings to rule the Crown of Aragon, conquered the kingdom of Valencia and its eponymous capital city. The *taifa* kingdom of Valencia was a rich prize indeed. With fertile and well-irrigated lands, the fabled *huerta* (garden) of Valencia, worked, after the Christian conquests, by the great husbandry skills of Mudejars, was one of the most fertile and productive agricultural regions in the entire peninsula. The capital city, Valencia, benefited from a great port and soon rose to be one of the great commercial entrepôts of Iberia, overtaking Barcelona in terms of population and commercial activity. Valencia was thus ideally located for forays into the western Mediterranean and North Africa. The city and kingdom also had a substantial Muslim or Mudejar population whose members remained important contributors to the Valencian economy. Instead of being expelled as was the case in western al-Andalus, the Mudejars remained on the land, to the great profit of their lords and the kingdom. Far more significantly, even though Valencia was conquered by an army of Aragonese and Catalans, James I chose not to annex his newly conquered kingdom to either Aragon or Catalonia or to partition it. Instead, he created a new political entity within the Union (the formal agreement joining Aragon and Catalonia). As such Valencia emerged as a distinct realm with its own laws, representative assembly, and equal status with the other two kingdoms.

Third, in the thirteenth century, the Crown of Aragon became deeply involved in Mediterranean affairs. Upon James I's death, the three realms of the Crown of Aragon (Aragon, Catalonia, and Valencia) went to his firstborn son, Peter (Pere, who ruled as Pere III in Aragon and Pere II in Catalonia), and the new kingdom of Majorca, with Perpignan as its administrative center, and rights to Montpellier and other lands north of the Pyrenees, went to his second son James (Jaume) II. Although faced with the usual unrest, Peter III soon pacified the Crown of Aragon, opening the door for ventures in the Mediterranean.

The most important of his moves was the capture of Sicily. Sicily was an important island in the Mediterranean, serving, once in Aragonese–Catalan hands, as a link between the Crown of Aragon's eastern and western Mediterranean markets. Sicily had a rich history and tradition. Under Frederick II, the great Hohenstaufen ruler and German emperor, Sicily had acquired a prominent place in Europe's political world. After Frederick's death in 1250, a coalition of French and papal forces hounded his successors and imposed, against the wishes of the Sicilian people, a French dynasty on the island. It did not last very long. On March 30, 1282, the people of Sicily rose up in arms against the French, put them to death, and called the Aragonese king to come and claim the island (Peter III had claims to the island through his marriage to Constance, Frederick's descendant). In reality, it was not so simple. The Aragonese king had been preparing for the conquest of Sicily for more than a year and, under the cover of a crusade in North Africa, an Aragonese–Catalan fleet was strategically placed off the coast of Sicily ready to land. It was, as Thomas Bisson has argued, one of the easiest annexations of a realm to the Crown of Aragon. Far more significantly, the Sicilian Vespers allowed Spanish entry into the Italian peninsula.[15]

But the annexation of Sicily was not necessarily a painless process. The Papacy had long sworn eternal hatred against Frederick II and his descendants, and the usual papal weapons of excommunication, interdict (of Sicily), and releasing Peter III's vassals from any allegiance to him was soon followed by an invasion of Aragon by French troops in 1286. Parallel to this, noble disturbances and an urban revolt in Barcelona created havoc in the Aragonese–Catalan realms. Against all these enemies, Peter triumphed. The French were beaten back and internal enemies and revolts were put down forcefully. But his victory did not mean an enhancement of royal authority.

The Aragonese nobility protested vehemently that they had not been consulted on Sicilian matters. Organized into a union and meeting at Zaragoza, the rebellious nobles wrested from the king a confirmation of their ancient privileges and liberties in 1283. From this challenge to royal authority originated the office of the Justicia of Aragon (see also below and chapter 6), a sort of ombudsman whose authority, as protector of Aragonese liberties, would play a central role in Spanish politics into the early modern period. The Catalans soon followed suit. In December 1283 the Catalans demanded that all royal legislation and taxes be approved by the Catalan Corts (or representative assembly), and that meetings of the Catalan Corts be scheduled annually. The king, facing papal opposition and a French invasion, acquiesced to the demands.

Unlike other realms in the medieval West, which in the late thirteenth and early fourteenth centuries underwent dramatic transformations that allowed for a greater centralization of power in the king's hands, in the Crown of Aragon, Peter III's victories were followed by a series of concessions which formalized the relationship of the Crown to local institutions and elites. Thus, from then onwards the Corts or parliaments of the three constituent kingdoms exercised a great deal of autonomy, and Barcelona retained its traditional liberties. The kings of the Crown of Aragon saw henceforth their powers limited by the "constitutional" arrangements that emerged from the conflicts of this period.

Peter III's sons, Alfonso III (1285–91) and James (Jaume) II (1291–1327), inherited the motley territories of the Crown of Aragon. Alfonso received the Crown of Aragon proper, while James inherited Sicily, pointing to the institutional fragility of the Aragonese and Catalan realms and the difficulties of breaking away from a long tradition of partible inheritances. With their respective possessions, they also inherited the continual unrest of the Aragonese, always ready to rebel on the issue of their traditional liberties and rights, and of French and papal animosity against the Aragonese–Catalan presence in Sicily. As Thomas Bisson has noted repeatedly, the kings of the Crown of Aragon were not forceful in establishing their unchallenged rule in Aragon, choosing compromise again and again for the sake of a free hand in the Mediterranean. Alfonso III acted no differently in bowing to the demands of the Union in 1287 when he confirmed its privileges. But the king's reign was not without success, conquering Majorca, and in 1287 Muslim Minorca. The Balearic Islands, with their strategic location in the western Mediterranean, now became a natural bridge for the Crown of Aragon's involvement in Sicily and, eventually, Sardinia, Corsica, and southern Italy.

Upon Alfonso's death, after successful campaigns in the Balearic Islands, James II inherited his brother's domains and Frederick or Federico, a younger brother of Alfonso and James, became the viceroy of Sicily. But Frederick soon claimed the throne of Sicily for himself. For the next two decades, the Crown of Aragon's political life was dominated by the affair of Sicily and by the conflicts between the different branches of the Aragonese–Catalan ruling house. As an aside to these internal conflicts, Frederick sponsored a Catalan expedition to the eastern Mediterranean. In the early fourteenth century, Catalan soldiers and merchants gained a foothold in Greece, establishing the Duchy of Athens. It remained in Catalan hands late into the fourteenth century. Ramón Muntaner, one of the most distinguished chroniclers of the age and a soldier in the eastern campaigns, wrote a lively account of the Catalan–Sicilian expedition to the East. It remains one of the monuments of Catalan literature.

James II (1291–1327)

Meanwhile in the peninsula, James II proved to be, in spite of his difficulties with his brother Frederick over Sicily, one of the Crown of Aragon's most resourceful kings. He restored royal authority in Aragon (as much as it was possible to do so within the "constitutional" nature of Aragonese kingship). James II also cooperated with the kingdom of Castile in attacks against Granada and extended Aragonese–Catalan influence in North Africa and the Levant. And, after a long series of conflicts and diplomatic negotiations, he gained control of Sardinia in 1324, driving the Pisans out of the island and challenging Genoa for hegemony in the western Mediterranean. James II was a tireless and capable administrator and diplomat. His labors provided the Crown of Aragon with a fairly sophisticated bureaucracy and an efficient administrative structure (see chapter 6). His diplomatic efforts led to the addition of the counties of Urgell and Empúries to Catalonia and, through exhaustive negotiations with the French, he gained control of the economically and strategically important Val d'Aran. James II also formalized the relationship between the king (or count in the case of Catalonia) and the Corts or parliaments of the respective realms which were part of the Crown of Aragon. Working with the Corts and making them subject to an annual royal summons, James II was thus able to defuse a great deal of the latent opposition to royal authority and to provide a regular forum for dissent and complaints. Upon his death in 1327 he left a realm fairly at peace and in the midst of a brilliant cultural renewal.[16]

Alfonso IV (1327–1336)

James II's son, Alfonso IV, succeeded him to the throne in 1327. He was almost as capable as his father, but his reign was plagued with unfulfilled expectations. His alliance with Castile to conquer Granada came to nothing. His second marriage to Leonor, a Castilian princess, was fraught with difficulties and conflict about the inheritance of Peter, his son by a previous marriage. Leonor, wishing to advance the claims of her own children, tirelessly conspired against the rightful heir and became a troublesome disruption for Alfonso and for the Realms of Aragon. In the early 1330s the king gave way to his wife's insistent pleas for her son Ferrán, settling on him Tortosa, Alicante, Elche, and other important towns on Valencia's western frontier with Granada. The citizens of Valencia, however, raised serious objections at the partitioning of their kingdom and the damage done to the rightful heir's rights. In some respects, while the peculiar rights and liberties of each of the kingdoms of the Crown of Aragon made centralized rule difficult, in this particular case and other similar ones these same liberties helped to preserve the integrity of the Aragonese Union. Alfonso IV had no option but to relinquish his projected settlement on Ferrán. But the bitter animosity between the queen and her stepson bore harsh results in Peter's enduring animosity toward Castile once he ascended the throne.

Alfonso IV's willingness to step back from his original decision also reflected his Mediterranean-dominated foreign policy. The unfinished business of Sardinia loomed large in the king's concerns. Once again eastward expansion and the commercial interests of Barcelona and Valencia trumped peninsular concerns. By compromising on the home front, the rulers of the Crown of Aragon, James II, Alfonso IV, and Peter IV, while not fully preventing pervasive violence or noble and urban unrest, avoided some of the extreme situations found in neighboring Castile. That the Crown of Aragon escaped troubling minorities also had a great deal to do with its relative stability and the ease of dynastic succession. Nonetheless, the last years of Alfonso IV's short reign were also shaped by the economic crisis sweeping the peninsula and the rest of Western Christendom. Although at the Corts of Montblanch (Catalonia) in 1333, the king's and the Corts' representatives were keenly interested in regulating the activities and salaries of royal officials, limiting torture and mutilation, some of the ordinances, for example those dealing with livestock (sheep and lambs), reflected growing concern with the economy. At the end, suffering from severe illnesses and with most of his ambitious program unfulfilled, Alfonso IV died in 1336.[17]

Peter (Pere) IV (1336–1387)

His successor, Peter IV, known to historians as Peter the Ceremonious, ruled the Crown of Aragon for over 50 years, placing his powerful imprint on the Crown and on Iberian history. A formidable ruler and a learned man, Peter IV faced crucial challenges. First and foremost was how to avoid the fragmentation of the Crown of Aragon's lands into particular realms. Although the union of Aragon, Catalonia, and Valencia was essentially secure, the kingdom of Majorca (including Perpignan, the growing elusive rule over Montpellier, and the Balearic Islands of Majorca, Minorca, and Ibiza), plus Sardinia, Sicily, and parts of southern Italy, were on the brink of developing autonomously. In the case of Sicily, its rulers were willing to enter in direct competition with the Aragonese kings. Peter IV also faced increased conflicts with Castile, mostly as the result of his stepmother Leonor of Castile's schemes to advance the fortunes of her son within Valencia and other areas of the realm. And, as had been the case with his father, Peter IV had to deal with deteriorating social and economic conditions, highlighted by the Black Death that devastated the Crown of Aragon's lands in 1348–50, above all Catalonia.

What is remarkable is how very successful he was in advancing his agenda on all fronts. In dealing with the kingdom of Majorca, he used the refusal of James III, the almost independent ruler of the southern French and Balearic realms, to attend a summons to Peter's court to charge him with breaking the oath of fidelity owed by a vassal to his lord and thus forfeiting his kingdom. This was followed by an invasion of the island of Majorca, supported by a Barcelona fleet, and by the annexation of Majorca, Roussillon, and Cerdagne (the last two lands located along the border between Catalonia and France and part of the putative kingdom of Majorca). Thus, his actions prevented the emergence of an independent realm in the Mediterranean and northern flanks of Catalonia and of a fierce commercial competitor to Barcelona's mercantile activities.

His successes in the western Mediterranean and in the north were marred by widespread civil wars in Aragon, Catalonia, and Valencia. Difficulties with his own brother (yet another prince named James) led to the Aragonese nobles reviving the Union and clamoring for the protection of their vaunted liberties. Once again, Peter IV ran into the fierce opposition of the individual kingdoms seeking their liberties and taking sides on the complicated politics of succession. His two half-brothers James and, above all, Ferrán served as a rallying point for the king's enemies. In the 1340s, the kingdoms were racked by violence, and it was not until 1348, when the plague led the rebel armies to disband, that Peter IV gained the upper hand. His victory over the Unión, as the league of rebels called themselves, in 1348 was tempered by the king's confirmation of the traditional rights (*fueros*) of Aragon and by further autonomy granted to the Justicia of Aragon. By 1350 his rule was secured throughout the realms and consolidated by the birth of a male heir. Victory over rebellious subjects in Aragon was countered by new royal confirmations of Aragonese rights. In Valencia, however, a kingdom without a long political tradition of dissent, Peter IV harshly punished the rebels and revoked – though only temporarily – many of the city's liberties.

Peter IV faced other difficulties. The first was a war against Genoa. The conflict was waged not only in the western Mediterranean over Sardinia but also in the east, where Sicilian and Catalan troops in the Duchy of Athens engaged Genoese forces. The war ended with the Crown of Aragon maintaining a fragile hold over Sardinia throughout most of the king's life. Far more successful were his campaigns and diplomatic policies in Sicily. They yielded closer relations between the peninsular and insular kingdoms, when Peter IV's second son, Martín, married the heir to the Sicilian throne and became the viceroy of the island.

By the mid-fourteenth century, the Crown of Aragon and its king, Peter IV, faced yet another set of peninsular problems. The Black Death played havoc with the social and economic life of the three kingdoms. Barcelona, which had long been the center of the Aragonese–Catalan economy, began its slow and inexorable decline. In the east the Crown of Aragon became entangled in the Castilian civil war and in the spreading violence which accompanied the expansion of the Hundred Years conflict into the peninsula. For the succeeding decades, the Crown of Aragon's rulers were drawn into a series of debilitating clashes with their Castilian neighbors, to the detriment of their Mediterranean enterprises. These are topics which will be covered from the Castilian perspective in the next two chapters. The difficulties of the last years of Peter IV's reign cannot obscure, however, the king's many accomplishments. These include his enduring patronage of culture and his far-reaching administrative reforms. His rule marked an important landmark in the fortunes and development of the Crown of Aragon's social, political, and cultural life.[18]

Conclusion

We should not conclude this chapter without a brief look at other Spanish realms. During most of the thirteenth century, Navarre was either ruled by great French lords such as Thibault, count of Champagne and king of Navarre (1234–53) and his children, Thibault II (1153–1270) and Henry I (1270–4). After the marriage of Henry's daughter Jeanne to Philip the Fair, the kingdom came into the hands of the Capetian and Valois kings of France, and later the Evreux family. Only in 1425, with the marriage of the Infante of Aragon, Juan de Trastámara, to Blanca, did the kingdom somewhat revert into the world of Spanish dynastic politics (see chapter 5). Although commercially, linguistically, and culturally Navarre had more in common with Castile than with France, throughout the fourteenth century it was within France's political sphere.

The other great Spanish kingdom was Granada. After the disasters of Las Navas de Tolosa, Granada withstood the Christian thrust into the south that led to the conquests of Seville and Valencia. A combination of Christian weaknesses (due to internal conflict) and Granada's resilience and prosperity made the Nasrid kingdom an important player in peninsular affairs right up to its surrender in 1492. It could mount successful military campaigns against its Christian neighbors, though by the fourteenth century any hope of real success rested on alliances with North African rulers. In spite of a shared religion and language, the Moroccan connection proved consistently distasteful. The other problem was one of constant internal strife within Granada's royal family. Succession to the throne was always a risky business and the most perfunctory glance at the chart of Granada's kings between the early fourteenth century and the late fifteenth shows how problematic and confusing an orderly line of descent could be. Palace politics and coups, assassination, or exile led to unsavory alliances with putative enemies, and excessive concessions. It undermined Granada's natural advantages and strengths.

To contemporaries, the two core political entities in Spain in this period, Castile and Aragon, must have seemed quite dissimilar, from their language of administration (the Catalan Corts' ordinances were in Latin, those of Castile in Castilian) to their political institutions. Though Castile was far larger and had greater demographic resources throughout the period, the Aragonese kings never had their rule as seriously imperiled as those in Castile did. And the Crown of Aragon made such gains in the western Mediterranean – holding the promise of great profit and intellectual rewards – as to equal or surpass those made by Castile in the peninsula. The Crown of Aragon of course faced problems that were distinct from those of Castile and of such long-term consequence that they cross the chronological boundaries of these chapters on political developments.

Chapter 4

Toward Trastámara Spain, 1350–1412

As Spain rulers strove to meet the challenges of plague, violence, demographic losses, and economic upheavals, they also sought to fulfill their multi-pronged political agendas. First and foremost among them was expansion and crusade. It is difficult for us in the twenty-first century – or perhaps not so difficult considering the present political climate – to think that the sure, and most often invoked, answer to a deteriorating economy and to social crises was yet another raid against Granada or a campaign against Moroccan forces in the south, as was the case with Alfonso XI, or even more ambitious military enterprises, such as those of James II, Alfonso IV, and Peter IV in the Mediterranean and the Levant. Territorial expansion and crusades thus remained a vital expression of kingly authority. And there were, after all, clear benefits to such adventures. As noted earlier, substantial financial gains could be obtained on the frontier or in the Mediterranean. A restless nobility could be distracted from its challenges to the Crown into the pursuit of glory and profits elsewhere. Warlike kings were always praised by the chronicles, even if their actions mired the kingdom in endless troubles. Peaceful ones were always bitterly criticized. In the years after the Black Death, leading to the rise of the Trastámaras as the sole ruling family in Castile and after 1412 in the Crown of Aragon, rulers in these two polities engaged in a variety of moves aimed at maintaining control over their respective realms, while continuing to advance the Reconquest in southern Spain or to expand in the Mediterranean. Things did not always work as planned. Castile sank into civil war, while the Crown of Aragon reaffirmed its Mediterranean vocation, even though it also developed further along the lines of a federated model.

The Crown of Aragon from Peter IV to the Compromise of Caspe (1412)

Peter IV, the Ceremonious (1336–87)

Peter IV's long rule accounted for many successes but also some serious and, at times, long-felt reverses. While the Black Death seriously impaired the economy of the Aragonese realms and their ability to contribute to the royal fisc, Peter IV had also to deal with a debilitating insurrection in Sardinia and with the enmity of other great Mediterranean seafaring powers. At the Corts of Perpignan in 1350, while still in the midst of the devastation of the plague, the king notified the procurators from the different realms attending the meeting of the extent of the Sardinian revolt and its implications. While protesting his own poverty, the king requested a subsidy to meet the expenses of a Sardinian military campaign.[1]

After the mid-fourteenth century, Peter IV, the author of a formidable chronicle, a patron of the arts, and a ruler with a keen sense of his own dignity and of court protocol (thus his sobriquet), was drawn even deeper into a series of debilitating conflicts. Rebellion in Sardinia led to renewed conflict with the Genoese in both the western and eastern Mediterranean. Catalan victories over Genoa at sea and successive campaigns to quell resistance in Sardinia yielded only an uneasy peace. Far more troubling, continuous warfare had ruined Sardinia, denying the Crown of Aragon any substantial return for the many years of war and expense. Moreover, in spite of Genoa's defeats in 1352 and 1353 in the Bosporus and off the coast of Sardinia, the Genoese kept providing support for Sardinian rebels. Furthermore, their commercial presence in the western Mediterranean, and especially in Castile, was not seriously diminished. In fact, Peter I of Castile had strong ties with the Genoese, and, in the early years of his reign, the Castilian king was eager to flex his muscles and test his rivals. Thus, he sought to exert Castilian control over disputed territories (Murcia, Alicante, and others). Added to these growing difficulties, there was the long-lived feud, which was noted in chapter 3, between Peter IV and his contentious stepmother, Leonor of Castile.

The usual armed incursions, failed or half-hearted attempts at peace, and renewed warfare in the late 1350s led to a Castilian attempt to land in Majorca and a Castilian naval attack on Ibiza. By 1363 the Castilians, now allied with Navarre, Portugal, and the count of Foix, renewed their campaigns along the Castilian–Aragonese border, forcing Peter IV to go begging to the Corts for further subsidies.[2] With the coming of the French into the peninsula and Peter IV's alliance with France and the Trastámara pretender, Henry, the Castilian threat was temporarily deflected. A change of dynasty in Castile in 1366 did not mean, however, an end to Aragonese problems, and Murcia, the Crown of Aragon's important territorial gain on the western Valencian frontier, was lost forever. Several lessons can be drawn from this short account of Castilian–Aragonese antagonism. Even though the Crown of Aragon had made significant inroads into the Mediterranean from the thirteenth century onwards, its western flank remained vulnerable. The Castilians could not only conquer frontier areas – part of the continual shifting of borders between the two realms – but they were able to capture such important Aragonese towns as Calatayud and Valencian towns such as Morvedre, and threaten Zaragoza, Valencia (the capital cities of Aragon and Valencia respectively), and even Majorca in the Mediterranean. Although Peter I of Castile faced serious opposition at home, the kingdom of Castile was far more capable of dominating the peninsula than was Aragon. This Castilian military (as well as demographic) superiority, though not always evident, would shape relations between the two realms until the Bourbon centralization of the eighteenth century.

Conflict with Castile was ended by the usual and tired dynastic marriage, but the last years of Peter IV's rule over the Realms of Aragon were also troubled by family dissension. After his third wife, Eleanor, died in 1375, Peter IV took as his mistress Sibilla de Fortià, a woman of lower rank. When he married her in 1377 and had her crowned queen four years later, the king did so without the approval of his two sons (by his marriage to Eleanor), John (Joan) and Martin (Martí). A noble uprising in the county of Empordà toward the end of his reign and enduring troubles in Sardinia marred Peter IV's final years. Neither these problems, nor Peter IV's reverses against Castile, diminished the Crown of Aragon's gains in the Mediterranean or the administrative and cultural accomplishments of his reign (see chapters 6 and 8). Peter IV also left two sons, who followed him in rapid succession. John I had long been a king in training, reaching his thirties with ample administrative experience but always in his father's shadow. John sought to carve his own space, breaking away from the king because of Peter IV's fourth marriage to Sibilla and over differences on whom to support during the Great Schism of 1378 (John supported Clement VI, the French pope).

John I (1387–1396)

When John finally came to the throne, he did so while suffering from serious illness (most probably epilepsy) and had little of his father's diplomatic skills. At the Corts of Monzón (1388), Aragon's, Catalonia's, and Valencia's urban representatives requested a thorough judicial and administrative reorganization of the Aragonese realms. John had little patience – loving to hunt far more than the burdensome affairs of government – or taste for these parliamentary battles. His responses to the Corts' demands antagonized and rallied urban representatives against the monarch. Only the intervention of the queen, Yolande de Bar, prevented the worse. John I was indeed fortunate in his queen, for she proved to be a loyal and resourceful asset throughout his troubled reign.

In the Mediterranean his delay in responding to threats imperiled Catalan control over Sardinia, though in Sicily he moved forcefully to secure Aragonese–Catalan interests through the marriage of his nephew, Martin (son to his brother of the same name), to María, heiress to the island's crown. Although this was a good first step, restoring Aragonese–Catalan control over the island was a far more difficult task. John I also neglected his relations with Castile, favoring a French alliance and antagonizing the former without any substantial gains from the latter. On his southwestern flank, a revived Granada made feints into Valencian territory. There the large number of Mudejars, together with Granada's military presence, made for a potentially explosive combination. In 1391, to add to John I's many misfortunes, waves of violence against the Jews swept the peninsula. In the Crown of Aragon, the cities of Barcelona and Valencia, and areas in Majorca, were the sites for some of the most violent attacks on and killings of Jews, who were given the choice between conversion and death – a story to be told in greater detail in chapter 7. These events revealed deep fissures in Spain's social fabric. As Philippe Wolff pointed out in a short but influential article more than 35 years ago, the attacks against the Jews resulted in part from growing social tensions. Long-term anti-Jewish antagonism joined resistance against royal power, and anger against emerging social and economic differences to create a volatile and violent conflict. The Crown and substantial segments of the nobility and clergy rallied to protect the Jews, correctly perceiving the menacing quality of religious violence. In the end, growing social unrest and violence intersected with rising tensions between the king and his respective Corts over issues of administration, the perception of royal incompetence, legal policies, and taxation. Meanwhile, the critical issue of a divided Church, exacerbated by the election to the papal throne of Pedro de Luna as Benedict XIII (an Aragonese subject and fairly active in Aragonese politics) complicated international matters further since Benedict XIII was one of two or three elected popes contending for legitimacy in the late fourteenth century. John I's support for the Luna pope, who was a rather eccentric character at best, caused many complications. When the king died in 1396 in a riding accident, he left no direct male heirs to the throne and a weakened Aragon, at least in comparison to the state of the kingdom at the height of the reign of his formidable father, Peter IV.[3]

Martin I (1396–1410)

John I was succeeded to the throne by his brother Martin I known as the Humane. Such appellations, as noted in the previous chapter, were often not a good sign of effective kingship in the Middle Ages, meaning that kings who were too good or "humane" may not rule with the necessary force required by rebellious estates and nobles. Martin I did try, as did his wife, to address some of the problems he had inherited. While the king remained in Sicily, his wife, María de Luna, a relative of pope Benedict XIII, traveled to Barcelona to preside over the meetings of the Corts and to deal with the claim to the throne of one of John I's daughters (or rather of her husband Mateu de Foix). Since the Crown of Aragon rejected female succession, even though some of the best rulers of the period were consort queens, María de Luna was able to negotiate the Corts' acceptance of the new king and to gain a substantial subsidy from them as an incentive for Martin to return to the peninsula.[4] Having left his son, Martin the Younger, and his wife in firm possession of Sicily, the king returned to Barcelona in 1397. His peripatetic wanderings through the different capitals of his respective kingdoms – Barcelona in 1397, Zaragoza shortly afterwards, and Valencia in 1402 – is revealing of the political requirements of ruling such a federated monarchy as that of the Crown of Aragon. Visiting and residing in each of these political centers, swearing to uphold each of his kingdoms' liberties, confirming their *fueros* was a requirement. But Martin I was, for all his good intentions, drawn deeper into the Great Papal Schism's complicated politics. His family connections with Benedict XIII through his wife made him the sole ally of the pope at a time when all other European powers had abandoned the Luna pope's cause. In the end, the pope, besieged and isolated in Avignon, moved his court to Barcelona in 1409.

At home Martin I addressed three fundamental problems. The first was the dramatic losses experienced by the royal domain through Peter IV's and John I's grants to the high nobility. Following developments elsewhere in Europe, Martin I strove to recover as much of the royal domain as possible and to emphasize its inalienability (see chapter 6). Second, the king sought, not always successfully, to restore order and to curb municipal and noble abuse of their dependants. Finally, as Bisson has pointed out, the kings of the Crown of Aragon could no longer live on their personal income. The business of government had to be negotiated with the individual Corts and subsidies obtained from them if the king's policies were to be carried out at all. In that sense, the long process of organizing the governance of the realms in terms of an accepted "balance of political forces" had come to full bloom. "The king's power," in Bisson's insightful formulation, "had become that of one privileged estate among several, a power that for most public purposes could only be exercised through negotiation with the nobles and urban politicians."[5] I will have a great deal more to say about these developments in a later chapter, but for now it may be useful to note that this was perhaps the most efficient form of governing the disparate realms, and that, in doing so, the medieval kings of the realms of Aragon proved to be far more cunning than their early modern successors. In fact, when Philip IV and his prime minister Olivares sought to impose a Castilian model on the Crown of Aragon, the result was open rebellion and the wrecking of Spain.[6]

Toward Trastámara Spain

Martin I's death in 1410 marked the end of a dynasty that harked back to Sancho III the Greater (1000–35) and even earlier to Wilfred the Hairy (873–98). The king's own son, Martin the Younger, had died a year earlier in 1409, and no direct descendants remained alive. A constitutional crisis threatened the wellbeing of the realms, as several candidates to the throne either came or were put forward by different political forces within the federation of kingdoms. These candidates included Jaume d'Urgell, a great-grandson of Alfonso IV, and thus with claims to be part of the royal family. Jaume may have counted on Catalan support but faced stiff Aragonese opposition. Louis of Anjou, the French candidate, was himself a grandson of John I, and he enjoyed some Aragonese support. But the eventual successful candidate was Ferdinand (Fernando), regent of Castile and grandson of Peter IV, the Ceremonious. After a great victory over the Muslims at Antequera in 1410, he became known throughout the land as Ferdinand of Antequera, joining his military and political prestige to his rightful family claims. Emerging as a compromise candidate and with the support of Pope Benedict XIII, Ferdinand, because of his deep involvement in Castilian affairs, presented peculiar problems of his own. Representatives of the Corts of Aragon, Valencia, and Catalonia met at Caspe in 1412. After months of debate, Ferdinand was elected king in the so-called Compromise of Caspe. With his election the political history of the two core-realms in the peninsula, Castile and the Crown of Aragon, became even more intertwined. The Trastámaras, the bastard descendants of Alfonso XI, now ruled over most of Spain.

Castile, 1350–1410

Peter I (1350–1369)

The chaos and disorder which Castile had endured during Ferdinand IV's and Alfonso XI's minorities were replayed with a vengeance in the second half of the fourteenth century. Although royal minorities took, once again, their dismal toll (the minorities of Henry III and John II), the main cause for political upheavals came from fierce intra-familiar conflicts for control of the Crown and from the aggressive role of a new nobility born out of the disorder and civil wars of the 1360s. As we saw in the preceding chapter, the capable Alfonso XI had given his entire affection to his high-born mistress Leonor de Guzmán, a woman of great ability and fecundity, and to his large brood of bastard children (mostly males and troublesome). His wife, María of Portugal, and his only son and legitimate heir, Peter (Pedro), Alfonso XI mostly ignored. On his second family the king bestowed the highest honors and juiciest land grants and benefices. In fact, he created a rival power to that of his son, and his decision to benefit his bastard children over his own rightful heir brought, as already noted in the previous chapter, untold grief to the realm. His illegitimate children, known collectively as the Trastámaras (from the holdings of the eldest male, Henry, count of Trastámara), began to challenge the power of the newly named king from the beginning. When Peter I, known in history mostly because of the propaganda of his opponents as the Cruel, came to the throne in 1350, he faced the disasters of the plague, the growing political complications of the Hundred Years War, and the power of his half-brothers, led by Henry, count of Trastámara, and by Fradrique, the powerful master of the Order of Santiago. Peter I was not helped by the actions of his mother, María of Portugal. After years of neglect at the hands of her husband, María saw the death of Alfonso XI and the ascent to the throne of her only son, Peter, as a golden opportunity for revenge, Leonor of Guzmán was imprisoned and then put to death, adding resentment and hatred to what was already an untenable situation.[7]

Peter I has been much maligned by historians, but the sobriquet of 'the Cruel' was, to a large extent, justified by some of his actions. His love for his mistress María de Padilla also created abundant problems, but he may not have been as evil and violent a king – most kings in this period were violent – as later chronicles, highly partisan to the Trastámaras' cause, depicted him in later years. Faced with the devastation of the plague, he sought to restore order to the realm, calling a great meeting of the Cortes in Valladolid in 1351. Attempts to place a ceiling on wages and to survey the resources of the realm (the *Becerro de behetrías*), though not too successful, reflected a willingness to respond to the crisis in a meaningful ways. Nonetheless, his abandonment and imprisonment of his wife, Blanche of Bourbon, shortly after their marriage in 1353 and his passion for María de Padilla led to opposition not only from the Trastámaras but also from urban centers and factions in the nobility. María de Padilla's family showed an insatiable thirst for material gains, further antagonizing urban elites. As an influential presence in Peter I's court, the lesser-born Padillas – members of a low aristocratic Sevillian family – did not help the king's cause. All came to a head in 1356 when Peter was victorious over a coalition led by his half-brother Henry of Trastámara. He exiled Henry and subdued the rest; other problems, however, were building, and were soon to confront him.

Shortly after Peter's defeat of his half-brother, Castile was drawn into the conflict between England and France (the Hundred Years War). Around the same time (1357), Peter launched an offensive against the Crown of Aragon over disputed territories in the region of Murcia and the taking of Genoese ships and merchants sailing in Castilian waters (near Cádiz) by Catalan ships. This conflict, which was also tied to the Aragonese–Catalan support for Henry of Trastámara (then exiled in Aragon) and the Castilian support for a disaffected Aragonese prince, became a general peninsular war, drawing also on allies from beyond the Pyrenees. Castile forged an alliance which included Granada and Portugal, while the Crown of Aragon benefited from the support of the Trastámara interests and from rebellious Castilian nobles. The drama of the period was accentuated by Peter I's execution of some of his half-brothers, among them Fradrique and his cousin Juan. The latter's murder, as reported by Pedro López de Ayala, a hostile chronicler of the king's deeds, was particularly savage, involving the defenestration of the Infante Juan's dead body. He had been lured to a meeting with the king by false promises of a profitable appointment and reconciliation, only to meet his death. These actions, not untypical of the age, only added to the growing legend of Pedro's cruelty.

As we have seen above, Peter I had great success in his campaigns against Aragon, showing Castile's superiority in peninsular affairs. Castilian ships sailed into the western Mediterranean and threatened the Valencian coast, Ibiza, and Barcelona, while Castilian troops occupied important border towns in western Aragon. When Henry of Trastámara, Peter IV's ally, invaded Castile during Peter I's foray into the western Mediterranean, the Castilian king returned home, ordered the execution of two additional half-brothers, Juan and Pedro (he must have taken a particular pleasure in killing a half-brother named after him), and gained an impressive victory over Henry at Nájera in 1360. That year it seemed as if Peter I's star was on the rise. He had soundly defeated the Crown of Aragon and shown Castile's power within the peninsula. He had violently thinned the ranks of his half-brothers by killing three of them. He had quelled noble threats to his power; his legitimate wife, abandoned two days after the wedding, was securely confined, while his mistress María de Padilla was, for all practical purposes, the queen. Peace with Aragon was signed in 1360. The settlement provided considerable gains to Castile which kept some of the territories gained on the Aragonese border and in Murcia. Henry of Trastámara and his allies, no longer protected by the Aragonese kings, fled to the safety of France. In the meantime Peter I's legitimate wife was executed, while the king claimed that he had secretly married his mistress, making the four children born from her lover legitimate. Peter was not unique in these outrageous actions – his namesake in Portugal behaved in the same fashion. Moreover, these accounts only gloss lightly over the many crimes and excesses of the period. Marital and succession questions had a way of spilling over into the broad political arena and of bringing widespread disorder throughout the realm.[8]

Conflict against Aragon was renewed in 1362 with Peter I of Castile's successful invasion of the Crown of Aragon's southern flank, leading to the occupation of towns in the Valencian hinterland. A peace treaty, signed in 1363 at the insistence of the Pope, only postponed further hostilities. In 1365 Henry of Trastámara, now a claimant to the throne and enjoying widespread support within Castile from towns and nobles and abroad from the Crown of Aragon and the king of France, forged a broad alliance against Peter the Cruel. The main element of their plans was to bring the French constable Bertram Du Guesclin and his mercenary troops into the peninsula at the very high cost of 300,000 gold florins. A very capable military leader, Bertram, by refusing to engage in pitched battle and by harassing the English troops with hit-and-run tactics and small skirmishes, had been able to reverse the earlier English gains in the Hundred Years War. His troops were composed mostly of mercenaries (the *routiers*) who, after a temporary peace treaty between France and England, caused havoc in the area around Paris. Their expedition to Spain served two purposes: providing a well-seasoned armed force against Castile's king and removing their troublesome presence from France. Faced with these enemies, Peter I sought an English alliance and lured Edward the Black Prince (son of Edward III of England and heir to the English throne) to Spain with the promise of important territorial grants in the Bay of Biscay region. On April 13, 1367, Prince Edward and Peter I inflicted a severe defeat on the invading Franco-Aragonese-Castilian armies at Nájera. Bertram was captured and Henry of Trastámara had to flee the battlefield.[9]

Peter I's desire to kill those captured at Nájera, his inability to fulfill his agreements with Edward the Black Prince, and the latter's illnesses led to the English withdrawal from the field. By 1369 Henry of Trastámara, once again with French and Aragonese support and with widespread recognition of his claims to the throne from most of the important urban centers in northern Castile, invaded the realm. This time their combined forces defeated Peter I at Montiel. In March of that year, the Castilian king was lured to a parlay with Bertram Du Guesclin, and there he was murdered by his own half-brother – his body left unburied and exposed to public mockery. Henry now became king of Castile, the second of that name, and a bastard branch, that of the Trastámaras, came to rule the kingdom of the castles and lions. But, after such widespread disorder, the future looked uncertain indeed.

The Trastámaras in Power

Henry (Enrique) II (1369–1379)

Henry II came to power at a time when the Castilian realm was at a crossroads. While the kingdom had undergone serious crises and transformations (see chapter 2), it had also experienced a vigorous cultural flowering and dramatic developments in its administrative and legal structures (see chapters 6 and 8). The new dynasty came to power having given lavish grants and titles to supporting nobles, and territorial concessions to their royal allies in France and the Crown of Aragon. Henry II's initial hold on the crown was a tentative one. New men came to the fore demanding a share of the victory, and the king also granted them substantial privileges and lands. Historians have long argued that the first decades of Trastámara rule witnessed the disappearance of the old nobility, a nobility dating to the late eleventh and twelfth centuries, and its replacement by a new nobility. In reality, the transformation was signaled by the rise to prominence of lesser branches of the great old noble houses, with a few new lesser nobles rising to very high status. This promotion in rank was tied to the granting of large estates and to extensive royal privileges. Such erosion of the royal domain and authority had, in turn, disastrous consequences for Castile over the next hundred years. Not unlike France or England in the late fourteenth and fifteenth centuries, the rise of the nobility led to waves of violence and instability. Securely grounded in their new economic power and high standing, the Castilian nobility challenged royal authority and even coveted, as was the case in the reigns of John II and Henry IV, the control of the Crown. In many respects, however, the nobles did not have to look too far for a model. The Trastámaras, using the positions, titles, and income given them by their father (Alfonso XI), rose to the throne. But many of these developments were still to be played out in the future. In the early 1370s, Henry II still had to consolidate his position against a host of new enemies.[10]

Restoring order and securing his throne were not easy tasks. Henry II faced the armed opposition of Peter I's followers. It did help considerably that Peter had left no legitimate male heir in the peninsula (though in Castile, unlike France, women could inherit the crown) who could be raised as a legal alternative to him. Nonetheless, Peter's supporters controlled some important strongholds around the country. Not only those resisting from within, but also the rulers of Portugal (King Fernando, 1367–83), the Crown of Aragon (Peter IV), Navarre (Charles II, the Bad, who had played such a sorry role in France's disturbances of the mid-fourteenth century), and Granada (Muhammad V) saw Henry II's internal trouble as an opportunity to dismember Castile. Portuguese armies invaded the area of Galicia, while the Navarrese entered the Rioja region and Granada's forces raided the south, taking Algeciras. By resisting some of these invasions and by adroit marriage alliances between the Trastámaras and the ruling houses of Portugal, Navarre, and the Crown of Aragon, Henry II was able to withstand the initial storm and to lay the foundations of Trastámara hegemony in Spain; yet, as the frontiers became stable, a new claimant to the throne appeared. John of Gaunt, Edward III of England's son and a younger brother of the Black Prince, had married Peter I's daughter, Constanza. John now claimed the Castilian throne on behalf of his wife. Henry II's response was to seek closer ties with the French, and the Castilian navy, a formidable naval force during this period, played a significant and victorious role against its English counterpart in the 1370s.

From just holding on to the throne he had just usurped, Henry now turned to the offensive, recovering lands lost to Navarre, invading Portugal, even threatening the English lands in Gascony and defeating, in alliance with the French, an English fleet in a great naval engagement in 1375. Far more significant, Henry II of Castile and Peter IV, ruler of the Crown of Aragon, agreed to marry their children. Leonor, a princess of Aragon, married the Infante John (Juan), heir to the throne of Castile. This union eventually led to Trastámara control of most of the peninsula and to the union of the realms in the late fifteenth century. This did not mean, however, that amicable relations prevailed between the two kingdoms, but the matrimonial alliance allowed Henry to advance his political agenda internally and to embark on territorial expansion against Navarre and Portugal. In less than ten years, and after very uncertain beginnings, Henry II was able to establish his rule throughout the realm and to leave the kingdom to his heir without too many challenges. This he did by claiming to descend from de la Cerda family. Thus, the Trastámaras traced their lineage back to Alfonso X, while branding Sancho IV and his progeny as usurpers. That Peter I the Cruel was represented as an ally and protector of the Jews, and, in some of the most virulent propaganda, as the illegitimate son of a Jew, only helped discredit the legitimate line while exalting the Trastámaras. In the end a large prize had to be paid nonetheless for this favorable outcome. As noted earlier, lavish grants, given to the nobility as the means to secure their support during the civil war, led to untold violence by the nobility in the succeeding years.[11]

John (Juan) I (1379–1390)

The last years of Henry II's reign and the early years of John I were dominated by the struggle against Portugal and by the Trastámaras' attempts to dominate the peninsular political agenda. These murky conflicts, shifting alliances, and open warfare took place in the context of the Great Schism and of the continuing conflict between England and France. Loyal to their long alliance with France, John I had to fend off the English advances in the peninsula while attempting to intervene into Portugal. The Portuguese king Fernando died in 1383, opening the door to Castilian claims to the Portuguese crown through John's marriage to Fernando's daughter, Beatriz. The union of the two realms was, however, not yet to be. The majority of the Portuguese people rallied behind João, the illegitimate son of king Pedro and half-brother to Fernando. Chosen to be king by the Portuguese Cortes in 1385, João I reignited the long-term Portuguese alliance with England and blocked Castilian incursions on Portugal's eastern frontier. John I of Castile did not accept his defeat quietly and invaded Portugal in 1385. At Aljubarrota, the Castilian army suffered a crushing defeat, insuring Portuguese independence and the success of the new ruling house of Avis. After the reverses in Portugal, John I had to face other threats. John of Gaunt, now the father of the new king of England, the first Lancaster monarch, made yet another claim to the throne of Castile. Although John of Gaunt successfully invaded Galicia, he was unable to make any progress into the Castilian heartland. One gets the impression of endless conflict, but in reality the Trastámaras, John I of Castile in this specific instance, were able to weather the frequent political storms and international antagonisms and achieve some modicum of peaceful relations with other Iberian kingdoms and even to begin plans for expansion. In terms of John I, these plans were cut short by his unexpected death in 1390. In many respects, John I, as his father Henry II had done, was able to solidify Trastámara control of the realm, to gain, albeit through exorbitant bribes, the reluctant support of the nobility, and to pass his kingdom to his son without too much dissent from either the nobility, the urban representatives to the Cortes, or the high clergy. That he left a minor son, Henry III, as heir was something he could not help, but there would be a heavy price to pay, as was always the case, for extended royal minorities.[12]

Henry (Enrique) III (1390–1406)

When Henry III came to the throne at the age of 12, the usual scramble for control of the regency took place. While threats from the outside were not as pressing as in previous minorities – John of Gaunt's claims had been settled by a dynastic marriage and the Lancaster family had far more important business to attend to in England – a fragmented regency and the Castilian Cortes' attempts to settle the affairs of the realm led to further disturbances. No one, however, could have predicted the eruption of anti-Jewish violence throughout Castile in 1391. Beginning in Seville and swiftly spreading to other towns in Andalusia and northern Castile – Cordoba, Cuenca, Burgos, most notable among them – thousands of Jews were either killed outright or forcefully converted to Christianity. The violence and the social tensions underlying the attacks against the Jews did not bode well for the young king, as the Crown made futile efforts to stop the carnage and destruction of Jewish property. Assuming power in 1393, Henry III, barely 14 years old, proved to be, in spite of his continuing ill health, a forceful ruler. His main goal was to curb the ambitions of the high nobility and, specifically, those of his uncle Fradrique of Benavente, one of the original regents. During Henry III's rule, the Castilians gained a firm hold on the Canary Islands, establishing a Castilian outpost in the Atlantic. On the crucial issue of the papal schism, Castile, as had been the Trastámara policy, sided with France in calling for Benedict XIII's resignation.[13]

It is difficult for us today to recognize fully how much energy medieval rulers deployed on the issue of the papal schism, or how very troubling the existence of two and, at times, even three contending popes was for medieval Christians. Their deep concerns serve as a constant reminder of the links between politics and religion and the impact which the Great Schism had on the late medieval West. But besides the Castilian king's interest in the end of religious strife within the Church, Henry III also faced a resurgent Granada. As he made preparations for a campaign to respond to Granada's invasion of Murcia, he died, a mere 27 years old, in 1406.

The Perpetual Minority of John (Juan) II (1406–1454)

Leaving a small son of 2, John, as his heir, Henry III's death opened the gates to a turbulent period in Castilian history, with episodic violence that would not abate until the reforms of the Catholic Monarchs. In contrast to the usual patterns seen in the regencies of unfortunate Castile – in the short span of time covered by this book, if one counts Ferdinand IV and Juana la Beltraneja as bookends, Castile endured five minorities – John's minority proved to be a great deal less troublesome than previous ones. The late king's brother, Ferdinand, later Ferdinand of Antequera and king of the Crown of Aragon in 1412, was a forceful and capable regent, though not without larger ambitions and not without a desire to further his own and his children's fortunes at the expense of the Crown. He shared the regency with John II's mother, Queen Catalina of Lancaster, a vain and ineffectual ruler. Following an old and well-tried formula, Ferdinand marched south to meet the forces of Granada and to profit from raids and contributions to his crusading efforts. His victory at Antequera over the Granadian armies in 1410, followed by a spectacular triumphal entry into Seville, provided Ferdinand with the prestige and resources for his bid to be selected as the next king of the Crown of Aragon. But Ferdinand shrewdly built for himself and his children an unassailable power base within Castile. The troubles of the next five decades bore sad witness to his ambitions. It is to them that we now turn.

Chapter 5

Spain in the Fifteenth Century
Toward the Rule of the Catholic Monarchs, 1412–1469

In 1412 Castile and the Crown of Aragon came to be ruled by closely related members of one family, the Trastámaras, with Ferdinand of Antequera as king of Aragon, and John II, his young nephew, as king in Castile. Illegitimate by birth, having come to the throne by assassination, the Trastámaras – Isabella and Ferdinand were direct descendants of Henry of Trastámara – fought against great odds while slowly building the foundations of Spain's hegemony in Europe and the known world in the early modern period. If the particular histories of Castile and the Realms of Aragon were strongly linked in cycles of familial alliances and violent antagonisms before 1412, by the early fifteenth century their histories became inexorably intertwined. In spite of frequent marriages between the two branches of the family throughout the fifteenth century – incestuous ties one may call them – of which the fabled union of Isabella and Ferdinand was only the most productive, the relations between the two realms were anything but peaceful. In reality, any hope of a working partnership seemed nearly impossible.

In the Crown of Aragon each distinct realm had needs which were quite incompatible with those of Castile. As the Trastámaras came to rule Aragon, Valencia, Catalonia, and their Mediterranean possessions, their interests and policies shifted to reflect their subjects' trans-Pyrenean and Mediterranean concerns. Nonetheless, for the more than half-decade between the Compromise of Caspe and the marriage of Isabella and Ferdinand the histories of these two realms needs to be seen as a whole, even though, for the sake of clarity, they are presented here as distinct. Paradoxically while the violence of the nobility became an endemic scourge in Castile during the first seven decades of the fifteenth century, and high nobles made serious attempts to either control the Crown or despoil the realm, the kings and the high nobility could also engage in extravagant excesses and fanciful displays across political boundaries. All these took place while the peasantry in both realms suffered greatly from violence and growing economic difficulties. Decline and disorder in one area were matched by new and unprecedented sources of income. The wool trade that had begun in earnest after 1350 now brought a flood of money into the pockets of those nobles, ecclesiastics, municipal councils, and members of the royal family, which owned large flocks of sheep. It brought instant wealth to merchants, generating for the Crown huge tax income collected on the movement and grazing (*portazgo* and *montazgo*) of the transhumant animals. It also generated considerable tithes on the export of wool and the import of textiles and other luxury items.[1]

In the Crown of Aragon endemic social and political conflicts in Barcelona, violence in northern Aragon, and the *remenças'* rebellion throughout most of northern Catalonia in the fifteenth century had, as their counterpoint, the Aragonese–Catalan control of Naples from the mid-fifteenth century onwards, the reception of Italian humanism, and profitable trade with Italy and North Africa. The period was a turbulent one, but it was also dazzling in its accomplishments and gaudy displays.

Castile, 1410–1469

John II (1406–1454)

John II's long, tormented, and fairly incompetent rule was marked by the growing power of princely factions and by the long and debilitating struggle between these princely and noble pretenders and John II's long-time favorite, the enigmatic and cunning Don Alvaro de Luna. Until Ferdinand of Antequera's death in 1416, the king's uncle and regent, remained a custodian of the Castilian king, even though he was already the king of the Crown of Aragon. He served as co-regent with Catalina of Lancaster, and the affairs of both kingdoms marched in unison without too many complications. The queen followed Ferdinand to the tomb two years later in 1418; only then did John II assume the throne. An indolent man, John II was an easy prey to the influence or intimidation of others. And there was never in Castile an absence of those who wished for far more than they had – whether power, dignities, or possessions. Fabulous fortunes were built at the expense of the Crown, and king-makers, or those who wished to see themselves as king-makers – or, even worse, as kings – would be around in such numbers and with such ambitions as to inflict severe damage on the stability of Castile.[2]

One of the most insidious problems was the close link between ruling houses. When Ferdinand I of Aragon died, he was succeeded by his son Alfonso V, the Magnanimous (1416–58). The new king spent most of his life either trying to conquer Naples or, after succeeding in his plans, living there and mostly concerned with Italian affairs. His two brothers, John (one must admit that there are too many Juans or Johns in this story) and Henry (too many Henries as well), collectively known as the Infantes of Aragon, had been granted huge possessions and titles in Castile by their father while he was regent of Castile. Henry, for example, was master of the Order of Santiago, with control over its extensive holdings and military resources. To complicate matters even further, John of Trastámara, the Infante of Aragon, also became, though his marriage to Blanca, heiress of Navarre, king of the Pyrenean kingdom in 1425. And then John II of Castile married María, the sister of Alfonso V of Aragon and the Infantes. John II of Castile's own sister, yet another María, also married Alfonso V. Incestuous, as noted earlier, is a good word to describe their close and dangerous intimacy.

I realize how very confusing this is all getting, but if I have descended into these intertwining family histories it is to highlight how very much of a family affair the politics of Castile became in this period, though, in many respects, this was not very different from what happened in England or France around this time. John II of Castile was the cousin of the king of Aragon and the troublesome Infantes and twice over their brother-in-law. All were, more or less, of the same age, but most certainly not of the same ability or disposition, with poor John II of Castile overwhelmingly the less gifted in every department. Thus, John II's authority was immediately contested, and Castile became a battlefield for the ambitions of these political players. The Castilian king became more often than not a captive of one of the factions vying for control of the kingdom or, when not under the control of his enemies, in thrall to his favorite.

Luis Suárez Fernández's account of the period in his *Nobleza y monarquía* provides a rich guideline to the political complexities of the first half of the fifteenth century. Shifting alliances, to the point of distraction, betrayals, foreign conflicts followed each other so swiftly that a scorecard would be needed to keep track of all the players, all the changing of sides, and all the events. Nothing was simple. For example, the Infantes of Aragon could and did work against each other, for individual ambitions trumped any sense of family loyalty or political sense. By 1425, when the Infante of Aragon, John, became king of Navarre, the Infante Henry had two brothers and a cousin (and brother-in-law) who were kings. Surely, there must be a kingdom somewhere in the peninsula for him, and why not Castile? In 1420 the Infante Henry imprisoned John II of Castile, two years removed from his long minority, and for several months ruled Castile on behalf of his prisoner. The king of Castile escaped in November of that year, partly because of the Infante John's mistrust of his brother and partly because of Alvaro de Luna's forceful intervention.

An illegitimate son of a minor noble but connected to the important Luna family – his grand-uncle was Pedro de Luna, who as Pope Benedict XIII was the main protagonist of the Great Schism – Alvaro was born in 1388 and sent to the royal court at the age of 20 to make his fortune. A young man of great physical abilities (in spite of his slender frame), intelligence, and charm, and with an iron will, Don Alvaro, as he is usually referred to in the chronicles, became the inseparable companion of the much younger John II. Their relationship became so intimate that the queen regent, Catalina, had Don Alvaro removed from the court, only to bring him back at the pleading and insistence of her son. When John took sole possession of the throne, Don Alvaro's mastery over the young king brought endless complaints from the high nobility and intense resentment from the Infantes of Aragon.[3]

Most contemporary opinion, often hostile, depicted Alvaro de Luna as a man of base origin and mostly concerned with building his own fortune. Lacking a modern biography until Nicholas Round's recent formidable study of Don Alvaro's life, we may see him as someone who did indeed make a fortune at the expense of the royal domain, but who also fought mightily for over four decades to restore and assert royal authority over a selfish nobility and to focus Castile's resources on the war against Granada. It was Don Alvaro who freed the king in 1420.

Between 1418 and 1420, on the road to the first of John II's many humiliations at the hands of his cousins the Infantes of Aragon, different factions emerged at court and throughout the land. Some high nobles sided with the Infantes of Aragon, or at least with one of them; others sided with the king's favorite. Most sought their own advantage and changed sides as needed. The cast of characters on one side or another of the political spectrum was always fluid and shifted according to political circumstances and the ability of one faction to offer more than its enemies.

The great noble houses of Castile – Velasco, Enríquez, Manrique, Quiñones, Pimentel, Mendoza, Stuñiga, Medinacelli, Villena, Fajardo, Guzmán, and others – made fabulously rich by the Trastámaras' gifts during the civil war, now took sides in the conflict. The Enríquez, López Dávalos, Manrique, and others supported the Infante Henry, while Gómez de Sandoval, Hurtado de Mendoza, and even Alvaro de Luna supported the Infante John in an earlier phase of the antagonisms between the two brothers. Yet the Infante Henry was able to attract Alvaro de Luna's support by granting him the title of count and by sponsoring Alvaro's marriage to the wealthy and well-connected Elvira de Portocarrero. By the late 1410 and early 1420 the Infante Henry seemed to be the undisputed winner. He had control of the king, acting as a shadow king on John II's behalf. He had outmaneuvered his brother and accumulated titles and possessions that made him uniquely powerful within Castile. But, as Suárez Fernández has argued, it was not in the nature of the high-born Castilian nobility to allow any great noble – and the Infante Henry, though of royal blood, was essentially just another great magnate – to gain the upper hand. Their unrest allowed Alvaro de Luna to rescue the king on December 10, 1420, though the rescue meant essentially placing the king under the strict control of Don Alvaro.

The next few years witnessed continual conspiracies, shifting alliances, and threats of war between Castile and Aragon as Alfonso V tried to check Alvaro de Luna's increasing power. As Don Alvaro's enemies gathered strength, signaled by a truce between the Infantes of Aragon at their brother, Alfonso V's, prompting, John II's favorite went into yet another exile. In many ways, one of Don Alvaro's most remarkable assets was his ability to retreat and accept defeat temporarily and thus to thwart his complete destruction. Yet neither the king nor the kingdom could do without Don Alvaro. The Infantes of Aragon were great at creating trouble, but not too competent at ruling. Their identification with Aragon and Aragonese interests did not make them overly popular in Castile either. By January 1428, Don Alvaro, by then constable of Castile, was back at the side of his king. The return of the constable and the visit of Leonor, the daughter of Alfonso V, on her way to Portugal to marry the heir to the Portuguese throne, provided the setting for a whole month of festivities in Valladolid during May 1428. This fantastic cycle of festivals (which I have examined in detail elsewhere), undertaken in the squares of Valladolid in front of throngs of citizens and visitors and costing fabulous sums of money, was partly orchestrated by the constable for specific political purposes. In the rich iconography and symbolism of the feasts, the clothing of the participants, and the esoteric literary references, political points were scored and fought over. We will have an opportunity to look at the significance of festivals as cultural artifacts later on (see chapters 6 and 8), but the outcome of the festival is what concerns me here.[4]

After all the festivities and symbols had been played out, the Infante Henry was ordered to remove himself to the frontier and to reassume his duties as Master of the Order of Santiago in the struggle against Granada. His brother, the Infante John (already king of Navarre since 1425) was equally requested to leave the kingdom because, as the chronicle tells us, there wasn't room in Castile for two kings.[5] Alvaro de Luna's significant victory was followed immediately by royal (by which I mean Alvaro's) attempts to curtail noble power and to erode noble support for the Infantes of Aragon; decisive victories, however, were elusive in Castile's complex political landscape. Alfonso V, reluctant to give up his influence in Castile, summoned his two brothers to his court and ordered them to put rivalries aside and to mount a joint attack on Castile. Attempts at internal risings against the constable's government failed, as did the Aragonese invasion in 1429. Don Alvaro, always prudent or calculating, did not press his advantage, agreeing to a truce with the Aragonese.

The real victims of this continual strife were the royal fisc, the Castilian economy, and the people. Devaluation of the coinage, heavy fiscal demands on the Church (on the pretext of a crusade against Granada), and large subsidies extorted from the Cortes did substantial damage, while Don Alvaro bestowed lavish gifts and concessions on his supporters and on himself. Nonetheless, by 1432 the Aragonese branch of the Trastámaras had been forcefully removed from Castilian soil; Don Alvaro, securely ensconced in his position as favorite and constable, began his personal rule. The king gave himself completely to the hunt and chase, indolently leaving the government of the realm in the hands of his favorite. As Suárez Fernández has astutely pointed out, however, Alvaro de Luna's rule was not a despotic but an oligarchic one. Rather than rule on his own, he presided over and guided a significant group of magnates, most of them connected by blood. This high nobility, including the Velasco, Ponce de León, Stuñiga, Manrique, and other families, received extravagant new titles and lands, the latter either those confiscated from the Infantes of Aragon and their supporters or, worse still, from continuous raids into the royal domain. In that sense, one must qualify an earlier statement as to the role of Don Alvaro in strengthening monarchical rule. While he did save Juan II from his predatory cousins and heighten royal prestige at home and abroad, the price was high indeed.

Such a rule as that of Don Alvaro after 1432 implied continuous struggles, conspiracies, and shifting alliances. It was good enough for the constable to rally and lead the nobility into yet another attack on Granada. It was another matter for the nobility to accept Don Alvaro's leadership without question or opposition. Thus the political situation was always tense; and the romance and lavish displays of chivalrous feasts and military actions could not always obscure the political violence lurking under the surface. Be that as it may, the constable enjoyed substantial victories. He had supported the winning papal candidate at the council of Basle in 1436, guaranteeing papal support for his program. Aragon, with Alfonso V deeply engaged in his Neapolitan venture, had been removed, at least temporarily, from interfering in peninsular affairs. Portugal was mired in troubles, and a settlement had been worked out with the Infantes of Aragon. The most important aspect of the latter was the marriage of the king of Navarre and Infante of Aragon John's daughter, Blanca, to the Infante Henry, son of John II of Castile.

From this position of relative strength, Don Alvaro sought to curb the growing power of his noble allies. Instead, the constable faced widespread noble rebellions throughout the realm, encouraged and supported by the always troublesome Infantes of Aragon, above all with the king of Navarre's continuous political intrigues. The Navarrese king saw this as an opportunity to further his power and to dominate the political life of Castile. A noble league against the constable was formed, and when the king of Navarre joined its ranks formally, Don Alvaro de Luna, once again, withdrew from the court and went into exile in 1439. The triumph of the noble league marked the collective victory of the noble class and the defeat of the monarchy and the Cortes. During all these civil commotions, the Cortes had played a sorry role, either neglected or forced to acquiesce in the constable's plans. Now a triumphant nobility began to distribute land and titles to the chagrin of the towns, which suffered fiscally and territorially from such excesses.

Within months rivalry and envy emerged among the high nobles, allowing the constable to organize his own league with some urban and noble support and, most of all, with the king's unwavering loyalty. As these factions fought for control of the king, Crown, and royal council, the constable plotted his return. In many respects, though a great many of these internecine struggles were about power, they were also about the governance, or the type of governance, of the realm. The great magnate families wished for a weak monarch. An impotent king – and John II was as clumsy a king as one could have – allowed the high nobility to accumulate wealth, titles, and power at the expense of the Crown. Alvaro de Luna fought for a strong monarch, because in the 1420s, 1430s, and 1440s royal authority was in fact synonymous with his own authority. The high nobility, however, lived in fear of weakening the Castilian king so much as to allow one of the Infantes of Aragon, specifically the king of Navarre, to lord it over them and to put a stop to their raiding of the royal domain. Urban elites did not profit from civil strife and preferred a strong monarchy, although they were not always of one mind as to who should be the king. In any case, in the first half of the fifteenth century municipal councils were unable to reprise the role they had played on behalf of the Crown a century and a half earlier.

In many respects, this question of how to organize and distribute power was at the center of the long century and a half of civil conflict plaguing

Castile. Although in the next chapter I will attempt to deal with these matters in a more cogent fashion, one may preliminarily argue that in the early fifteenth century the struggle was also about the extent of royal power and the role of the high nobility in emerging national monarchies. Medieval kings always ruled with the consent of their subjects, whether noble or urban representatives. While this central principle of medieval statecraft had been forcefully reasserted in the Realms of Aragon to the detriment of the Crown, in Castile, as was the case in France and England, the transition to new monarchical forms was still in play and would not be resolved until the reign of Ferdinand and Isabella and their Habsburg descendants. Even then, the resolution would only be partial.

This is why in Castile the great noble houses, mistrusting each other, fearing each other, were willing to deal with Don Alvaro de Luna, their worst enemy. In this free for all, the Infantes of Aragon were even willing to make a deal with Don Alvaro (and, of course, as ready to betray him), as they fought factions of the high nobility for control of the king and the realm. By 1443, John II of Castile had become, once again, a virtual prisoner of the Infantes of Aragon, as John, king of Navarre and now a widower, married Juana Manrique (the future mother of Ferdinand the Catholic), sealing his alliance with one of the most influential factions of the Castilian high nobility. The confusing situation of the early 1440s imperiled monarchical power and the realm, prompting some nobles, bishops, and urban representatives to push for a political compromise that would prevent Castile from sinking into complete anarchy. Complicating matters, the Castilian heir, yet another Infante Henry, already dominated by a favorite (at that time Don Juan Pacheco, a high nobleman who would visit incredible disorder on Castile for the next few decades) also joined the oscillating game of supporting and opposing his own father.[6]

On May 19, 1445, those hoping for a noble oligarchy and those in favor of a strong monarchy met on the battlefield at Olmedo, a battle which the *Coplas de Mingo Revulgo*, as has been seen in chapter 2, glossed satirically. At Olmedo, the royalist forces, with Don Alvaro leading them, soundly defeated the noble host. The leaders of the revolt were captured. The Infante Henry (one of the Infantes of Aragon) was severely wounded and later died. The constable was once again firmly in control. And yet his victory was, once again, short-lived. The heir to the throne, influenced by Pacheco, now became the standard-bearer of noble privilege. A general pardon and a fresh redistribution of grants to Don Alvaro's noble supporters further weakened the outcome of the battle of Olmedo. John II's marriage to a Portuguese princess (the future mother of Isabella the Catholic) brought new faces and intrigues to the court that would prove the constable's undoing in the end. The great noble houses now rose to greater distinction and power, benefiting from the new round of antagonisms. It is perhaps a reflection of the great wealth Castile was able to generate in this period that such gifts and concessions to the high nobility and Church could still be given after almost a century of unrestricted raiding of the royal domain. Far more remarkable was the ability of the realm to bounce back from such spoiling of its resources.

Olmedo, for all its significance, solved nothing; from 1447 onwards, the constable, now in open warfare with the heir to the throne, Henry's favorite Pacheco, and Queen Isabel, began slowly but inexorably to lose his power. The next few years witnessed the ebb and flow of Don Alvaro's remaining influence at the court and on the king. Frontier wars with Granada, Aragon, and Navarre did nothing to rally Castilians to the flag. By 1452 the game was over. Betrayed and abandoned by his king and queen, Don Alvaro was captured and placed in prison by royal order. On June 22, 1453, in a public ceremony in Valladolid, Don Alvaro de Luna was beheaded. John II's official chronicle describes his death in almost hagiographical terms. Although the constable is taken through the streets of Valladolid while the charges of tyranny are read to the throngs lining the streets and the square where he was to be executed, the chronicler emphasizes the constable's piety, comparing him to a martyr. The crowd cries at the sight of the constable on the stage in Valladolid's main square. Don Alvaro dies the good Christian death, but he also dies with extraordinary dignity and courage, an exemplary, chivalrous death. From the stage, Don Alvaro's last words are for John II, and he admonishes the king "to give better reward to those who serve him [John II] than he has ordered for him [the constable]." Swiftly and cleanly beheaded by the executioner, his head was displayed for nine days and his body for three. In a silver bowl placed in front of his head, the people of Valladolid deposited alms to pay for Don Alvaro's burial. In time his body and head were moved from one burial place to another until ending at a sumptuous chapel in Toledo. The long hold that Don Alvaro had exercised over his king, the realm, and the culture of Castile in the first half of the fifteenth century had come to a tragic end.[7] Having lived under Don Alvaro's tutelage most of his life, the king could not live without him, dying a year afterwards in July 1454, and leaving his poor realm in far greater disorder than he had found it.

Henry (Enrique) IV of Castile (1454–1474)

As troubled as John II's reign had been, Henry IV's rule was as chaotic or even more so. Born on January 25, 1425, the Infante Henry witnessed, and played a central role in, the political conflicts besetting Castile in the 1440s and early 1450s. Unlike his father, who remained fairly constant to his favorite Alvaro de Luna until the last two years of his life, Henry moved from one favorite to another. And although Alvaro de Luna was guilty of many political sins, including building his own fortune at the expense of the Crown, he did defend royal prerogatives and authority against the ambitious Infantes of Aragon and the high nobility. Henry's favorites, and he had many throughout his life, could never be accused of lofty ideals or any sense that they wished to advance the Crown's interests. They cared only about themselves.

An eccentric, much-maligned king, Henry IV may have been far more capable than he has been portrayed by hostile chronicles. There have been, in fact, several attempts to rehabilitate his historical standing.[8] An unfortunate king with aesthetic sensibilities rare in his world – his royal seal, for example, radically departed from the formulaic equestrian depiction favored by previous Castilian kings[9] – his behavior was thought unacceptable by most of the nobles vying for power. With great interest in the burgeoning culture of his age, Henry often dressed and ate in Moorish fashion and had, something unforgivable to his enemies, little taste for military conflict against Granada. This is in spite of having conducted several successful expeditions at the frontier early in his reign. His public life had begun on a very inauspicious note. Married in 1440 to the Infanta Blanca, the daughter of John II of Navarre (the Infante of Aragon – thus Blanca was a second cousin to Henry), the heir to the Castilian throne, then a mere 15 years old, fled the conjugal bed without consummating the marriage. The union had been of course part of a political settlement and a door for John II of Navarre's hope for further interference in Castile. Henry's response to his young bride, together with his well-known and much-criticized homoerotic relations with his young favorites, led to repeated charges of impotence – which would prove crucial in later years. Early in life he fell under the influence of Juan Pacheco, later marquis of Villena, a nobleman whom we have already met as someone deeply connected to the disturbances and civil conflict of John II of Castile's reign. Pacheco, or Villena, as he would be known, played quite a nasty role in Castilian politics until the reforms of Ferdinand and Isabella. In the 1440s and 1450s he used the Infante for his own purposes, weakening Alvaro de Luna and his king, and building an extensive domain in the area of Murcia (the Marquesado of Villena) and a fabulous fortune.

In 1454 Henry, already king, began, under the tutelage of Villena, to make plans for another royal wedding, probably to remove the bad taste left by his failed marriage with Blanca. In 1455 he wedded Juana of Portugal, while John II's two other surviving younger children (Henry's half-brother and

-sister), Alfonso and Isabella, remained putative rivals and claimants to the throne in the absence of an heir. For all his shortcomings and early difficulties, it seemed, in the early years of his reign, that Henry might still restore royal authority. The difficulties were many. His early campaigns against Granada, mostly raids aimed at weakening the Muslim stronghold, though prudent in conception and strategically wise, drew the high nobility's ire since they favored big campaigns providing immediate and large profits. Together with charges of impotence and sodomy, that of cowardice was now also hurled at the king. The other thorny issue was how to distribute the rich inheritance of Don Alvaro de Luna. On this issue Villena (Pacheco) overplayed his hand and drew growing noble opposition. It did not help that the king, though firmly in Villena's hands in the late 1450s, still surrounded himself with a retinue of young men of lowly origins, and that he bestowed upon them great titles and fiscal benefits to the displeasure of the high nobility. Such gifts were given in rapid succession to Don Miguel Lucas de Iranzo, who rose to the rank of constable of Castile in spite of his low origin, or to Beltrán de la Cueva, who amassed an immense fortune based solely on the king's favor.

The reality, of course, was that even a king of greater ability would have run into noble opposition. Though titles and fortunes were at stake, a greater issue was the constitutional (if such a word can be used in this context) structure of the realm. In many respects, the nobles had organized a league to thwart the emergence of a strong monarchy. That league, a kind of medieval Castilian Fronde (after the league against Mazarin and the young Louis XIV in seventeenth-century France), had its origins in the reign of John II, and now was reinvigorated by Henry IV's policies and behavior, and Villena's excessive ambitions. As always, Alfonso V of Aragon, based in Naples, and his brother, the surviving Infante of Aragon, John, king of Navarre, played their destructive roles in the mounting conflict. To counter this, in the late 1450s Villena sought alliances with the Aragonese faction, withdrawing Castilian support for the pretensions of Carlos, prince of Viana, who had challenged the rule of his father and uncle (see below), providing yet another example of how far the political life of both realms had become intertwined. Actions in one kingdom always had immediate repercussions in the other.

While all these confusing and shifting alliances were taking place, three significant developments occurred. One was the splitting of the noble oligarchy once more into opposing bands. On one side we find the marquis of Villena, already in firm control of the Military Order of Santiago (and its vast resources) and enjoying significant ecclesiastical and noble support, while on the other side the most powerful of all Castilian noble families, the Mendozas, worked out an agreement with the late Alvaro de Luna's remaining supporters and descendants on behalf of a strong monarchy. This development was of course soon negated by further betrayals and reversals, but it planted the seed for a segment of the nobility to support Isabella's cause later on.

A second significant development was the birth of an heir, the Infanta Doña Juana, in 1462, seven years after the marriage between Henry IV and Juana of Portugal. Since in Castile women could inherit the throne, the Infanta was sworn by the Cortes as the legitimate successor to Henry. The birth and legal recognition of his daughter as heir came at a time when Henry had gained important victories on Navarre's frontier and when the Catalans, by then in open revolt, offered him the rule over Catalonia on August 11, 1462 (see below). But all these promises for a restoration of royal authority came to nothing, as the marquis of Villena, once again, betrayed the king and made his own independent settlements elsewhere. The king's political, as opposed to his alleged sexual, impotence was quite evident to everyone by 1463; from there the road into anarchy descended quickly along a sharp slope.

Third, as the king fell under the nefarious influence of Beltrán de la Cueva, Villena and his allies began to raise questions as to Juana's legitimacy. By 1464 charges that the Infanta Juana was in reality the daughter of Beltrán de la Cueva began to surface in an attempt to transform the Castilian political landscape. Within this context of ever-shifting alliances, slanders, and intrigues, one may summarize some of the salient events. By 1464 noble factions fought each other, changed sides, and betrayed one another as often as possible. Led by Villena, the great aristocratic clans of the Mendozas, Enriques, de Haros, and other powerful lineages sought to institutionalize a noble oligarchy as the main political order within the realm. They could not do so, however, without a king; thus, part of their policy was the aim to control the king or, after the Infanta Juana's legitimacy was called into question, to control either of John II's two remaining children, Alfonso and Isabella, or both. This led to the preposterous and abhorrent proposal to marry Isabella to the much older and corrupt Girón, a member of the Villena clan, and to actually abduct the Infante Alfonso and proclaim him king.

Meanwhile the ever weaker Henry IV came to lean further on Beltrán de la Cueva, now Master of the Order of Santiago – whom the king misguidedly saw as another Alvaro de Luna – and on a bevy of "new men" (a good number of them conversos) and university-trained bureaucrats. Remarkably, the monarchy still had an extraordinary reservoir of goodwill among the peasantry and the lower orders of society. In that fateful year of 1464, as Villena and his forces prepared to assail the king, thousands of peasants armed with pitchforks, knives, and staves rallied around the king and escorted him to the safety of his beloved Segovia. This deep-rooted and popular understanding of the king as the final preserver of order and justice came to full fruition during Isabella's first years as queen.

Popular support for the monarchy, however, was not yet fully articulated. The king was, after all, not capable of leading a popular movement permanently. A gathering of nobles and ecclesiastics in Burgos in 1464 drew up a list of charges against the king and his favorite. The charges – that the king was too friendly to the Muslims, that he minted bad coins and distorted justice, that he had relinquished his powers to his favorite Beltrán, plotted to kill his half-brother and half-sister, and, most damning of all, that the heir to the throne, Doña Juana, was illegitimate – resonated deeply throughout the realm. The king, as always, sought to compromise. He sacrificed Beltrán de la Cueva, who was forced to resign as Master of the Order of Santiago, while also surrendering the Infante Alfonso to the nobility. This, however, did not prove to be enough. In 1465, at Medina del Campo, a commission dominated by the rebellious nobility ordered the exile of the king's supporters and the recognition of the Infante Alfonso as the legitimate heir to the throne. The king finally reacted. As the two contending factions prepared for a resolution in the field of battle, the monarchy sank to its nadir. On June 5, 1465, outside the walls of Avila, in a theatrical performance already brilliantly interpreted by Angus MacKay more than a decade ago, an effigy of Henry had its crown, sword, and scepter ritually removed, and then was rudely kicked off the stage as the Infante Alfonso was proclaimed king.[10]

The "farce" of Avila, as this event came to be known, represented the lowest point in the history of the Castilian monarchy, but it also marked a turning-point in the history of Castile. Not all the great noble lineages recognized Alfonso as king. Vast regions of the realm and many of the kingdom's popular elements remained faithful to Henry, showing at this impasse the enduring power and prestige of the monarchy. Others rallied to the king as well. Led by Segovia, the Castilian towns, which had proven to be particularly passive through the long decades of unrest, organized themselves officially into a general Hermandad (see chapter 6), providing, as they did for Isabella in the early 1470s, new strength to the royal cause. After Henry IV's symbolic dethronement and ritual humiliation outside the walls of Avila, the next decade witnessed a slow dance between the different political actors, as they sought to clarify the succession issue and define who was going to rule Castile. In many respects, these were the same issues that were disputed during Isabella's early years and not settled until the Catholic Monarchs' decisive victory over their noble rivals and other claimants to the throne in the late 1470s.

With three possible candidates to succeed Henry IV, each faction embraced one or other of the candidates at least once. The king's daughter – whether legitimate or not – had been recognized by the king and the Cortes as the rightful heir, though this decision was later revoked. The Infante Don Alfonso, the king's half-brother, had already been raised as king by the rebellious nobles in Avila, and Henry had been forced to acknowledge him as his heir. Finally the Infanta Doña Isabella became the object of innumerable marriage plans by which different noble clans sought to advance their own political agendas. The young princess was even for a while in the hands of Villena. Obviously the magnates supporting or advancing a particular candidate seldom thought of advancing the monarchical cause or restoring order. Rather, their aim was to firmly control these putative royal heirs and to advance further their own individual or family designs. In the meantime, the royal domain and rents continued to be dismembered by the nobles' insatiable appetite. General disorder prevailed.

On July 5, 1468, the Infante Don Alfonso, or King Alfonso XII to some of his supporters, died of a sudden illness. That left Isabella as the most logical heir, leading to hurried realignment of the kingdom's political forces. Suárez Fernández, whose careful reconstruction of this turbulent period has been one of the main guides for this brief summary of events, has argued perceptively that the problem at hand was not necessarily that of the royal succession, that is, who had the legitimate right to succeed Henry IV; rather, the issue was whether the authority of the nobility or that of the Crown would finally prevail in Castile.[11] I will argue in the next chapter that the eventual triumph of monarchical ideals was foreshadowed in the institutional reforms and transformations of the previous two centuries, but one glance at France shows that the final triumph of kings could be delayed for quite a while, and that the nobility not only proved resilient but capable of bouncing back even after strong kings. That, however, was not the case in Castile.

As these issues were debated, Henry IV's queen, Doña Juana, who had been given as a hostage to one of the noble families, became pregnant by another man. The queen's notorious sexual misconduct further weakened the Infanta Juana's claims, and Isabella moved boldly to delegitimize her niece and to gain recognition for her own claims. After a long series of negotiations between the king and Isabella's supporters, an agreement, known as the Pact of the Toros de Guisando (from the place where it was signed), was reached on September 18, 1468. The king declared his recognition of the Infanta Juana as his heir null and void and named Isabella as his rightful successor. In return Isabella and different noble factions renewed their allegiance to the king. Henry IV's disastrous concessions acknowledged the Infanta Juana's illegitimacy which, after years of scurrilous attacks on her legitimacy and on the queen's sexual behavior (or misbehavior), was not difficult to believe. The question that remained was: who was going to control Isabella? On the assumption that Princess Isabella (as she titled herself after the settlement) could be managed, those plotting to that end were wrong.

One of the conditions of the Pact of the Toros of Guisando was that Isabella was to be married soon. The choice of her husband and future king of Castile was indeed a weighty political decision. Portuguese, French, and Aragonese candidates emerged immediately; each of them with his own promise of significant diplomatic and political gains, but also with great disadvantages. Isabella, acting with growing independence, rejected the Portuguese alliance and later on the French one as well, strongly inclining to a union with Ferdinand, the heir to the Crown of Aragon. An Aragonese marriage brought fears to many of Castile's magnates, as the memory of the role played by the Infantes of Aragon remained very much alive in Castile. After all, Ferdinand was John I, king of the Crown of Aragon's son (the former king of Navarre and, in an earlier incarnation, king-maker in Castile). John's nefarious interference in Castilian affairs for over four decades had left a rather sour impression among Castilians. After protracted negotiations between Isabella and Ferdinand defining the extent of each other's power in their respective realms – negotiations which belie the romanticized version of their wedding – and a cold assessment of what Aragon could contribute to Isabella's cause in Castile, the princess fled the grip of her noble captors to the safety of Valladolid. Ferdinand traveled to Castile, and on October 18, 1469, under the protection of a forged papal bull allowing the marriage, the fate of the two great Iberian kingdoms was sealed, and everything in Spain was changed.

Since the marriage had been undertaken without the king's approval (one may read here without Villena's approval), attempts were made to reverse the agreement of the Toros de Guisando. Denying the validity of his previous oaths, the king, joined now by his unfaithful wife, declared Isabella's succession rights void and recognized the poor Infanta Juana (a veritable football in the political struggles) as the legitimate heir. Anarchy prevailed as the great noble lineages sought to carve out independent regions under their control. The civil war that followed, or rather a war that pitted different noble factions against each other, is described in detail in John Edwards' volume in this series and summarized in chapter 9 below.[12] As we come to the end of this political narrative for Castile, one must acknowledge that while the marriage of Ferdinand and Isabella is rightly considered a watershed in the political history of the peninsula, for contemporaries the union in 1469 represented yet another chapter, and not a promising one, of Spain's troubled late medieval history. It would take another decade to restore some semblance of order in Castile, and this could not have been possible without Ferdinand's cunning political skills and Aragonese contributions. The son of one of the most notorious troublemakers helped lay the foundations of an ordered and well-policed society as Spain, and above all Castile, was propelled into the modern world.

The Trastámaras in Aragon, 1412–1479

The history of the Crown of Aragon in this period was a very different one from that of Castile. Ferdinand of Antequera's ascent to the thrones of the diverse realms of the Crown of Aragon in 1412 was never an easy process. His capture of Antequera in 1410, a signal victory in the long history of peninsular Reconquest, and his steady hand as co-regent for his young nephew John II had propelled him to a prominent place in Iberian affairs. When Martin the Humane died without heirs in May 1410, Ferdinand became one of several candidates to the throne of the Realms of Aragon. The closest familial claim was that of Frederick (Federico), the bastard son of Martin the Younger, that is, the grandson of Martin the Humane, but Federico's illegitimacy, long connection to Sicily, and general lack of support in the peninsula made him an untenable candidate. Other main contenders emerged along with a bevy of foreign and local pretenders to the Crown. The first of the two main candidates was Jaume d'Urgell, a descendant of Alfonso IV. The second, and successful, candidate was Ferdinand of Antequera, who also had strong family connections to the last Aragonese king. Ferdinand's mother, Eleanor, was Martin the Humane's sister.

The period between 1410 and 1412 witnessed fierce factional warfare in Aragon and Valencia between the partisans of both candidates, while the Generalitat, in unusual behavior for the always rebellious Catalans, kept order within the Principality and pushed for a political compromise. Ferdinand's influential role in Castilian affairs raised fears among the independent-minded Aragonese and Catalans, but his ability to deploy Castilian resources – the object of Aragonese fears – also allowed him to muster troops (diverted from following up on his victory at Antequera with an attack on Granada) to strengthen his hand within Aragon and Valencia. At Caspe in June 1412, commissioners selected by the three different political entities comprising the Crown of Aragon (including the powerful and charismatic preacher, and later saint, Vincent Ferrer) gave the nod to Ferdinand as the new ruler of the Aragonese Realms. As we already know from the discussion of Castilian history in the early half of the fifteenth century, the Aragonese, Catalans, and Valencians had little to fear in reality. If anything, it was the Infantes of Aragon who interfered in Castilian polit- ics and not the other way around. Yet one can also read the history of the peninsula in this period as the hegemony of Castile's royal family, the Trastámaras, over all of the Spanish realms. Moreover, the Trastámaras' obses- sive attention to Castile's internal politics had a detrimental effect on the neglected realms of Aragon. The rule of one family over most of the Iberian realms increased rather than diminished the conflicts between the different kingdoms.

Ferdinand I (1412–1416)

The new king moved swiftly to consolidate his rule and to insure a smooth succession. His son Alfonso was sworn as heir to the throne shortly after Ferdinand's coronation, while his second son John (the Infante of Aragon and eventual king of Navarre and of the Crown of Aragon) became lieuten- ant general in Sicily, in an attempt to prevent Sicily and Sardinia from breaking away from Aragonese–Catalan rule. Shortly before his untimely death on April 2, 1416, Ferdinand I took decisive steps to end the Great Schism by withdrawing his support for Benedict XIII, the Luna pope. This represented a courageous or treacherous step (depending on which side of the issue one was), considering that the pope had strongly supported Ferdinand's candidacy to the throne and his policies in Sicily. Ferdinand's death, after only four years as king, opened the way for Alfonso V the Magnanimous's long and complex rule. Alfonso, besides ruling over the Crown of Aragon and its Mediterranean possessions for many years, qualifies as one of the great Renaissance princes. Choosing to live in Naples, he was keenly interested in Italian affairs and culture and an important art patron.[13]

Alfonso V (1416–1458)

Born in 1396, the eldest son of Ferdinand of Antequera and Leonor de Albuquerque, the richest heiress in Castilian history and the quintessential *rica hembra* – it was said of her that she could ride from Castile's frontier with Aragon to that with Portugal without ever stepping out of her lands – Alfonso benefited from a substantial inheritance in Castile, as did his troublesome brothers. This gave him a very high stake in Castilian affairs, as he had in the Mediterranean through his Aragonese inheritance. Married to Maria of Castile, John II's sister, as one of his own sisters was married to the king of Castile and another to the Portuguese heir to the throne, Alfonso's life was deeply woven into the fabric of peninsular dynastic politics, and these familial ties and properties in Castile drew the Aragonese king inexorably into Spanish affairs, even though his heart and body were firmly settled in Naples. Because of his interest in Italy, Alfonso V was throughout most of his long reign an absentee ruler, though his wife represented him most effectively in Catalonia during more than two decades of his rule, while his brother John served as his proxy in Castile. Yet, regardless of Maria of Castile's considerable abilities and the conflicts between the Infantes of Aragon and Alvaro de Luna which effectively prevented Castile from interfering in the eastern kingdoms' politics, ruling the Crown of Aragon was no easy task. Nor was managing rivalries with Genoa in the western Mediterranean or handling the pope or Italian politics any easier.

In the Crown of Aragon proper, Alfonso V met the immediate resistance of Catalonia's civic leaders, always jealous of their liberties and privileges. The discontent was replicated in Aragon and Valencia, which voiced, on very specific grounds and for very good reasons, their mistrust of Alfonso's Castilian advisers. The Corts of the Realms of Aragon also expressed the desire to have the king respect traditional liberties, showing great reluctance to finance his ventures in Italy, and making repeated requests for his return home. Complicating matters further, the political machinations and erratic behavior in Castile of the Infantes of Aragon prompted Aragonese armed interventions (1425) which, to add insult to injury, did not prove very successful. The king responded promptly. In Aragon and Valencia, either through fiscal and political concessions or through an occasional show of force, Alfonso V was able to secure some steady support for his Italian campaigns. This he did mostly by bowing to the long-established Aragonese and Valencian tradition of *foral* (from *fueros* or charters) rights and "constitutional liberties," though from time to time, as was the case in Aragon in 1442, the king met stiff resistance. In that instance, Alfonso V agreed to enhance the powers of the Justicia of Aragon (a sort of ombudsman who kept a careful watch on Aragonese liberties), together with other reforms which, while limiting royal authority, provided the king with a free hand in Italy.

Catalonia, as always, was another matter. Caught in the factional struggles between the high nobility and urban representatives, the king faced stiff resistance from both camps, insistent on diminishing royal power and creating rival centers of power. Though Alfonso navigated these troubled waters rather diplomatically, making strategic concessions when needed to avoid open confrontation, the demands of each of the branches represented at the Corts amounted, in Bisson's words, to "a veritable constitutional programme."[14] At the Corts of St. Cugat and Tortosa (1419–20), the Catalans asked for the power to veto royal appointments to the king's council, judicial independence, and the precedence of the *Usatges* (the old *foral* codes of Barcelona and Catalonia) over new royal legislation. In return the king was to receive a substantial subsidy. Again, citing Bisson, the Catalonian pactists (from pact or constitutional agreement with the Crown) sought a share of power unprecedented in the medieval West.[15]

Even if the negotiations came to nothing, and both sides were left with accumulated ill will toward their opponents, the negotiations between the Corts and the king set the boundaries for the political aspirations of different political forces within the realm and highlighted the serious difficulties present in ruling the Crown of Aragon in general and Catalonia in particular. Alfonso V, however, was willing to concede a lot as long as he could focus on Mediterranean affairs. But this was a long-term project at best. His policies in the Mediterranean and Italy would take more than two decades to bear fruit, at great human and fiscal cost. Alfonso's strategy can be summarized as follows: first and foremost, the Aragonese king continued the long struggle against Genoa for control of Corsica and trade in the western Mediterranean. Genoa's power had been ebbing as other Italian principalities or republics rose to prominence in the Italian peninsula. Genoa had, in fact, come under the suzerainty of the Visconti (the rulers of Milan). Although Genoese merchants and seafarers still played a significant role in the commercial exchanges of the western Mediterranean and in the expanding Atlantic trade, the city's glory days as a pre-eminent naval power were already on the wane. Corsica was central to Genoa's influence in the Mediterranean; it soon became a battleground. Alfonso V's invasion of the island in 1420 led to a series of Aragonese victories and reverses, and the uncertain outcome of these campaigns kept both powers engaged in a long and debilitating struggle. Snatching victory out of defeat, Alfonso V, after being badly beaten at the naval battle off Ponza (August 1435) and carried away to Milan as a prisoner, was able to charm the Milanese into a treaty, opening the door to a final and conclusive Aragonese victory in 1442.[16]

Alfonso's policies and eventual success in his struggle against Genoa and eventual control of Corsica were deeply bound up with Catalonia's long-term strategy in the western Mediterranean and in line with Alfonso V's wishes to either secure or maintain Catalan control over Sardinia and Sicily, and the even greater price of ruling over the kingdom of Naples. Recognized as heir to the Neapolitan throne by Queen Giovanna in 1421 (and then disowned as the queen chose René of Anjou instead), Alfonso committed all his energies to establishing his rule over what would become his beloved Naples. Alfonso V's policies drew him further away from the internal affairs of the Crown of Aragon and Spain, that is, from having to deal with economic decline in Catalonia, endless bickering over "constitutional liberties," and endemic troubles with Castile. The possibility of starting anew as an Italian Renaissance prince appealed strongly to Alfonso V's political ambitions and aesthetic sensibilities.

To do that, however, required great effort. First, Sicily had to be secured by Aragonese–Catalan contingents in 1435 after fresh agreements with Milan. Alfonso V landed in the island and remained there for two years while seeking to assert royal control over Sicily's restless inhabitants. But Naples beckoned. Once again, as had been the case after the Sicilian Vespers in 1282, the French and Aragonese were matched against each other for control of southern Italy. Besieging Naples in 1438, Alfonso V led a four-year campaign against the city until in 1442 the Aragonese–Catalan army breached Naples' defenses and captured the city. Invested as king by Pope Eugenius IV in 1443, while his bastard son Ferrante was recognized as heir to Naples, an event marked by lavish celebrations (see chapter 8), Alfonso V was now a true Renaissance prince. As such, he was drawn into the endless tug of war of Italian politics. Turning his back on his Visconti ally, Alfonso overextended his reach in his ambition to control Milan, while his long-suffering peninsular subjects yearned for his return.

One could look at Alfonso V's balance sheet and attempt to assess the impact of his Italian ventures on Spain. In hindsight, Aragonese–Catalan rule in southern Italy and in the great Mediterranean islands of Sicily and Sardinia projected Spanish power into Italian affairs. Ferdinand the Catholic's policies in 1494 and Spanish intervention in Italy in the late fifteenth and early sixteenth centuries had their foundation in Alfonso V's struggles for Naples. The new Neapolitan king was astute enough to foster Catalan (and Valencian) commercial outposts throughout the Mediterranean, establishing secure and profitable foundations for Catalan and Valencian trade. Rule over Naples provided a direct link between Renaissance Italy and the Iberian peninsula; the reception of humanist learning in both the Crown of Aragon and Castile – in the latter kingdom through the Trastámara connection – had important consequences for Spanish culture and politics in the late fifteenth century.

Yet, Alfonso V's single-minded preoccupation with Italian affairs had a deleterious impact on the different realms of the Crown of Aragon. As gifted as Queen María or the Infante John, despite his stubborn interference in Castilian affairs, were as representatives of their husband and brother respectively, they could not fully compensate for the long absence of the king. Barcelona's, and with it Catalonia's, economic decline continued apace. In return, the region's progressive impoverishment had dire social and political consequences. Aragon did not fare much better as the frequent royal requests for subsidies to pay for the Italian campaigns and the governance of Naples badly drained much needed resources. In Catalonia a veritable class struggle devastated the Principality. Magnates against knights, urban elites against those below them, landlords against their servile peasant population, and in Barcelona the old and endless rivalry between the Biga and the Busca, all of these conflicts flared up to new and higher levels of intensity. By the mid-fifteenth century, peasant (*remenças*) agitation against harsh conditions and the absence of freedom under which they toiled became the central issue of the period.

The Remenças

If I may be allowed to digress, we should here briefly examine the rebellion of the *remenças*. The long-lasting rebellion of Catalan peasants, seeking to gain the right to purchase their freedom, drew elements of the high nobility and urban commercial interests into the conflict. Everyone, at the end, had a stake in the rebellion, and most of all the Crown. As such the war of the *remenças* was not typical of fourteenth- and fifteenth-century popular risings elsewhere in Europe, which pitted those on top against those below, and certainly not typical of Castile. The Catalonia *remença* rising was indeed part of a complex political process, and the outcome was a political one as well. Its roots lay in the period just described. The *remença* peasants' status and the harsh conditions under which they labored were completely out of step with developments elsewhere in the medieval West and in the rest of Iberia. The *remenças* were serfs and, as such, bound to the soil. As has been noted earlier, they toiled under harsh social and fiscal burdens, their wives and daughters open to assaults from the nobility, a source of grievance compounded by the use of peasant women as wet-nurses for the nobles' children. As will be seen below, at the Sentencia of Guadalupe in 1486, shortly after the chronological terminus of this book, the recently crowned Ferdinand the Catholic granted peasants the right to purchase their freedom.

Alfonso V played both sides of the political spectrum in confronting the *remença* revolt. And when the king entertained freedom for the peasants as a possibility – as long as a substantial amount of money was added to the royal coffers – he opened the door to the *remenças'* long and successful struggle to gain their freedom. In doing so, he also opened the door to endless years of civil war.

In the end Alfonso V, by giving prominence to Naples over his peninsular realms, diminished the significance of the latter. By bequeathing Naples to his bastard son Ferrante, Alfonso also failed to create a true Mediterranean empire. The timing was also inauspicious. By casting his lot with the Mediterranean, Alfonso V joined the fray at a time when the Ottoman Turks, fresh from their historical conquest of Constantinople in 1453, were beginning their more than century-long bid for supremacy in the Mediterranean. Alfonso V was wise enough to settle Italian affairs for a while by co-signing, together with Florence, the Papacy, Venice, and Milan, the other four great Italian powers, the treaty of Lodi, which sought to prevent any of the main political players in the peninsula from establishing a hegemony. It gave Italy a breathing space for four decades; it did not prevent, however, the entry of foreign powers into the peninsula in 1494 and Italy's eventual domination by Spain and France. When Alfonso V died in 1458, admired by poets and those he so liberally patronized at his lavish court in Naples, his son Ferrante inherited the Neapolitan kingdom, while the king's brother, John, who was by then 60, inherited the Crown of Aragon.[17]

John II (1458–1479)

From disruptive high nobleman in Castile and Infante of Aragon to king of Navarre, the life of John II, Ferdinand of Antequera's second son, spanned most of the fifteenth century. Born in 1398 and benefiting from his father's influence in Castilian affairs as regent of Castile and from his mother's extraordinary wealth and position, John was, first and foremost, a great Castilian lord. As such, even after becoming the consort king of Navarre in 1425, he kept throughout most of his long life an unwelcome finger on the pulse of Castilian affairs. We have already met the Infante John, as one of the proud Infantes of Aragon, and described some of his conflicts with Alvaro de Luna, with his own brother, the Infante Henry, and with an ever-changing cast of noble factions for almost three decades before becoming the count-king of the Crown of Aragon. But although Castile remained uppermost in his mind, John engaged vigorously with the affairs of the Crown of Aragon's expansive world and with Navarre's troubled inheritance.

Having become king of Navarre through his marriage to Blanca in 1425, he held on to the Navarrese throne even after his wife's death in 1441 and against the opposition of his own son and rightful heir Charles (Carlos) of Viana. From 1441 to Charles' early death 20 years later, John struggled to maintain his control over the Navarrese realm. When he died in 1479, Navarre devolved to his great-grandson, Francis (Francisco), a grandson of Gaston of Foix (who had married Leonor, the last living descendant of

John and Blanca). With this Navarre returned to French rule for a short while until annexed by Spain in 1512.[18] Besides his Navarrese duties, John served as representative of his brother in Aragon in the 1430s and beyond. He fought at the side of his brother in the disastrous defeat off Ponza in 1435 and, together with Alfonso V, was carried off to Milan as a prisoner. At his brother's behest, he served as royal proxy for Aragonese interests – though it was mostly about his status in Castile that he worried – until the Infantes of Aragon were soundly defeated (with the Infante Henry dying of wounds suffered in the battlefield) at Olmedo in 1445.

Inheriting the Crown of Aragon from his brother in 1458, he still retained, by the terms of Alfonso V's will, rule over Sardinia and Sicily, though Naples, which had drained so much of Aragonese–Catalan resources, went, as noted earlier, to Alfonso V's bastard son. John II's long battle with his own son, Charles of Viana, over the Navarrese succession spilled over into the internal affairs of the Crown of Aragon and broader peninsular politics. Siding with Charles or aiding him became a way for Catalans, French, Castilians, and others to undermine John II. Through his many years of scheming and troublemaking in Castile and in the service of his brother, John II had failed to make many friends in Aragon. His concession of Roussillon and Cerdagne, traditional Catalan lands, to Louis XI, king of France, at the treaty of Bayonne in May 1462 only increased Catalan anger – particularly since the treaty was to provide John with French support in crushing his own subjects.

What followed was confusing indeed. The Catalans, rightly incensed by John II's actions, offered the rule of Catalonia to Henry IV of Castile, renouncing their fealty to John II. Though Henry IV was the wrong choice in many ways, this act of defiance and rejection of John II was symptomatic of the wider political problems confronting the king; even more, it reflected the intractable nature of the Crown of Aragon's internal political structure. If to these problems one adds the continuing economic difficulties in Aragon and, most of all, in Catalonia, one could see that John II had his hands full. When Henry IV of Castile abandoned the Catalan interests at Louis XI's request, Catalan leaders sought to make other deals. First they tried Louis XI himself, but his price, the annexation of Catalonia to France, was too steep for Catalan pride and independence, as it proved to be again in 1640. And then they turned to Portugal for a ruler. When that also failed, they sought out René of Anjou, count of Provence and Alfonso V's former rival for Naples. It was a quite hopeless enterprise.

As Bisson has argued, this political and "constitutional" crisis – for after all the conflict was also about the right governance for the Principality and the nature of the relationship between king and subjects – turned into a civil war.[19] Early in the struggle, opposition to John II and support for Charles of Viana was so adamant as to unite the fiercest of rivals, the Busca and the Biga, in defense of Catalan liberties. This did not bode well for the king.

All these confusing sets of alliances and betrayals opened the door to war in Catalonia, as John II sought to impose his undisputed rule in the region only to meet fierce Catalan resistance. Armed conflicts, which drew outside powers at different stages in the long and protracted struggle, were further complicated by the Crown's ambiguous position regarding the *remença* rebellion. And to add one more ingredient to the pot, the Queen Juana Enríquez (second wife to John II and a member of a powerful Castilian magnate family) and their son Ferdinand, heir to the Realms of Aragon, also took prominent roles in these shifting political alliances. In the end, with Barcelona besieged, the city surrendered in 1472, and John II, with some exceptions, proved to be a magnanimous and intelligent winner, ratifying most of the Catalan liberties. By then, however, Barcelona's economic life had been crushed; its population had fallen precipitously. In the meantime, Ferdinand had been married to Isabella of Castile for three years. Although Valencia and Aragon broke briefly away in rebellion, and the old king tottered slowly toward his death, the marriage changed everything. With John II's passing a new era opened: one dominated by Castile's military superiority, Atlantic ventures, and the taming of the Castilian nobility. The Realms of Aragon would suffer from then onwards from benign neglect. But that is yet another story.[20]

Chapter 6

The Sinews of Power

Administration, Politics, and Display

Disorder and repeated challenges to royal authority, the selfishness of the nobility, and the enduring free-for-all to grab as much of the resources of the kingdom as possible seem to have been the only discernible pattern of political life throughout the Spanish realms, though Castile seems to have fared the worst during the period between 1300 and the reign of the Catholic Monarchs. Nonetheless, in spite of the perception of doom that pervades most political narratives of that century and a half, certain trends and innovations – both in the Crown's actual political program and in its administrative innovations and reforms – provide a more positive counter-narrative to the previous relentless accounts of rebellions, wars, and disasters.

For one, throughout the period under examination kings (or their favorites acting in their own interests) sought to expand and assert their authority over their subjects and over the rather unyielding institutional structures of their respective realms. Noble factions, responding to these royal policies, attempted to thwart these efforts and to accumulate as many privileges and as much property (at the expense of the Crown) as possible. But note that privileges and material gifts came from the Crown, and what could be wrested from kings by force or as part of political deals could also be taken away – as the Catholic kings did – in those periods when royal authority was in the ascendant. Urban elites and representatives assemblies (Cortes, Corts) worked their own deals, equally seeking to advance their own privileges and oligarchic interests. Yet, agreements between Crown and cities were, on the whole, far more beneficial to the kings than dealing with the numerous noble factions vying with each other for a share of profits, lands, privileges, and other goodies. The immense majority of the people, often voiceless in these political processes, just hoped to avoid getting caught up in the crossfire as the three main political actors – Crown, nobility, and urban interests – competed for the prize.

One should note that ecclesiastics, who had representation in both the Cortes and the royal court, do not appear prominently in this story. By the fourteenth and fifteenth centuries high Church dignitaries had become fully part of the internecine struggles of the nobility. The scions of great noble families, these bishops and great abbots' political aims and actions often reflected those of their own familial clans. Church reform, when it came, did not spring from ecclesiastical concerns with the plight of the people below. Rarely were these high Church officials real shepherds to their flocks. As we may remember from chapter 2, those at the bottom were represented as sheep, those at the top as wolves. Bishops, archbishops, and powerful abbots were, more often than not, among the wolves. Their flocks, spoiled and tortured by the nobility, taxed to death by kings and their masters, pinned their hopes on a strong monarch.

We must digress here for a bit. From the thirteenth century onwards – and this was indeed one of the main issues of contention throughout the two following centuries – the Spanish realms stood at a crossroads (which seems like a long time to stand at a crossroads). In general terms this meant defining the very nature of governance. Was there a sense of public responsibility, of the "public," that is? Were there lands that belonged to the kingdom, lands that could not be alienated, as opposed to lands belonging to the king qua individual? Surely if the history briefly told in the three previous chapters teaches us anything is that the nature of royal holdings was always contested in this period, and this fluidity depended on political circumstances, the weakness of the king, and other factors. Nonetheless, the sense of Castile and the Realms of Aragon emerging as territorial entities and the growth of regional and kingdom-wide identities worked as powerful incentives for the slow emergence of new ways of conceiving the kingdom and royal authority.

New feelings and ideas about *patria* (fatherland or motherland) or *tierra* (the land) found echoes in ambitious legislative programs – as for example the failed legal reforms of Alfonso X in the mid-thirteenth century and the successful legislation of Alfonso XI in 1348 – or in the assertive claims of the Aragonese and Catalans to their ancient "constitutional" privileges or to a monarchical authority based upon a commonly agreed pact or contract. What was being decided (and re-decided in a constant give and take) in the thirteenth century and afterwards was the nature and extent of royal power and the relationship between the king (or queen) and his or her people. In the mid-thirteenth century, it appeared that kings would win the day, but the ascendancy of rulers such as Ferdinand III and James I was either short-lived, as in the case of the former, replaced by his politically ineffectual son Alfonso X, or did not have staying power, as was the case in the Crown of Aragon. Noble, and in Catalonia urban, resistance to royal encroachment and claims to power filled the interstices created by royal minorities, social and economic upheavals, and international strife. The outcome was never certain. The final success of Ferdinand and Isabella in Castile (for the Crown of Aragon was just too difficult to reform and was left to the enjoyment of its ancient privileges and to enduring neglect) was never a given. Yet the kings of the Spanish realms, like their counterparts in other medieval realms, had tools at their disposal which eventually tilted the conflict in their favor. None was as powerful a tool as the incipient royal bureaucracies.

We should not proceed without a caveat. In this chapter and throughout this book, I have used terms such as Crown, kings, monarchs, royal authority. All these terms can and should be problematized. By kings I of course also mean queens. After all, both Castile and the Crown of Aragon had some very successful queens. Some of them ruled completely on their own, as was the case with Urraca and Isabella in Castile. In the Crown of Aragon, queens served as lieutenants or almost viceregal representatives quite effectively, as we shall see below and as we have seen in previous chapters. Other queens in Castile and Aragon were effective regents, as was the case with María de Molina, and they proved to be far more capable than many of their male counterparts. It may not be an exaggeration to say that the best kings in Spain were usually female. The terms king, Crown, and monarch are always meant here to encompass that complex system, often implying co-rulership, that was medieval kingship. It was never as simple as I have conveyed here for the sake of brevity. Much more so when the craft of ruling was so deeply dependent on, and embedded in, the workings of royal bureaucracies.

Administering the Realms

Collecting taxes and restoring order bring us face to face with the manner in which Spanish kings or their agents laid the foundations for new ways of ruling, administering the realm, and placing the Crown on a more secure fiscal footing in the late Middle Ages. In the midst of what seemed like undisputed anarchy in Castile and weakening royal power in the Realms of Aragon, innovative administrative transformations took place. These measures strengthened the rulers' hand over the next century and a half and made possible, at least in Castile, significant political reforms. These institutional developments, veritable sinews of power, were not always obvious to contemporaries and were slow in the making. They can be grouped in broad categories: administrative practices, fiscal reforms, military and territorial innovations, and regulating and defining the relationship of the Crown with other orders within the realm. As is always the case, the boundaries between these categories were always fluid; it is indeed not easy to study these developments without reference to other aspects of a broad range of transformations propelling the Spanish monarchies into the early modern period.

Bureaucracies

Most of the bureaucratic structures found in Castile and the Crown of Aragon had long histories. The appearance of early administrative institutions and functions was associated with the royal court (*curia regis*) and the emergence in the central period of the Middle Ages of specialized offices – constable, chancery, seal keeper, and the like – in response to the needs of war, taxation, and the preservation of order. Many of these offices, especially in Castile, had been created in imitation of Muslim administrative practices and to the present day retain their linguistic association with their Muslim origins. Such offices as those of the *alcalde*, *alguacil*, *almotacén*, and others are obvious examples of this cultural and institutional borrowing.

Although bureaucracies are synonymous with the emergence of royal power in the medieval West,[1] the great Christian conquests in the south and the Aragonese–Catalan expansion into the Mediterranean in the thirteenth century made necessary new administrative practices and led to innovative approaches to the administration of the realm.[2] Writing on these themes, I am guided, most of all, by Luis García de Valdeavellano's magisterial *Curso de las instituciones*.[3] As was the case elsewhere throughout the medieval West, kings, or in the case of Catalonia counts, led and supervised, at least in theory, the entire administrative structure. But, as bureaucracies became larger and more sophisticated, the idea that kings could keep their hand on all governmental affairs became ludicrous, especially considering the peripatetic nature of medieval kingship or the exigencies of the Reconquest and Mediterranean affairs. Alfonso V, as we already know, spent most of his reign in Naples. His wife, María of Castile, acting as his lieutenant in Catalonia, effectively ran the Principality with the help of royal agents. Rulers, therefore, began to delegate power, while at the same time assigning inspectors (*inquisitores* or *pesquisidores*) to guarantee compliance with royal edicts. Although royal inquisitors did not prevent the breakdown of order, they projected royal power throughout the realm and served as a deterrent to the growing autonomy of royal bureaucrats. Keeping royal administrators in check could take several forms. Alfonso XI had some of his most important servants executed for malfeasance or too much independence. Henry II (Trastámara), fresh from his victory in the civil war against his brother Peter, sought to assert firm royal control over royal officials, having his measures endorsed by the Cortes.[4] In fact, the Cortes of Toro in 1371, as well as others of the early Trastámara Cortes, showed a remarkable desire, albeit often unsuccessful, to reform administrative structures and to set the realm in order. Later rulers benefited from these efforts. Along the same lines, royal officials – now slowly on their way to becoming public officials – had to render accounts of their years of service. Called *residencia* in Castile and *purga de taula* in the Crown of Aragon, the law commanded royal officials to render careful accounts of all the transactions undertaken during their period of office.[5]

The royal court

Around the Spanish kings a series of important offices evolved from earlier times and became formalized from the 1280s onwards. Including the constable, royal notary, *chancillería*, and treasury, as well as other offices directly associated with court ceremonial, the royal court had gained a formidable number of prominent royal agents by the early fourteenth century. Not only did these powerful men – most of them representing either great magnate families or Church dignitaries, though, as was the case in the fifteenth century, others were newcomers – provide, with the help of university-trained lesser bureaucrats, administrative continuity and long-term planning, but they also enhanced the prestige and "public" image of the monarch. The downside to this was that some of these offices became points of contention for great families, competing with each other for direct access to the king or, as was the case in Castile, for control of the monarch himself. In some cases, some offices became associated with one family, as the powerful de Haro family did with the office of constable in the fourteenth century or as the great noble house of the Moncada did with the position of senechal in Catalonia.

The royal court was a powerful administrative and political structure. In her formidable book, Rita Costa Gomes describes a Portuguese court populated by representatives of the great noble families in the kingdom and adjacent realms, ecclesiastics, merchants and urban representatives, Jews, Muslims, numberless servants, children and adolescents brought up at the king's expense. She has identified by name as many as 265 individuals in 1462, and one must suppose that an equal or greater number could be found in the royal entourage of Castilian and Aragonese kings. In fact, the Castilian accounts of 1293–4 yield a large number of names of servants and higher royal officials, providing the tools for partially reconstructing Castile's royal court staff at the end of the thirteenth century.[6]

There is another aspect of royal courts that is pertinent to this discussion. The itinerant Spanish royal courts served as sites for noble exchanges. As Costa Gomes has shown, the Iberian nobility circulated among the peninsular courts. Their interests, connections, and political agendas transcended the confines of emerging "national" kingdoms. By the fifteenth century, with the increasing popularity of knight-errantry and *pas d'armes*, one could speak of an international noble class. Catalan knights could be found in English jousts. French and German knights-errant traveled and fought throughout the peninsula. Marriages between great noble houses across the boundaries of kingdoms strengthened these ties and ran counter to the interest of centralizing-minded kings. Yet these noble connections mitigated, to a certain extent, the bitterness of conflicts between Iberian realms. In many other ways as well, royal largesse and protection for noble visitors to individual courts legitimized and enhanced royal power. Rituals of hospitality, gift-giving, and patronage of courtly events such as jousts, *pas d'armes*, and other festivities became indispensable parts of the complex mechanisms by which kings did eventually overcome noble resistance and gained or forced their collaboration with, and obedience to, royal authority.

To summarize, bound by growing court ceremonials and festive cycles after 1300 (see chapter 8), one could easily see the significant role that court society – and the court itself – played in giving a decisive advantage to Spanish kings, as it did to other late medieval rulers, in overcoming what seemed the insurmountable opposition of other orders in society. In addition, though the entire court did not always accompany the king in his travels throughout the kingdom, royal itinerancy, as Costa Gomes shows, helped fix the territory and projected royal power throughout most of the realm or, at least, to strategic or sensitive regions of the kingdom. Subjects liked to have their kings around. Alfonso V's long stay in Naples was the cause of endless bickering by his subjects, who clamored for his return, though in reality his wife was a far better administrator and ruler than he could have been.

In Castile, the cities of Valladolid, Burgos, Segovia, Avila, Toledo, and Seville served as "hosts" to a monarchy without a fixed capital (there would not be an official capital in Castile until the designation of Madrid as such in the second half of the sixteenth century). In the Crown of Aragon, Barcelona, Zaragoza, and Valencia had long been traditional administrative and ritual centers. They drew frequent visits from the king or his representatives. This peripatetic behavior also provided Spanish kings with excellent opportunities to supervise the workings of local administrators, maintain or renew relations with local elites, and strengthen alliances with local nobles throughout the territory. In the same manner in which ritual and festivals bound the high nobility to the Crown, royal visits were part of complex negotiations between the king and his people that reiterated principles of mutuality and well-defined responsibilities. Royal visits were expensive affairs, threatening and exhausting the local economies, but they were part of a quid pro quo in which towns and local elites received rewards for their hospitality in the form of new or renewed privileges or individual grants. And since royal visits were always accompanied by elaborate ceremonies and festivities, they provided the Crown with yet another opportunity to display its superiority or symbolic advantages over rivals. Although many of these patterns can be found in earlier centuries, it was only after 1300 that such events became formalized and recorded in the chronicles in a systematic fashion. And even though the kings faced endless opposition from nobles and cities (the latter certainly in Catalonia) during this period, itinerancy, entries, and festivals lay the ground work for later political developments which clearly benefited the Crown. Yet, at the end, the power of kings rested on the mundane and day-to-day business of running the realm.

Local Administration and the Law

If the court and royal bureaucracy, as they perambulated through the Spanish realms, gave great advantages to the Crown, it was the continuity of royal agents on the ground doing their work, collecting taxes, giving judgments, keeping the peace, and other such activities that firmly established the flow of government and accustomed subjects to compliance with royal edicts. These subjects would, of course, rebel from time to time; and in the century under study more than from time to time, but there was seldom any serious questioning as to the right of kings to order their realms. Even more effectively, royal administration was replicated at the local level by municipal and village councils. Although quite litigious and often at odds with the Crown about their privileges, tax exemptions, and royal agents' disregard for these grants, local governments fully accepted the hierarchy of power established by law, tradition, and practice. In doing so, they also buttressed the superiority of the monarch within the realm. Again, struggles occurred, but everyone agreed on the rules. And these rules on how to govern, who owed what to whom, and other such elements of medieval rulership rested upon a long tradition of *fueros* (charters) granted to localities at their foundation or reconquest. Ranging from the great *Usatges* of Barcelona to the ancient *Fuero juzgo* (a translation of the *Lex visigothorum*), or to quite novel legislative initiatives, such as Alfonso X's *Fuero real* or Alfonso XI's *Ordenamiento de Alcalá de Henares*, these texts became tools in the struggle for (and against) local autonomy. Reliance on them, however, only reiterated the unique power of kings to make law. In addition to this, the frequent ordinances of the Cortes or Corts provided a continuous body of rules and regulations for the governance and legal existence of the kingdom.

The fourteenth and fifteenth centuries were particularly fertile in enunciating principles for the governance of the realm and in establishing structures of power that led, at least in Castile, to stronger monarchical authority. But even where this was not the case, as in Aragon and Catalonia, legislative actions and royal edicts helped to define the relations between kings and their people. When Alfonso XI carried out his ambitious legal reforms, the *Ordenamiento de Alcalá de Henares*, in 1348, or when Catalan rebels placed humiliating limitations on royal rule and reasserted the primacy of the *Usatges* and the Corts' monitoring power over royal decisions, we witness what Weber, in a felicitous phrase, described as the "routinization of power." The setting of rules of governance fully agreed by all (or almost all) parties and the relations between ruler and ruled became part of mutually accepted administrative routines. One can list the benchmarks of this legal evolution in Castile: from the setting of the appropriate hierarchy of legal texts in 1348 with the reintroduction of the previously rejected *Siete partidas* as a supplemental code, to the king's reserving to himself the power to make, change, and interpret the law.[7] Thus, in spite of the cycles of violence and challenges to royal power, these legal and administrative reforms propelled the Spanish realms into a very different political world from that of earlier centuries. Legal developments, however, would have been useless without those enforcing the law and promoting an expansion of royal power and prerogatives throughout the land.

The king's men

In a soon-to-be-published book, Francisco Hernández (one of the most insightful scholars of thirteenth-century Castile) explores the royal bureaucracy's complexity in this period. One gets a strong sense of the growing sophistication of royal administration in the royal accounts of 1293–4. The same, perhaps to an even greater degree, could be said of the Crown of Aragon. In the eastern kingdoms there was a strong notarial tradition and Mediterranean-influenced bureaucratic practices. But the questions remain: what were these offices, who were these royal officials, and how did they administer the Spanish realms?

One of the most important positions in the Crown of Aragon was the governmental lieutenancy. Ruling over motley kingdoms and possessions ranging from Aragon, Catalonia, Valencia, and the kingdom of Majorca to the Italian Aragonese–Catalan possessions, the Crown of Aragon's kings found it impossible to rule directly over these dispersed and different kingdoms. Even their perambulation from one realm to another could not satisfy the needs of government, nor please its people. From the thirteenth century onwards the Crown of Aragon had developed a system which delegated power to a member of the royal family to rule specific realms in the absence of the king. Heirs to the Crown or princes of the blood were often the people designated to hold the position. Peter III did so in Catalonia between 1258 and 1276, just before assuming the throne. John II, Ferdinand's father, did so for four years between 1454 and 1458. Royal brothers might also be called on to fulfill this function, as was the case with the aforementioned John II (who was also the heir to the throne), or of the two Peters who held the lieutenancy of Catalonia in 1289–95 and in 1354–5 respectively. The uniqueness of this institution, however, rests on the fact that queens were as often given these tasks. Seven of them held the lieutenancy of Catalonia between 1310 and 1477, and two of them, Violant de Bar and María of Castile, did so for a considerable span of time. As such, these lieutenants functioned as representatives of the kings and fulfilled all the functions of the ruler in the absence of their husband. María, who ruled Catalonia at a critical time (between 1420 and 1453, with some interruptions) while Alfonso V remained in Naples, did so far better than most of her male counterparts.[8] Clearly such practices were put to very good use by the Catholic Monarchs and their Habsburg descendants through the office of the viceroy. In the peninsula, in Italy, in the Low Countries, and in the New World, the Aragonese–Catalan administrative model became essential to the running of the Spanish empire.

Other positions, though not as glamorous or influential as that of the administrative lieutenancy, played significant roles in the managing of the realms. One of the most important royal agents was the *merino*. A regional administrator, tax collector, judicial official, and, at least in theory, careful watchman over royal prerogatives, the merino had jurisdiction over a territorial unit (the *merindad*), an area comparable to the English shire or French *bailliage*. As such the merino – an office that existed under different names in Castile, Aragon, Navarre, and Catalonia (there with the name of *veguer*) – exercised wide powers in a well-defined political and fiscal territory. First and foremost the emergence of the *merindad* signals the Spanish realms' division into well-defined administrative units for easier governance and, most of all, to prevent the concentration of power in the hands of a royal official administering a territory too large or rich for the comfort of the Crown.

In 1351, in the wake of the plague, Peter I of Castile ordered an extensive survey of the royal, ecclesiastical, and seigniorial rights and fiscal resources of all of northern Castile. The *Libro becerro de las behetrías*, as the manuscript (and now published) record of the inquest is known, reflects the ability of the Crown to send numerous royal agents into the most isolated villages in northern Castile. In the mid-fourteenth century, this incomplete survey of northern Castile listed fifteen *merindades*. Some, such as the *merindad* of Aguilar de Campoo, extended over vast territories in the nearby mountains and plain and included 262 different villages.[9] What the *Becerro* reveals is the division of the realm into regions whose contours were determined by geography and history. These northern *merindades* corresponded to earlier stages in the historical development of the kingdom and reflected the ways in which traffic, commercial and military, flowed from one town to another. It was a topography of wayfaring as much as a topography of power.

Responsible for such vast and diverse geographical spaces in a region in which transportation was not always easy (as was the case in northern Aragon and Catalonia), the merinos were organized in a hierarchical scheme. The merino *mayor*, or head merino, supervised the administration of regional officials. Each merino or *bajuli* (another term used in Catalonia) worked in turn with a bevy of subordinates, known, depending the period, as *sayones*, *tenientes*, or *honores*. This elaborate territorial organization was replicated in the semi-autonomous urban centers with *alcaldes*, merinos, *sayones*, and a complex system of subordinate offices. In some cases, certainly after 1300, royal *alcaldes* bridged the distance between kingdom-wide and local administrative structures. In Castile, from the mid-thirteenth century onwards, the *adelantado de la frontera* (a military official in charge of defending border areas) rose to a prominent position within the royal administration. Because of the fluid conditions found in the liminal territories between Christian and Muslim Spain, the *adelantados* exploited the position to their own advantage, as did Don Juan Manuel in 1320s and 1330s Murcia.

Castilian administrative arrangements could be found, with some local variations, throughout the Spanish realms. There were of course exceptions. In the Basque provinces (part of the larger kingdom of Castile), peculiar institutions existed. They were grounded in ancient privileges and reflected the aristocratic character of Basque society. In Aragon the kingdom's regional administrative units were called *honores* or universities (from the concept of guilds) and also *merindades*. *Juntas*, a form of *hermandad* or league of

Aragonese municipalities or communities, became a fixture of Aragonese royal administration and civic life from the late thirteenth century onward. In addition, because of the frequent absences of the monarch as he attended to the needs of other realms, in Aragon, Catalonia, and Valencia, a royal representative, usually a member of the royal family, stood, as already noted, in representation of the king. In Catalonia the equivalent of the merindades were the *vegueries*. By the early fourteenth century there were 18 such administrative units: each of them with a *veguer*, fulfilling the same role as that of the merino in Castile. Because of the fierce claims to autonomy upheld by most Catalan communities, the *veguer* shared responsibilities with a local magistrate, the *battle*. A whole subset of lesser functionaries or parallel fiscal bureaucracies developed from the thirteenth century onwards, buttressing royal authority at a time when the monarchy faced stiff resistance from nobles and cities.

The fourteenth and fifteenth centuries represented a critical period in the formalization of administrative and fiscal institutions. Without this, the political reforms of the late fifteenth century could not have taken place. These developments, in spite of frequent setbacks and reversals, took place along parallel tracks: (1) the growing assertion of royal prerogatives and new legal elaborations defining the relation between Crown and people; (2) the introduction of new administrative practices and offices which became an integral part of statecraft; (3) the inroads made by kings, certainly in Castile, in controlling the fiscal and political resources of urban centers and in curtailing their autonomy. Although the Castilian monarchy proved to be the most successful – if a somewhat centralized kingdom is the measure for success – the Crown of Aragon was, by far, the most innovative, the most prescient in imagining a federation of realms, in limiting royal authority, and in working out, through the system of lieutenancies, a collective and geographically far-reaching monarchy.

The Crown and the cities

One must dispel once and for all the notion that medieval kings (or queens) could rule autonomously, without interference from their subjects. There were no absolute rulers in Spain until probably the eighteenth century, and then only as a French import. What we witness in the late Middle Ages is a tug of war between different groups in society, which in Castile eventually led to the Crown gaining the upper hand, while in the Crown of Aragon, and above all Catalonia, resulted in a reassertion of municipal autonomy and local government. Allow me to present just one single example of what is a very complex topic and which we may be able to explore below from the perspective of the relation between the Crown and the Cortes or Corts.

In Castile the Crown had a long-standing alliance with the cities. From the twelfth century onwards the Castilian kings bestowed on the cities and on their urban ruling oligarchies numerous privileges. In return the king benefited from the military support of urban militias in raids against Muslim lands and, by 1300 and afterwards, in opposing rebellious nobles. After the conquest of Seville the Castilian rulers entered into a partnership with the urban centers to oppose the nobles' growing ambitions and power.[10] But the Crown conceived of this partnership as an unequal one. Under Sancho IV the Castilian Crown tried to intervene in municipal affairs by creating a parallel municipal body, the *Jurado* or jury (jurymen), or by remitting to the royal court or to royal judges (*alcaldes del rey*) many judicial matters hitherto under local jurisdiction. Growing fiscal needs as the economy collapsed and rising unrest within the cities – disfranchised citizens opposing ruling elites or internecine warfare between patrician factions – led Alfonso XI to name *regidores*, royal agents who now became municipal administrators, throughout Castile in 1345 and afterwards. Although in reality most of the *regidores* were selected from the same oligarchic groups that had already monopolized power within the cities, Alfonso XI made sure to appoint enough outsiders to guarantee a royal oversight of municipal councils. Moreover, even if the same elites still preserved their power within the cities, they did so now as agents of the Crown: their power coming directly from the king and not from their own social and economic standing within their respective cities.[11] With all the caveats that such sweeping assertions deserve, one could still argue that municipal autonomy in Castile came to an end by the mid-fourteenth century. This is confirmed by the sorry role that representative assemblies played in the turbulent years ahead. In the Crown of Aragon, as always, the story was different.

The king and the Cortes (Corts)

The contractual nature of the Spanish realms was most evident in the ebb and flow of relations, agreements, and disagreements between the Crown and the kingdoms' representative assemblies. The late Middle Ages witnessed dramatic shifts in these relations as royal prerogatives and the rights, privileges, and duties of each of the different orders within the realm became either defined or redefined according to political circumstances. This is not a monochrome story since each of Spain's political entities – Castile, Navarre, and the different kingdoms comprising the Crown of Aragon

– had its own representative assembly, its own language of governance, and different administrative styles and structures.

Spain had the longest tradition of representative assemblies in the medieval West, pre-dating by a century or more similar developments in England and France. In brief, emerging from the gathering of the *curia regis* (the king's court), these assemblies became general Cortes or true representative assemblies when urban centers sent procurators to their meetings at the request of the king. This happened in León, the site of the first official Cortes for which we have extant evidence, in 1188. The presence of urban representatives provided a convenient forum in which to air grievances, and brought representatives from leading towns together with each other and the king. Far more important, urban procurators approved subsidies for a monarchy which always had an insatiable appetite for new funds, and voted on taxes and other fiscal matters essential for the realm's governance. Historians have long argued that representative assemblies came into being because of fiscal necessities, above all, the maintenance of a stable coinage. And this serves as a reminder that in the Middle Ages, rulers raised funds and imposed taxes with the consent of the ruled. I know that the classical formulation, enunciated by Bartolus in the mid-fourteenth century – the famous *quod omnes tangit . . .* , roughly rendered as "that which touches all, should be decided by all" – evokes "constitutional" arrangements and "democratic" participation. These medieval arrangements were far from that. Those who paid taxes – merchants, artisans, peasants, and the like – also often (especially the oligarchic elites) collected tribute and profited from their role as interlocutors for a vast sea of those below who had no representation. Urban procurators, who from the late twelfth century onwards represented only the upper levels of urban society and nobody else, also engaged in direct negotiations with the Crown and received frequent confirmations of their privileges – an important symbolic and real requirement in the uncertain world of the Middle Ages – tax exemptions, and other grants. It was often a ferocious negotiation, and the ordinances of the Cortes, sent to all the towns for keeping in their respective archives, do not fully reflect the give and take of these meetings, often held during very troubled times.

Of course, the tone of the ordinances and, far more significant, the results, changed from year to year, reflecting political contexts. They also changed from realm to realm. In Castile the Crown's relations with the Cortes swung from almost total royal dependence on urban procurators and leagues of cities to neglect and abuse of the institution by rulers safely ensconced in their power base. In the Crown of Aragon, above all in Aragon and Catalonia, the kings and queens dealt with their respective Corts gingerly.

These representative assemblies could prove quite cantankerous and demanding; the Crown had little leeway and often had to abide by the Corts' demands. Many of the privileges granting wide autonomy and jurisdiction to the Corts had been wrested from the Aragonese kings or, in some cases, given quite freely at a time when the Crown of Aragon's Mediterranean ventures required a free hand at home and some semblance of military and fiscal support. Reversing the contractual nature of the relationship was very difficult and, at times, as Olivares and Philip IV found to their chagrin in 1640, impossible.

The Cortes or Corts had gained, often after a great deal of conflict, the right to be summoned on a regular basis. The frequency of their meetings, however, changed from kingdom to kingdom and depended on many different factors. For example, in Castile the Cortes were to meet every two years. At the gathering of the three orders at Palencia, held in 1313 in the midst of widespread violence and conflict over the regency of the young Alfonso XI, the regents agreed to call the Cortes into session at least every two years between the feast of St. Michael (September 29) and All Saints (November 1), giving the right to high ecclesiastics and royal advisers (which by that time also included urban representatives) to do so if the king or regents failed to meet this obligation.[12] This, of course, often fell by the wayside or was utterly ignored. In times of crisis, these representative assemblies could meet as often as twice a year, as they did in 1313, and contending factions within a regency could, and did, call competing Cortes on their own. Or they could not meet at all, as was the case when the Castilian kings had the upper hand and a firm control of the realm. For example, there were around eight Cortes held during Alfonso XI's minority between 1312 and 1322, a very troubled time indeed, and only nine between 1322 and 1350, when the king had restored some order. For most of the 1330s Alfonso XI did not summon the Cortes even once.

In the Crown of Aragon, the Cortes of Aragon was to meet every year in Zaragoza according to the Royal Privilege of Aragon (1283), or every two years anywhere else in the kingdom as mandated by a royal edict in 1307. Catalonia's Corts also alternated between mandated meetings every year or every three years. Both in Aragon and, far more so, in Catalonia the time span between regular meetings of the Cortes or Corts did not mean the absence of a strict surveillance of royal actions by the Corts' representatives. Unlike Castile, where the king enjoyed a fairly free hand in the affairs of the realm while away from the Cortes, in the eastern kingdoms the Corts selected representatives to a standing committee, which served as a permanent representation of the assemblies' authority and as a standing deterrent to royal policies which these representatives considered harmful to the realm, or to royal claims to unrestricted authority. An innovation of the late fourteenth and early fifteenth centuries, the Diputació del General (Corts) or Generalitat, as it was known in Catalonia, or Diputación in Aragon, these smaller and permanent offshoots of the Corts became a true counterpart to royal power and the embodiment of an emerging Catalan and Aragonese sovereignty (if one can truly use the term of this period). In Catalonia, for example, the Generalitat's jurisdiction extended through a wide-ranging field of activities, from fiscal and administrative to judicial and military. Similar institutions, though less powerful than in Catalonia, emerged in Valencia as well. I would like to re-emphasize the significance of these developments within the context of Spanish and western European history. In Barcelona today the building of the Generalitat (a modern substitute for the ancient original building) still dominates the civic spaces of the city, proudly attesting to its enduring presence as the embodiment of Catalan political identity. This is quite a remarkable development for an institution born during the fourteenth-century crises and struggles against royal authority.

As to membership in the Cortes/Corts, in Castile the three orders of society – the high nobility, the high Church dignitaries, and urban representatives – constituted a full and legal meeting of the Cortes. Not all cities and towns had representation at the Cortes, and as the Castilian kings gained the upper hand they sought to limit the number of towns represented, as well as the number of representatives. As we saw in chapter 3, in 1315 as many as 100 towns sent representatives to the gathering of the Cortes at Burgos. Some localities, such as Avila, sent as many as 16 representatives (though the representation also reflected the factional division of the city's ruling oligarchy). At the Burgalese Cortes of 1315 a wide *hermandad* of town representatives and lesser nobility (*fijosdalgo*) joined forces against an unruly high nobility; the nature of the gathering and the ongoing strife may have accounted for the robust showing of Leonese and Castilian towns. Although the 1315 meeting was unusual in many respects, there is ample evidence that the number of towns sending representatives, or even the number of representatives from each town, varied greatly and depended on such factors as where the gathering of the Cortes took place, what issues were to be discussed, or even the individual towns' willingness or unwillingness to foot the high bill of sending procurators to the meetings.

Throughout the fourteenth and fifteenth centuries, as the realm's political dynamics changed and the direct conflict between the Crown and the segments of the high nobility took center-stage, the role of the Cortes diminished, as did the frequency of the meetings or even the number of those in attendance. By the time of Isabella and Ferdinand – which in many respects stood as the culmination of a series of institutional developments with origins in the previous 150 years – only 18 towns could send procurators to the meetings of the Cortes, and these towns could not send more than two procurators each, as ordered by the Crown and accepted by the Cortes itself in 1429.[13] By slowly reducing the frequency of the meetings and by severely curtailing the number of representatives in attendance, the Castilian Crown ensured a more pliant Cortes, turning it into an effective tool for ruling.

In the Realms of Aragon representation varied. In Aragon the Cortes had four branches: one exclusively for the high nobility or magnates; a second for the lesser nobility and masters of the military orders; a third for ecclesiastics (bishops and influential abbots); and a final branch for urban representatives. Although Catalonia followed this model from 1388 to 1405, the Principality, together with Valencia, maintained the traditional representation by orders: nobles, ecclesiastics, and urban representatives. As was the case in Castile, the number of representatives in attendance varied depending on circumstances, but it was eventually set at two per urban location with the exception of the capital of each of the realms – Zaragoza, Barcelona, and Valencia – which insisted on sending five representatives each. Unlike Castile, where each town named its own representatives, in the Crown of Aragon procurators to the Cortes or Corts were either elected or designated by a lottery. This should not lead us to think that this yielded a more "popular" or "democratic" representation. Towns were fairly hierarchical societies, even in strife-torn Barcelona. Those elected or chosen by a lottery came, with few exceptions, from the ranks of the narrow elites in control of urban life.

The Language of Power: Castile

Comparing the language and tone of the Cortes' ordinances over time provides different perspectives. As noted earlier, the use of the vernacular in Castile contrasts with the use of Latin in the Realms of Aragon (often mixed with the vernacular, Catalan or mostly a form of Castilian in Aragon). The differences, however, go beyond the language of administration and level of political participation. The ordinances of the Cortes in Castile describe how the king called the gathering of the three orders of society, summoning a specific number of delegates from the towns, as Ferdinand IV did to the town of Avilés in 1305 when he requested two representatives, or an undetermined number, as was the case in 1307 and on other occasions.[14] Urban procurators came with their lists of complaints. The king listened, agreeing with some of the requests (he cannot have agreed to all), and then ordering the drafting of the ordinances that summarized the urban requests and demanded compliance with the king's response. When a ruler had fairly firm control of the realm, as Alfonso XI did in 1348, he could summon representatives to the Cortes, not to listen to their petitions and pleas, but, with "their consent," to enact a new and comprehensive body of laws, the *Ordenamiento de Alcalá de Henares*.[15]

By the late fourteenth century and afterwards the protocol in the give and take between urban representatives and the king (or queen) at the Cortes had changed. The Cortes of Madrid in 1393 met as Henry III's troubled regency came to an end, and the young king reached his majority. The ordinances included language symptomatic of the changes that had taken place in the previous half-century or so, in spite of what appeared to be a weak monarchy. The ordinances, drafted by royal scribes and copied to most towns throughout the realm, include the response of procurators to royal questions rather than royal responses to urban complaints:

> Most excellent and Catholic king, and most high and powerful prince, and most *esmerado* [accomplished] and fearful lord. The knights and squires who are in your Cortes as procurators of the cities and towns of your kingdom, humbly and with great humility answer to your high and noble three reasons [points made by the king] that you proposed to your Cortes on the first day of your attendance . . .[16]

Although not every Cortes included such sycophantic language, there is little to gloss here. Such forms of addressing the ruler would have been inconceivable a century earlier and now had become part of a formulaic language of respect and obedience which, if not always fully realized by the king's rebellious Castilian subjects, articulated new discourses of power.

The Crown of Aragon

The meetings of the Corts in the Crown of Aragon, above all in Catalonia, were serious business. Not only do we get a mixture of Latin and Catalan, a day-to-day account of what transpired at the meetings, that is, something close to actual minutes of the sessions (as opposed to Castile's summaries presented in the final ordinances sent to towns), but the formulaic listing – and adhesion to the proceedings – of all those present, providing a very different feel from the Castilian experiences. In the long gathering of the

Corts in Girona and Barcelona in 1358, Peter the Ceremonious came cap in hand to request a subsidy for the "defense of the realm and of the land" (*pro defensione Regnorum et terrarum*). A formulaic listing of all those present details each of the different individuals and orders represented at the meeting. After months of deliberation and fierce back and forth, and a 225-page transcript (published in the nineteenth-century edition of the Crown of Aragon's Cortes), the king received a modest subsidy.[17] It is no wonder that the kings of the Crown of Aragon in the fourteenth and fifteenth centuries preferred the Mediterranean to this endless haggling with three different Corts. In fact, queens, holding the lieutenancy of the realms of the Principality, were the ones who often had to do business with the Corts, as María de Luna and María of Castile did for their respective husbands. And the Habsburg rulers of Spain often chose to go without substantial tax income and military conscriptions to avoid having to deal with such recalcitrant subjects.

In the end, whether in Castile or in the eastern kingdoms, the Spanish kings' relations with their respective Cortes set a pattern for a working relationship between the Crown and the different orders. The meetings, whether held frequently or not, provided a site for political exchanges, negotiations, and complaints. Grievances and royal responses to the petitions of urban procurators always focused on some vital area: justice or the absence of it, relations with, and control of, religious minorities, abuses by royal officials, and taxes. To explore each of these categories would engage us in an endless and, perhaps, tedious discussion. Instead, I would beg the reader's patience to briefly examine the question of taxes. Fiscal policy was, after all, one of the key responses to the crisis of late medieval society. Royal innovations in terms of tax-collecting and expansion of royal resources was at the root of the increased power of kings.

Taxes

As has been seen in chapter 2, new forms of warfare and governance, and the extravagance of the royal court, engaged all medieval kings (and queens) in endless struggles for new sources of income in the late Middle Ages. The Crown and its agents entered into frantic, and often brutal, attempts to raise funds. What were their methods? What were the results? Though medieval practices of raising revenue do not come close to the thoroughness of the modern age, the Spanish rulers had at their disposal multiple, and important, sources of income. In the late Middle Ages, while facing a decline in the number of taxpayers and a serious economic downturn, royal administrators demonstrated an uncanny ability to find new ways of raising funds. Their conscious actions on fiscal matters, dull as they may seem to most readers, were central to royal efforts to thwart noble attempts to emasculate the power of kings. Beyond that, as reluctant as the Cortes or Corts were about voting new subsidies, urban procurators understood that the king needed money. It was the obligation of the Cortes or Corts to provide it and/or to cooperate in finding it. Further taxation was a continual and painful reminder to the population at large of royal prerogatives and authority.

Spanish kings had long established their right to collect specific taxes throughout their territories. A long time before such practices became common in other Western realms, the kings of Castile and of the Crown of Aragon collected territorial taxes, that is, contributions paid through-out their realms not just from the royal domain. These taxes received the name of *terratge* in Catalonia and *marzadga* and *martiniega* (from the time of year when they were collected, either in March and/or on the feast of St. Martin, November 11) in Castile. These dues on either households, hearths, or arable measures were collected by royal agents or their local representatives at set times of the year and complemented the substantial income kings derived from their own lands. These traditional tributes had suffered greatly over the passing of the centuries. Nobles and clerics were exempted from most direct taxes. Sometimes they had appropriated many of these sources of revenue for themselves. Members of the urban elites, especially those with horses and weapons and belonging to the mounted urban militias, also enjoyed extensive tax exemptions, as did their servants. The very poor paid no taxes either. Moreover, over the long centuries of Reconquest and raids against Muslim lands, the king had granted extensive tax exemptions to those settling on the advancing frontier. All these different exemptions from taxes became an endless source of litiga-tion as royal agents sought to tax those who claimed to hold royal grants. Clearly new sources of revenue were needed.

One new source of income that proved particularly profitable was taxes related to the use of woods (*montazgo, forestatge*), a natural resource rapidly on the wane throughout most of Spain. Another was the right to pasture one flock's (*herbazgo*). Although these taxes had an earlier proven-ance, it was only in the fourteenth and fifteenth centuries that, prompted by the spectacular take-off of wool exports and the practice of trans-humance, they provided a steady and substantial contribution to the monarch's income. Kings had also regal rights over mines, salt-wells, and other natural resources. Far more profitable was the death-grip which Spanish rulers, Castilian kings most of all, had over the Church. Although royal dominion over ecclesiastical income had its origins in the twelfth and thirteenth centuries, by the late Middle Ages it was outright extortion. As Peter Linehan has brilliantly shown, the kings of Castile and, to a lesser extent, the Crown of Aragon had almost a free hand in tapping Church income under the pretext of launching a crusade against al Andalus, claiming as much as one-third of all ecclesiastical income for their own pockets.[18] Kings had also obtained from the Cortes a contribution to the maintenance of the coinage. That is, the king promised not to devalue the coinage in return for a contribution (*moneda forera*). Similarly, since in most parts of Spain everyone was, in theory, liable for military service, exemption was gained by paying a tax called *fonsadera* in Castile and *huest* in Aragon.[19]

The Crown also collected taxes on imports and exports of goods in and out of the kingdom. The accounts of 1293–4 are revealing of the fabulous profit made by Castilian kings from the import of textiles, but goods transported across the land were also taxed along the way at internal custom houses (*tablas* in Aragon, *puertos secos* in Castile) and upon entry into most towns. These taxes – which became really profitable only with the emergence of new patterns of trade in the late thirteenth century – reached unprecedented levels in the next two centuries since both imports and exports were subject to royal taxes. In the Crown of Aragon, Catalonia above all, a high proportion of these customs duties was collected by the Generalitat, though partially paid back to the Crown in the form of subsidies that had to be approved by the Corts. Another important profitable source of income and far easier to collect than customs duties was the head tax and special services imposed on Jews and Muslims. Paid annually as a direct tax by Jews and Muslims living under Christian rule, these substantial payments were further enhanced by the frequent tribute paid by the Nasrid rulers of Granada to their Christian royal overlords. In the late thirteenth century (1291) a limited number of *aljamas* or Jewish communities in Castile paid close to 930,000 *mrs.* (*maravedís*) in head taxes and service. The extant list of those localities paying the head tax did not include the Jewish community of Toledo or that of Andalusia, which might have doubled the amount raised in the north. In the Crown of Aragon (which included Aragon, Valencia, and Catalonia), payments were as follows: in Aragon, the Jewish *aljamas* contributed 60,000 *sólidos* (*ss.*) of *jaca*, while the Mudejars added 40,000 *ss.*; in Catalonia, Jews paid 100,000 *sólidos barchinonenses*; and in Valencia they paid 25,000 *sólidos regales*. Although most of this income was distributed to members of the royal family, royal agents, noblemen, and ecclesiastics, it represented an extraordinary contribution to the royal fisc *without* need to request funds from the representative assemblies.[20] By 1474, after the Jewish communities had been greatly diminished by the violence and waves of conversions in 1391 and afterwards, the income for the entire kingdom of Castile only amounted to 450,000 *mrs.*, a figure still formidable but far inferior to the income Jews (and Muslims) generated for the Crown throughout most of the fourteenth century.[21]

Among the most important fiscal innovations of the period was the imposition of the *alcabala* (a sales tax of around 5 percent on all goods purchased within the realm) as a regular source of income. A fiscal tool, both linguistically and institutionally, of Muslim provenance, the *alcabala* could be found before 1300, but it was not until Alfonso XI's reign that this sales tax became an established and renewable tax imposed throughout Castile to pay for the siege of Algeciras. As the Castilian Cortes agreed to extend the tax at each succeeding meeting, the *alcabala* became a permanent addition to a growing variety of royal fiscal tools. Finally, in this much-abbreviated listing of taxes, the subsidies voted at the meeting of the Cortes represented a substantial portion of the Spanish monarchy's income. As we have seen in previous chapters, getting the Cortes or Corts to vote a subsidy was not always easy. In early fourteenth-century Castile, when the Crown was battered by rebellious noblemen and ambitious regents, Queen María de Molina had to bargain very hard with the urban procurators and concede considerable privileges and tax exemptions to secure the towns' financial and military support. In the Crown of Aragon, the kings chose (or had no other option than) to work through the Corts. Although it did not always prove easy or agreeable and although these working agreements between Crown and representative assemblies often required significant concessions, these "constitutional" alternatives were perhaps the only possible solution to the always pressing fiscal needs of Aragonese kings. After all, the choice to work through the Corts in the motley eastern kingdoms had been made long before 1300; by then it had acquired the authority of tradition. Beyond that, the Generalitat had control of some of the Crown's revenues, and subsidies were often financed from these resources.

Control of the Cortes meant control of important tax assets. In the Realms of Aragon, although its kings enjoyed considerable independent fiscal power – counting as they did on the income of the royal domain, feudal or semi-feudal lordly rights, and territorial taxes – royal power was, by the very nature of the relations between Crown and Corts and between Crown and other orders of society (nobility and clergy), limited. In Castile the kings had learned early on that as much as they needed the Cortes and the cities to withstand magnate ambitions, their own autonomy was compromised by urban interference. When Ferdinand IV summoned the Cortes to Valladolid in 1312, the year of his death, he gave urban representatives a considerable stake in government, appointing some of their number to leading administrative positions in his court. The king chose 12 "good men" to serve as royal *alcaldes*, plus a series of scribes (*escribanos*) to serve them and to register officially their decisions. Those chosen for these positions came from the ranks of the urban patrician elites, providing a wide representation of different areas (and towns) throughout the kingdom. These towns were Burgos, Medina de Pomar, Vitoria, Sahagún, Benavente, Salamanca, León, Arévalo, Talavera, and Cuenca. Each of these new *alcaldes* received 6,000 *mrs.* annually and the scribes 3,000 *mrs.* in salary, a substantial figure indeed.[22]

Other kings thought differently. Although it was important to have urban representatives at court and in the royal bureaucracy, they should be subordinated to royal policies. Alfonso XI's naming of royal officials to administer the towns – the *regimiento* or *regidores* – was a move in that direction. So was the Castilian royal reluctance to summon the Cortes after the intense flurry of activity during Alfonso XI's minority at the beginning of the fourteenth century. Central to the political development of Castile in the fourteenth and fifteenth centuries was royal neglect of the Cortes. Urban interests might work temporary alliances with magnates factions and take sides in civil wars, or for one regent against another, but their collective fate lay always with the Crown. But why would kings, who in the thirteenth and early fourteenth centuries had forged such strong links with their cities, now forsake them and fail to summon the Cortes or to provide a collective setting for urban grievances and ambitions? The answer is a brutal one. In the fourteenth and fifteenth centuries, the Castilian kings, unlike their counterparts in the Crown of Aragon, benefited from autonomous sources of income. Between the ever-increasing amounts they received from taxes on the movement of livestock throughout the land and from the export of wool (the kings owned large flocks as well) to Flanders, the tax on Jews, and what they continually skimmed from the Church, the Castilian kings did not need to work too many deals with the cities or with the Cortes. Obviously, the relation remained important and a source of legitimacy and of fiscal and military support, but the substantial income kings now enjoyed independent of the approval of the Cortes allowed them scope to make extravagant gifts to the nobility and to put on excessive displays. Fiscal agility and some autonomy from institutional restraints were powerful solutions to the general crisis of the late Middle Ages.

Symbols of Power

Ruling in the Middle Ages was also the difficult art of projecting symbols, images, and gestures that reminded, and taught, those to be ruled about the authority of kings. In a world without TV, radio, e-mail, or newspapers, kings needed to construct an image of majesty and power superior in every sense to other symbols of power deployed by those competing with the Crown. Kings sought also to impress their subjects with the trappings and symbolic meaning of their office. These aims were achieved, though not always successfully, through an elaborate structure of rituals, ceremonies, cultural artifacts (such as palaces, art, literature, and other such cultural products), dress, and food. They also served as continuous reminders of the uniqueness of kings. That these symbols and ceremonies often failed and did not prevent opposition, armed resistance, and even the assassination or overthrowing of kings does not take away from the fact that these mechanisms were often very efficient at creating a sense of devotion to the Crown and at representing the king as the embodiment of the realm.

Sacred and unsacred monarchies

If one needed to emphasize further the differences between Castile and the Crown of Aragon, nothing would be as effective as to highlight the contrasts in how the rulers of each of these realms became kings. It has long been a trope in medieval historiography that the embryonic development of fairly centralized monarchies was unavoidably linked to the evolution of highly ritualized sacral kingship. That is, kings throughout the West developed ceremonials – some of them with roots in Roman, biblical, and Germanic traditions – that effectively helped to create what my teacher Joseph R. Strayer described once as a "religion of monarchy." Specifically I refer here to the rites of anointment and coronation which placed the king above his subjects and which granted an element of sacrality and ecclesiastical charisma to royal functions and powers. Kings were made by the grace of God, and anointment and crowning by ecclesiastics reaffirmed the close link between kings, the Church, and God. In many cases, these traditions, as seen in the so-called paradigmatic examples of France and England, allowed kings to claim that they could heal the sick (of scrofula) by the touch of their hands.[23]

So much for these broad formulations. Today we know that many of these English and French traditions were invented in the central or even late Middle Ages and given the patina of antiquity so as to command greater authority. We must not imagine these rituals and ceremonies to be immutable. One of the most remarkable features of Spanish ideas about the nature, limits, and rituals of power was their adaptability to new circumstances, and the willingness, certainly in the case of Castile, to embrace specific (though often modified to the individual king's taste) rituals, as Alfonso

XI did in his coronation in 1332, or to discard them altogether. Any serious study of royal ceremonial practices would focus on their differences and local peculiarities rather than on their uniformity. We know that the kings of the Crown of Aragon were crowned and anointed in the ancient capital of Zaragoza, although from time to time, and certainly after the ascent of the Trastámaras to the throne in 1412, anomalies occurred that departed from long-established models.[24]

In the twelfth century, the count-kings of Catalonia and Aragon had acknowledged papal suzerainty. Peter II had been crowned by Pope Innocent III in 1204 while at Rome. There is evidence that Aragonese kings clearly saw, as the French kings did, the connection between crowning, anointment, and the legitimating of the ascent to the throne. Peter III (1276–85), for example, did not assume his rightful title of king for almost a year until he was crowned at Zaragoza.[25] The great Catalan chronicler Ramón Muntaner describes in detail the events leading to the coronation of Alfonso IV in 1327, as well as the actual ceremonies marking his ascent to the throne.

> Once he had buried his father with all the solemnity due to a dead king, king Alfonso, with his brothers, ecclesiastical dignitaries, noblemen, and citizens [urban representatives] traveled to the town of Montblanch and held a meeting to decide where to travel first: whether to Aragon, Valencia, or Barcelona, for he wished to pay the debts he had with each of his kingdoms as his ancestors had . . . It was decided to go to Barcelona to hold Corts and assemblies with the Catalans. By Christmas he was in Barcelona, though he stopped along the way to visit different localities. In them, he swore to uphold all the uses, liberties, and privileges, and, in return, the Catalans took oaths to him as king [count]. On Easter Day, 3 April 1328, to bring happiness to his people as Christ's resurrection had brought happiness to his Apostles, the king came to Zaragoza, ordering that all the magnates, prelates, and urban representatives meet him there.[26]

The account is followed by a long list of those in attendance, including Muntaner himself as one of the six representatives of Valencia and accompanied, as was the case for Muntaner, by children and nephews. In Zaragoza, and as a prelude to the actual coronation, the king knighted many magnates. They, in turn, knighted many other lesser nobles and men. Muntaner counted at least 256 lesser nobles who were knighted that day and who, after the knighting ceremonies, paraded on horseback through the city from the cathedral to the king's palace. Later, in preparation for his coronation on Easter Sunday, the king kept vigil through the night of Good Friday. On Saturday the king and his court abandoned the clothes of mourning they had worn for the previous king, and the feasts began with abundant music.

In a ceremonial procession, the king traveled to the cathedral, surrounded by magnates, knights, and music, and he remained there throughout Saturday night. At dawn, the king "with his own hands" placed the sword and crown on the altar and dressed himself. Among his vestments, he also wore some ecclesiastical garments. The bishop of the city witnessed and helped in every detail of the ritual investment of the king: from the king taking his sword and girding it on himself to the placement of his spurs on his feet by his royal brothers to the appropriate prayers. The king, brandishing his sword, defied the enemies of the Catholic faith, promised to defend orphans, children, and widows, and maintain justice, offering his sword and his life to God. This was followed by the bishop's anointment of the king's shoulder and right arm. A mass followed after which the king took the crown from the altar and crowned himself.

Muntaner's chronicle continues with a detailed description of the festivities that followed, and I beg your forgiveness for this extended summary of the chronicler's account of Alfonso IV's self-crowning and ecclesiastical anointment. The actual story is far richer and takes almost 20 pages of the printed edition. The ritual program is quite different from French or English practices and, even more so, from those of Castile. First, self-crowning and anointment takes place after the king meets the Cortes or Corts and swears to uphold the liberties of Catalonia (and eventually those of Aragon). Second, the coronation is in Zaragoza, and the king, following the practice of Portuguese and Castilian kings, insisted on knighting himself. Third, there is an implicit association throughout Muntaner's narrative between the king and Christ – and this coming from an urban representative of Valencia! – and the choice of Easter Sunday for Alfonso's coronation, mixed with the ending of mourning and rebirth, sent a powerful message to those present. They, in turn, would go home and retell the story. Muntaner, who by this time in his life had seen and experienced much, cannot mask his admiration for all the festivities, for the quality of the horses, for the splendor of the royal sword and crown. Clearly these ceremonies, and Alfonso IV's crowning in particular, worked at the deepest level in binding social groups together and instilling loyalty to the king and kingdom – the magnates and knights rode through the streets crying "Aragon, Aragon." And finally, the king crowned himself, making it clear to all, and particularly the ecclesiastics, that the right to rule resided within him. The 1327 ceremonies tell us vividly of the differences between the Crown of Aragon and European northern realms. They tell us about how the Aragonese kings deployed rituals and celebrations to strengthen their power and to make claims to ecclesiastical roles not open to their many secular rivals. They tell us as well as how very different the Aragonese ways were from those of Castile.

Castile's non-sacral monarchy

There were also coronations and anointments in late medieval Castile, but they were exceptions rather than part of a well-established tradition. A few kings, Alfonso XI in 1332, Henry II, the new Trastámara king, after his ascent to the throne in 1365, were crowned (self-crowned) or partially anointed, but even the new Trastámara dynasty with its flimsy claims to the throne ignored those sacralizing ceremonies that marked the assumption of kingship in other parts of the medieval West. This is quite remarkable since the Trastámaras, once they began to rule the Crown of Aragon, demonstrated a healthy appetite for crowning, anointing, and royal rituals, as Ferdinand of Antequera's lavish coronation showed.[27] In Castile, however, there was not a clear relationship between ascending the throne and being crowned, even in those rare instances in which such ceremonies took place.

Alfonso XI had been king for two decades before organizing the spectacle of knighting, coronation, and anointment at Santiago and Burgos in 1332. By then he was already married, had an heir, and was as firmly in control of his realm as he would ever be in his long and distinguished rule. His coronation ceremony, which I have glossed elsewhere,[28] followed closely on the patterns we have already seen for the coronation of Alfonso IV in Zaragoza just a few years earlier. It may have been, in fact, inspired by the Aragonese example, with some peculiar differences. Alfonso XI was knighted by the mechanical arm of an image of St. James then at Compostela and which can still be seen at the monastery of Las Huelgas in Burgos. Peter Linehan has argued that this particular mechanical sculpture had come into Castile only in the first half of the fourteenth century, becoming, as it were, the foundation of an invented tradition.[29] Alfonso XI was crowned at Las Huelgas, a great Cistercian monastery and one of the sites, together with Compostela, Toledo, Seville, and León, vying to become a "sacral" center for the Castilian monarchy. Alfonso XI also crowned himself and was anointed only on the shoulder. The Church, as had been the case at Zaragoza, played a secondary role, and the *ordo* or script for the coronation, written by a Portuguese bishop and long deployed as an example of Castilian alleged sacral monarchy, was in fact discarded altogether and replaced by ceremonies scripted either by the young monarch or his agents.

Some scholars, notably Nieto Soria, have argued that even though the Castilian kings had chosen to abstain from ceremonial crowning and anointment, their rule had all the trappings of sacral kingship, as was the case elsewhere in western Europe. Whether in their hearts and minds these kings, or their ministers, believed that God had anointed and crowned them in spirit, or whether such propaganda was an attempt to explain the absence of such rituals, the argument misses the point altogether.[30] And that is that in Castile, where there was a rich tradition of crowning and anointing harking back to Visigothic and Asturian precedents and to the ceremonial crownings of Alfonso VI and Alfonso VII (late eleventh and early twelfth centuries), for a series of complex reasons the Castilian kings abandoned these practices by the second half of the twelfth century.[31]

Absence of ecclesiastically sponsored rituals of coronation and anointment did not mean at all that there was an absence of tradition or, far more important, of legitimacy in the Castilian kings' ascent to power. The Castilian monarchs developed a set of alternate and richly textured rituals that proved to be as successful in the long run as Church-related traditions. These included elevation on a chair or shield, exchanges of oaths between the king and his "people," the swearing of fealty by the Cortes, self-knighting, and most of all, the association of kingly power with the work of the Reconquest. It is quite remarkable how much mileage the Castilian kings extracted from the *ida contra los Moros* (the announcement of raids against Islam, or Crusades). We know that the royal military leadership of the Crusades against Muslims in the south or those in Granada brought substantial fiscal advantages since it allowed the kings to tap directly into the Church's income. And the same call to arms proved irresistible to the Cortes as well. Alfonso XI proved that repeatedly in the 1330s and 1340s when he requested funding for his campaigns against the Merinids in the south. Alfonso XI was a king without many of the political problems that plagued his descendants; yet later kings were also able to exploit their role as leaders of the host, the embodiment of the struggle against Islam, and defenders of Christendom.

Sumptuary Laws and Ceremonies of Power

Sacred or unsacred rituals associated with the making of kings underpinned a whole structure of other celebrations which, on the whole, sought to separate the figure of the king from that of his subjects. Although I could spend another chapter describing and explicating these additional tools of power, for the sake of brevity I will simply summarize them here. Dressing and eating were powerful markers of social distinction in the medieval world. They served to create a distance between the king and ambitious magnates. Sumptuary laws in mid-thirteenth- to mid-fourteenth-century Castile, although aiming to erect rigid boundaries between merchants and nobles, between Jews and Christians, also restricted certain furs, clothes, and colors to the use of the royal family. Similarly, under the pretext of imposing some austerity on a spendthrift nobility, the laws set out monetary guidelines as to how much was to be spent on food for the royal table and what types of food were to be consumed. At the same time, these laws also set limits on what magnates were to spend on their food on a daily basis.

The growth of court ceremonial and the enhanced importance of etiquette, a clear development in the fourteenth and fifteenth centuries, went far beyond the establishment of well-defined hierarchies of eating and dressing. We know that from the mid-fourteenth century onward chronicles, both royal and private, began to pay a great deal of attention to how people dressed at court. This was particularly the case in the descriptions of the royal family and great nobles. Similar attention was also paid to what and how much they ate. Muntaner already gives testimony to this new sensitivity. The anonymous *Hechos del condestable Don Miguel Lucas de Iranzo* overwhelms the reader with its descriptions of the banqueting, clothing, and festivities sponsored by the constable in 1460s Jaén.[32]

Increased attention to appearances was paralleled by a more punctilious observance of etiquette and by the triumph of a literary culture at court. We will explore some of these issues in greater detail in chapter 8, but here it may suffice to indicate that the transformation of Aragonese–Catalan and Castilian culture(s) under the influence of Renaissance models imported from Italy deeply affected the development of court society and helped legitimize kingly power. And kings through festivals also extended their power. Again we will examine some of these festivals in the context of cultural production (for they were cultural artifacts) in chapter 8, but one must remember the extent to which royal entries (an integral component of Alfonso IV's ceremonial tour of his realms), to give just one example, were among the most effective tools for the ruler. Royal (or princely) entries – the first ceremonial visit of a new king to one of the realm's cities – provided an opportunity for the display of royal power and to give lessons to subjects on obedience and respect for the king, and served as sites for intense negotiations between town and Crown. Even weak kings, such as Henry IV of Castile, could mount spectacular and theatrical entries to buttress royal authority.[33] Henry IV's royal entry into Jaén reflects the resources that rulers had even at a time when the monarchy was in peril. Already deep in trouble because of magnate rebellions, the king came to Jaén in 1464 to visit his former favorite, Don Miguel Lucas de Iranzo, constable of Castile. A short summary of this entry will give an idea of the manner in which powerful symbols were deployed for the benefit of a vulnerable king and an equally vulnerable constable:

The constable, riding a white horse with a scarlet damask banner in his hand and followed by a large contingent of men-at-arms, met the king at Alcalá la Real to escort him into the city. Half a league from Jaén, the canons of the cathedral chapter and municipal officials led a ceremonial procession. Five hundred knights with false beards [disguised as Moors], thirty others dressed as Moorish women playing tambourines and bells, four thousand children [an obvious exaggeration since the entire population of Jaén in the 1460s would have been barely over that figure] riding wicker horses, another thousand children armed with wicker crossbows and "many other men and women," the entire city, brought the king in ceremony into the city.[34]

In the spectacular cycle of festivities held throughout the month of May 1428 – festivities allegedly organized to welcome the Aragonese Infanta Leonor, passing through Valladolid on her way to her marriage in Portugal – beyond the public display of wealth, clothing, and courtly prowess, serious political issues were fought over between Don Alvaro de Luna, John II of Castile's favorite, and the Infantes of Aragon. The displays of elaborate costumes, artificial castles, *tableaux vivants*, wheels of fortune, jousts, and the like (all of them performed in the main square of the city for the edification of throngs of onlookers) were not empty gestures or just useless display. They were pregnant with ideological meaning and carried powerful messages to warring magnates and royal subjects about the authority of kings.

Chapter 7

Muslims, Jews, and Christians in a Century of Crisis

Unlike other parts of western Europe where Jews had been expelled by the end of the fourteenth century (1296 in England, early fourteenth century in northern France, and late fourteenth century in southern France), Spain had a substantial Muslim and Jewish population almost into the early modern period. Religious plurality and the manner in which the dominant Christian population dealt with religious minorities made Spain quite different from other realms in the medieval West. Although the history of relations between the three religions is an integral part of the larger peninsular history and it should not be compartmentalized, in this chapter and for the sake of clarity I examine the lives and travails of these minority religious communities and their interaction with each other and with Christians as a separate topic.

The late medieval crises shaped the conditions under which Muslims and Jews lived in Spain and animated the reactions of those in power and their policies against them. These crises also triggered violent upheavals from below. Restrictive laws against Jews and Muslims and widespread violence against them were part of that great sea-change that occurred in Spain from the early thirteenth century onward, transforming social relations, political structures, and Christian perceptions of non-Christians.[1] In many respects, the role and place of Jews and Muslims within Christian society serve as a marker for the historical evolution of Spain in the more than century and a half before Jews were exiled or forced to convert in 1492 and Muslims were equally compelled to accept Christianity in the early sixteenth century.

Because we know the denouement of this sad story, one is often led to believe that the history of Muslims and Jews in the late Middle Ages consisted of a series of benchmarks, leading inexorably to intolerance, exile, and/or forced conversion. It was not so, and the tragic final chapter to religious plurality in the Spanish medieval realms was not always a

given or even perceived as likely by contemporaries. For a long time the
traditional historiographical position has been to see the lives of Jews
and Muslims, and Christian attitudes toward them, as generally a story of
rapid decline, growing intolerance, and violence from the early thirteenth
century onwards. For Jews the landmarks are sporadic but violent attacks
throughout the Middle Ages, culminating in widespread violence in 1391,
forced conversion, the birth of the Spanish Inquisition (officially in 1484
but already functioning in some parts of the peninsula in 1478), and exile
(1492). For Muslims the Christian conquest of most of Andalusia in the
mid-thirteenth century, the expulsion of Mudejars (Muslims living under
Christian rule) from western Andalusia in the 1260s after a failed rebellion,
a century and a half of raids against Granada, the conquest of the latter
city in 1492, forced conversion in the early sixteenth century, the brutal
repression of the Alpujarras rebellion (1568–70), and the final expulsion
of the Moriscos (Muslims who had nominally converted to Christianity)
in the first two decades of the seventeenth century are the high, or one
should say the low, points of this traditional narrative.

Today we know the story a bit more clearly. Recent historians have
drawn a far more complex picture of what the lives of religious minorities
were like and of their relations to each other and to their Christian neighbors. In truth the edicts of the influential Fourth Lateran Council (1215)
resonated throughout the Christian world. Its harsh and exclusionary policies
toward Jews and, to a lesser extent, Muslims, had echoes in Castile's late
medieval legislation aimed at restricting the lives of religious minorities.
Yet the anti-Jewish measures found in the ordinances of the Castilian Cortes
after 1250 also replicated ancient Visigothic edicts. Pejorative representations of Jews and Muslims in literary works of the thirteenth and fourteenth
centuries also echoed similar polemical writings of the eighth century. As
Jonathan Ray has shown in his excellent recent book on Jews in thirteenth-
century Iberia, they had settled in frontier areas and prospered in the late
thirteenth century and succeeding centuries in a wide geographical arc
ranging from Portugal to the Balearic Islands.[2] And this is in spite of what,
in most books on Jewish life in Spain, has been depicted as a period of
utter decline for Jewish communities. One of the communities in question
was that of Morvedre, near Valencia. Mark Meyerson has adroitly chronicled
their successes and travails through most of the fourteenth and fifteenth
centuries. Most remarkable is Meyerson's description of a Jewish revival
during the fifteenth century, a period long postulated as one of severe decline
in the Jews' social and economic status. That may have been the case in
some localities – and we know that Jewish communities were wiped out
in some important cities in 1391 – but not everywhere.[3]

David Nirenberg, in a deservedly famous book, has illustrated the give and take between the three communities and the manner in which violence against Jews became, at times, ritualized. Most of all, Nirenberg reminds all of us that these histories – those of Jews and Muslims in Iberia – need to be contextualized in a specific time and location, and that we see these histories in teleological terms only at our peril.[4] As I have shown elsewhere, Jews and Muslims lived different lives in Avila than they did in Burgos in the early fourteenth century. It should not surprise us, then, that when violence came in 1391, they experienced the waves of attacks against them very differently: Burgalese Jews were either killed or forcefully converted; Jews in Avila, in the same kingdom and not too far from Burgos geographically, witnessed little violence. Moreover, Avila's conversos drew little attention from the Inquisition.[5] We also know that, although Muslims were forced to convert in the early 1500s, Mudejars had lived, and continued to live in some cases, fairly peaceful and productive lives in the rearguard of the Reconquest for centuries without any noticeable pressure to convert or leave.[6]

One needs to unpack all these observations and generalizations while trying to understand what life was like for these religious minorities in the period after 1300 and to what extent their fate was wound up with the general late medieval crises and the response to these crises by different social groups within society. Were there substantial differences in these attitudes and parallel histories in Castile and the Crown of Aragon? Or between north and south? Long ago Ubieto Arteta noted the correlation between the downturn in economic cycles and religious persecution. The eerie relationship between economic stress and bouts of violence against Jews and, to a lesser extent, against Muslims is undeniable.[7]

Thus, in periods of severe economic setback or crisis, it should not be surprising that harsh measures against Jews and Muslims were enacted or that outbursts of violence disturbed the routine of daily exchanges between the three religious groups. Yet even these apparently obvious formulations must be taken with a grain of salt and rightly questioned. Royal minorities and political instability also triggered violence against Jews and Muslims. So did the edicts of the Fourth Lateran Council in 1215, which had a long and deleterious impact on these relations. The ebb and flow of violence and accommodation between the three religions reflected the complex contexts of local interests, social filiation, and economic needs. As Monsalvo Antón has shown, anti-Jewish sentiments differed according to where one stood within the hierarchy of a highly stratified society. Those on top, whether nobles, high ecclesiastical dignitaries, or even the royal family, showed on the whole (with the usual exceptions) far less animosity toward Jews and Muslims as individuals than the "middling sorts." The latter, though often in economic competition with Jews, may have been far more accommodating (probably because of their close business ties) than people at the bottom. Those on the lower rungs of society, that is, the majority of the people, had already absorbed the virulent attitudes toward religious minorities codified in the Fourth Lateran Council edicts, in popular anti-Semitism, and in economic resentment. All of these different and complex sets of opinions had been carefully fanned by Mendicant preaching and rumor.[8]

But these generalizations are also full of holes. Not only is it risky to argue that the upper social groups were less hostile toward non-Christians – individuals differed widely in their actions and beliefs – but it is also inaccurate to describe those at the bottom of society as universally intolerant. One must remember that a large number of the pejorative depictions and legal pronouncements that excluded Jews and Muslims from full participation in Spanish life came from those on top. Alfonso X could maintain cordial and protective relations with Muslim and Jewish scholars and with his lordly Moorish vassals at his court while, at the same time, sponsoring harsh anti-Jewish and anti-Muslim legislation in his great legal code the *Siete partidas*. The reality at the individual level or in specific localities was always different from these overarching constructs. Toleration or *convivencia* (a term meaning the three different religious groups living in rather cordial relations and one which I try to avoid completely) during the late Middle Ages, a period during which, when Christians were on top, they were seldom tolerant, should perhaps be understood as periods oscillating between policies of live and let live and ones of harsh treatment and persecution. Gregory Milton, in his study of the social and economic life of St. Coloma de Queralt (a large village in the Tarragona [Catalonia] hinterland), shows in vivid detail the extent to which Christians, Jews, and Muslims were intertwined in borrowing and lending, and how stereotypes about the Jewish monopoly of moneylending are just that: stereotypes with little reality in many localities throughout medieval Spain.[9]

Having argued against an easy reading of the relations between Christians, Jews, and Muslims, one should nonetheless make an attempt to gain some general understanding of what the situation was throughout most of the peninsula during the roughly century and a half discussed in this book. Before that, however, it may useful to provide a brief summary of the parallel developments of the three religions in medieval Iberia and how the relationship between the three changed over time.

Muslims, Jews, and Christians in Medieval Spain

The common and parallel histories of these three groups begins in Iberia in 711 with the Arab invasion and the unexpected and swift collapse of the Visigothic empire. Massive conversions of Christians to Islam took place during the first decades of the Muslim conquest. In this period and for centuries to come, the Muslims would be on top throughout most of Spain. Their power lasted fairly unchallenged until the demise of the Caliphate in the 1030s, and important centers for Muslim political, cultural, and social life remained vital until the 1230s and 1240s in western Andalusia and Valencia, and until 1492 in Granada. Christians and Jews, as people of the Book, were allowed to keep their religion and to function with a great deal of economic freedom within Muslim society for most of the early and late Middle Ages, though, as always, exceptions abounded.[10]

During the early centuries of the Muslim conquest, Jews benefited the most. The Visigoths had harshly persecuted Jews. A few years before 711, the Visigothic rulers and the great Visigothic Church Councils had pushed hard for conversion or expulsion in words which were to be eerily re-enacted 800 years later. The Muslim conquest of Spain came at the most propitious time for Jews. In the next three centuries under Muslim rule, the Jews enjoyed their Golden Age. As intellectuals, courtiers, royal officials, merchants, and in myriad other ways, the Jews prospered, built an impressive cultural legacy, and benefited from significant material success, all under the fairly benign Muslim rulership.

Although there were some episodes of Christians challenging Muslim rule and religion and episodes of Christian martyrdom in 800s Cordoba, Christians benefited as well. Both Christians and Jews gained considerably from the cultural and economic advantages that the Islamic conquest brought to the peninsula. We should not be deceived, however, by this somewhat idyllic portrait. Although the early Islamic rulers of Spain, specially after the foundation of the Caliphate of Cordoba in 929, allowed a great deal of latitude to Christians and Jews, it was not tolerance. Muslims were on top, and there was no question as to whose religion was dominant. Yet in many respects Spain was a rather unique place in comparison to other Western realms. For one, Christians and Jews lived together under Islamic rule in some sort of rough equality for centuries. People of different religions learned, or were forced, to share physical spaces and engage in common commercial ventures and cultural projects on a fairly equal level. After the collapse of the Caliphate in the 1030s, Christians began to make inroads into Muslim lands. In the wake of Christian conquests – most significantly the conquest of Toledo in 1085 – a substantial number of Muslims and many Jews came under Christian rule.

These Muslims, known in their new status as Mudejars, and Jews and their descendants lived for almost half a millennium in northern Spain under Christian rule. Although burst of violence against these religious minorities erupted from time to time as a grim reminder of who was now on top, the reality is that people of the three religions commingled, shared cultural events, bought and sold from each other, and lived in fair close proximity to each other. The contradictions inherent in the relations between Jews, Muslims, and Christians could range from savage attacks and pejorative representations – the latter growing in vitriolic intensity in literary works and legislative ordinances after the early decades of the thirteenth century – to long periods of fairly stable coexistence. Again, the local context dictated the types of relations between Christians and religious minorities. In Burgos, an important commercial center, the Christian ruling elite, deriving most of its wealth and economic superiority from long-distance and local trade, had been able to block most Jewish and Muslim economic activity, from local moneylending to artisanal pursuits. There the substantial Jewish and the far less important Muslim communities had their economic activities well circumscribed to kingdom-wide financial activities, medical practice, building trades, cloth dying, and husbandry. Jewish and Mudejar neighborhoods were clearly defined, and there is no clear extant evidence of widespread inhabitation in other parts of the city. In Avila, Salamanca, and other urban centers with a substantial number of religious minorities, Christian ruling groups drew their income mostly from land rents and transhumance. Jews and Muslims practiced a wide variety of trades and professions and lived in their own neighborhoods but also in any other part of the city if they could afford either the rent or the price (which some of them certainly could in the early fourteenth century).[11]

Four things need to be emphasized here. First, in general (though this may be at times contested) Jews and Muslims living within Christian society belonged legally to the Crown. As such, they were exempted from municipal jurisdiction. These exemptions from taxes and service were an endless source of conflict between municipal councils and the Crown. Whether through direct petitions to the king at the meeting of the Cortes or through individual appeals, urban representatives sought to exclude Jews and, to a lesser extent, Muslims, from all fiscal affairs, to restrict their mobility and contact with Christians, and to regulate their clothing and appearance. Jews and Muslims, because they often functioned as royal agents or enjoyed exemptions from local jurisdiction, became targets for popular unrest. As David Nirenberg, Mark Meyerson, and others have shown, attacking Jews and Muslims was a fairly easy way of assailing royal power without confronting the Crown directly or drawing its merciless wrath.

Second, as we move into the late Middle Ages, the old and tired argument that Jews and Muslims were restricted to a few specific trades or to a small field of economic activities is patently incorrect. Again local contexts dictated and either limited or opened up the possibilities for pursuing a whole gamut of occupations and economic pursuits. Although the legislation of the Cortes and Corts sought to control the economic life of religious minorities, the frequency of these injunctions reveals that things went on more or less as they always had. Third, this meant that in Spanish society it was rare for anyone not to be familiar with Jews and Muslims, with their customs, and dietary and religious practices. This is by no means an endorsement of *convivencia*. Not at all: Spanish society could be quite brutal; tolerance was a rare medieval commodity. Historical circumstances had shaped the demographic and religious diversity of the Spains, and the long Muslim rule over most of the peninsula had provided models of coexistence and, far more significant, of the economic advantages of controlling and tapping the resources of minority religious communities for the benefit of the royal fisc. These communities had, in most cases, learned to live and let live. David Nirenberg's *Communities of Violence* shows how in the most sensitive of areas, that of sexual intermingling, regardless of harsh injunctions and penalties (including death) against sexual intercourse between members of religious minorities and Christians, even if they were prostitutes, such encounters were not uncommon. Gambling, fights, trade, crime, and other aspects of daily life brought members of the three religions into frequent illicit and licit contact. Often we know this because the case ended up in court, so we are only seeing the top of the iceberg and a far richer and more complex set of relations continued in spite of legal and religious prohibitions.[12]

Toward the End of Plurality, 1300–1469

But if this was so, what happened in the late Middle Ages that broke the fragile links that bound these groups into somewhat of a community? The road to expulsion and forced conversion was never an easy or an even one. In the midst of growing violence and tension, we find surprising reminders of what Spanish societies might have been like. Growing violence and legal restrictions coexisted with festive commingling of the three groups, with rituals of inclusion (even if these events often took violent or coercive forms). Jonathan Ray has shown the ambivalence of royal policies toward Jews at the southern frontier, the endless give and take in which attempts to police the boundaries between religious communities and Jewish activities were continually subverted by official inaction or disregard for the legal and religious edicts against such mixing. In northern Castile royal officials were active in evicting the owners from, and auctioning, farms owned by Christians who had defaulted on loans to the Jews. In 1330, Pedro Yeneguez (or Veneguez) the gatekeeper of the Jewish community in Medina de Pomar, acting in the name of the king and on behalf of John Martínez de Leyva, the *merino mayor* in Castile, sold the properties of peasants who had been unable to pay their debts to Jewish moneylenders in Medina de Pomar.[13] Such official support for Jewish moneylenders only exacerbated popular hostilities toward Jews.

Christians and Muslims also engaged in brisk commercial and real-estate transactions. Jewish and Muslim shopkeepers and artisans could not have survived by simply selling to their co-religionists, especially in small urban centers such as Avila. Thus we must assume that in the Spanish realms up to the expulsion and forced conversion of all religious minorities, members of the three religions interacted daily in business transactions, financial affairs, and the like. The evidence for such activities in the fourteenth and fifteenth centuries is overwhelming.[14] And these contacts extended to the physical spaces they shared. In 1297 Avila, Menachen, a Jewish dyer, and his wife Cimha sold a pair of houses in the main market of Avila to Pascual Sánchez, a cleric of the church of San Vicente, for 1,300 *mrs*. This is quite a large sum in terms of Avila's real-estate market and reflects the importance of the houses or, perhaps, other hidden agreements (an outstanding loan?) of which we are not informed by the extant documentation. The sale contract provides a good description of the houses and the neighborhood, and we can see how these three groups shared spaces and real-estate transactions. Menahen's houses had two doors. One opened toward the market and the other toward the cathedral. Thus, Menahen lived, at least until the end of the thirteenth century, in Avila's most prestigious Christian neighborhood (around the cathedral). His neighbors in 1297 were Mosse Merdohay on one side and a store for women's ornaments run by Ledicia, the wife of Mosse Amariello, on the other. Nearby we find the houses of Rabbi Yhuda, also a dyer, and of Mencia. Other Jews served as witnesses, while Christian surveyors, judges, and witnesses guaranteed the legality of the transaction.[15]

During Holy Week processions and ceremonies, Jews and Muslims played a significant ritual role in the late Middle Ages. As adroitly explored by David Nirenberg, we can see how different and contradictory messages played out in these important Christian festivities in oscillating patterns

of exclusion and inclusion. Whether Holy Week events in the Crown of
Aragon or Corpus Christi processions in late fifteenth-century Madrid, the
forced participation of Jews and Muslims in these ritualized performances
reinforced Christian superiority and humiliated non-Christians, while
creating spaces of inclusion. They could also be dangerous. After all, Holy
Week celebrations usually involved stoning or attacks on the Jewish neighborhoods or *call*. But these highly symbolic and scripted festivities also
confirmed and sanctioned the insertion of religious minorities within the
wider Christian society. In a spectacular demonstration of the complexities of these relationships, the example of the Infanta Blanca's ceremonial
entry into Briviesca in 1440 is quite revealing. In this year Blanca, daughter of John, king of Navarre – whom we have already met as one of the
quarrelsome Infantes of Aragon, later king of the Crown of Aragon, and
father to Ferdinand the Catholic – came into Castile to marry the heir to
the throne, the Infante Henry (later the ill-fated Henry IV). On the outskirts of Briviesca she was met by elaborate festivities, jousts, hunts, and
other excesses typical of the age. After the delay caused by these celebrations, she continued her journey to Briviesca, a little Castilian town under
the lordship of the Count of Haro. Briviesca's only advantage resided in
its location along the road to Compostela. As Blanca entered the town to
a lavish reception by municipal officials dressed in their best finery, and
by the town's guild with their *tableaux vivants* and celebratory performances,
the Jews danced in the streets with the Torah, and the Muslims followed
suit with the al Qu'ram, sending Blanca in great style to her unfortunate
marriage in Valladolid. And this in 1440 when things had already gone
dramatically wrong in terms of relations between Christians and religious
minorities, especially Jews.

The above description, taken from one of the chronicles of John II of
Castile, teaches us that Jews and Muslims could be found even in small
towns throughout the realm. In fact such towns had become safer and more
receptive to religious minorities (because of lordly protection in times of
political disorder) than large urban centers. Jews and Muslims were expected,
following long-established traditions in the kingdom, to join in the celebrations; one must think that they did so mostly under compulsion. Nonetheless, in 1440 Christians, Jews, and Muslims could and did dance together
in Spain's urban spaces without excessive violence. In Morvedre, Jewish life
was always in a continuous ebb and flow, though peculiarly the fifteenth
century witnessed a veritable renaissance of Jewish fortunes. Thus we cannot
see the Christian treatment of Jews and Muslims as an inexorable descent
into intolerance and violence. It went back and forth and a harsh final outcome was neither inevitable nor foreseeable for contemporaries. Nonetheless,

the reality is that, for a series of complex issues, the tone of Christian discourse against religious minorities (above all the Jews) or recent converts became more and more strident. At the same time levels of violence and legislative initiatives to restrict religious minorities turned harsher and harsher as the end of the Middle Ages came into focus. In many respects that change in tone reflected new political realities and new responses to the ongoing social and economic crises. In the end, religious minorities paid a heavy price for the incompetence of Spanish rulers. They became scapegoats and victims of the growing frustration of the people and to political mismanagement; worse still, they were the victims of purposeful, government-sponsored persecution. Why, then, did this happen?

The Limits of *Convivencia*

Even if one were to agree that the relations between religious minorities and the dominant Christian majority were never one-dimensional nor the final tragic outcome unavoidable, something went quite wrong in the late Middle Ages. Political developments, social changes, and economic crises triggered a series of responses from those in power and from those below that had disastrous consequences for Jews and Muslims, and, one should add, for Christians and Spain as well. While always remembering that legislative programs, legal codes, and pejorative literary representations were not always echoed by similar responses in real life, there is no question that general attitudes toward Jews, Muslims, and, later on, conversos changed for the worse. If the kings of the Crown of Aragon could name a Jew as *bailli* of Morvedre in the late thirteenth century, such appointment would have been unthinkable a hundred years later. In the end, in the fierce competition over trade, credit, profits, and resources, Jews and Muslims lost out. Rulers, though always concerned with the fate of religious minorities, found it expeditious to side with Christian urban interests, or to look the other way when heightened violence erupted against Jews and Muslims. This they did even if, at times, they sought to prevent a breakdown of order or to protect the Crown's Jews. And since these minority religious communities were themselves not monolithic and often plagued by internal strife, social frictions, and religious antagonisms, this did not help at all. At Morvedre and elsewhere social tensions between rich and poor Jews, conflicts over religious issues, or over personal hatred or jealousy drew Christian municipal and royal officials into the fray, eroded these communities' authority and autonomy, and set the stage for even worse things.

In tracing growing changes in the Christian perception of other religious groups our evidence for Castile is easier to read and to present than that for the Crown of Aragon. There were far more Jews and, after 1391, conversos in Castilian cities than in the Crown of Aragon's urban centers, though Barcelona, Girona, and Valencia had a significant Jewish presence. Areas of Aragon and the Valencian countryside counted a large number of Mudejars, but a good number of them were engaged in rural labor and thus often left out of the extant documentation. Unlike Jews and conversos in Castile, who were often in direct contact with Christians and deeply embedded into the realm's social, economic, and administrative life, Mudejars in Aragon generated substantial income from their lords, benefited from their protection, and became quite insulated from the passions agitating the peninsula in the late Middle Ages.[16] In Castile, somewhat different from the Crown of Aragon, one can easily trace the construction of an ideological and legislative program that helped to create a climate for violence, mostly against the Jews, shifting popular dissatisfaction against existing conditions into increasingly negative and restrictive policies against religious minorities.

Beginning in the mid-thirteenth century, the meetings of the Castilian Cortes became a rallying point against Jews and Muslims. The legislation of the Cortes, repeated almost ad nauseam until the end of the fourteenth century and the violent pogroms of 1391, sought to regulate the social and economic relations of Christians with members of the other two religions. First and foremost, the ordinances of the Cortes attempted to restrict contact between Christians, Muslims, and Jews. Although many of the provisions (certainly those against Jews) echoed, as already pointed out, the Visigothic legislation six centuries earlier, the desire to segregate Christians from other religious groups responded to the dramatic mental changes sweeping over Western Christendom and articulated most profoundly in the edicts of the Fourth Lateran Council (1215). The injunctions against contacts between Christians and others, the desire to restrict religious minorities to specific areas within towns and to force them to wear identifying marks and other signs of their difference, were the outward manifestations of deep transformations in spirituality and in the sense of what being a Christian, a Castilian, or an Aragonese meant in this period.

Although not all the reforms of the Fourth Lateran Council prospered in Spain – certainly not those dealing with ecclesiastical chastity – the peninsula was not completely immune to the cultural and religious transformations affecting the rest of Europe. In Castile Christians were forbidden to have Jewish or Muslim nannies to tend their children, and the legislation forbade Christians from serving Jews or Muslims. Although often disregarded, the ordinances of the Cortes ordered religious minorities to wear identifying marks, to wear their hair cut in a special way, and other physical signs which would help Christians identify the religious other easily. One can easily see what the problem was. In the streets of Spanish cities it was not always clear who was what, and either a round yellow patch sewn onto your clothing or an identifiable haircut could help prevent that which ecclesiastics and others feared most: miscegenation, sexual relations, and pollution. As Nirenberg has shown, patrolling the carnal boundaries between religious groups was a matter of the greatest concern.[17] If it was so troublesome, it was because such contacts were possible and did happen.

In a society in which most people looked alike and spoke alike (though this was not the case with Mudejars who, mostly in the eastern kingdoms, preserved their language, eating habits, and dress), but who were different in what was the most fundamental way in the Middle Ages, in their religious convictions, constructing that difference by requiring people to look outwardly different had a dire cumulative effect. Added to other common stereotypes – from a propensity to sodomy (a common accusation hurled against Muslims), being sexually promiscuous, having too many children, smelling peculiar (something often said of the Jews), or eating differently – the legislative agenda created a fictional type easy to hate and to persecute. These pejorative representations endured and prospered in the public mind and underpinned a great deal of the violence that was to come. By making religious minorities so pointedly different and, of course, inferior to Christians (though laudatory representations of Muslims also coexisted with negative ones), this broad front of restrictive ordinances, popular opinion, and literary representation lessened the humanity of Muslims and Jews and made violence against them much easier.

The truth, of course, is that as damning as these representations were, they were not central to the antagonism between urban representatives to the Cortes and religious minorities – in this particular case, mostly the Jews. The real bone of contention was financial. The bulk of the Cortes' legislation in Castile on matters related to regulating the life of religious minorities aimed at driving out Jews from their role in the fiscal affairs of the realm and in squeezing them out from their long-held roles as tax collectors, tax farmers, and moneylenders. As we know, Christians and Muslims were also active in the credit market, and although often Christian lenders extended credit in partnership with Jews or used Jews as cover for their practices, they were also in direct competition with them. Nothing elicited Christian wrath as powerfully as control over tax collection. Collecting taxes, a very profitable activity indeed, was of special interest to Christian urban elites. Exempted from most taxes by 1300, municipal officials again and again demanded from the Crown that Jews be removed from these activities.[18]

The Crown, while agreeing in principle and endorsing the Cortes' ordinances, never fully acceded to these demands. The reality was that only the great Jewish financiers could actually generate the large loans necessary to run a government always in desperate need of cash.

What we see in the relentless demands to reduce the interest rates collected by Jews, cancellation of Christian debts to Jews, and other restrictive economic measures is the push from Christian mercantile elites to eliminate or reduce Jewish competition.[19] Perhaps it was also the desire to replace them as the main economic actors. But even this statement can be disputed. As noted earlier, Christian and Jews often cooperated in business ventures, or Jews provided coverage and/or lucrative partnerships for Christian money. One should also note that Muslims or Mudejars were not targets for these punitive economic ordinances. Clearly, Mudejars, engaged in either rural labor, small crafts, or shopkeeping, were not seen as serious economic rivals. It was not always about religion. It was also about wealth. In some areas of Aragon and Valencia attacks against Mudejars did occur, but there was no extensive economic legislation against them.

Moreover, although there were legal attacks against Jews and Muslims in the Crown of Aragon, the fiscal arrangements in the eastern realms made the Crown depend more on the Corts than it did on the income from religious minorities. In Barcelona and Valencia Christian commercial and financial elites had long gained the upper hand in their competition with Jews. This is not to say that Jews did not play a fiscal role in the Crown of Aragon. They did. Nor does it mean that Jewish and Muslim moneylenders, merchants, and others, as Gregory Milton, Mark Meyerson, and others have shown, did not play an important part in the local and kingdom-wide economy. They did that as well. But in Aragon it was never the pivotal role that religious minorities played in Castile. In the end, in Castile the issue was far more about defining the place of religious minorities in the economic life of the realm while in the midst of social and economic crises than about asserting religious purity, though religious affiliation and a deeply ingrained sense by most Christians in medieval Spain that their religion was superior to Islam or Judaism remained a constant and an important catalyst for religious violence.

Complicating matters was the reality that, in most cases, the Jews were the servants of the Crown and, as such, vulnerable to royal requests and whims. The kings' natural and most profitable tendency was to protect religious minorities from popular violence. Yet, when trouble arose, the kings eventually gave way to the demands of urban procurators or to the pressures of popular armed insurrection, or, if they were minors, as was the case with Henry III in 1391, they proved incapable of stopping persecution.

crown + persecution

Because they were not Christian and lived in a world that was hostile to religious plurality and because Mendicant preaching and Church pronouncements constantly reminded the general population of their difference, Jews and Muslims always lived in a highly exposed position. Some of the greatest Jewish financiers, figures such as Don Isaac ibn Zadok (known in Castilian documents as Çag de la Maleha (an influential figure in the court of Alfonso X and one of his most important fiscal officials), Abraham el Barchilon (in charge of finances under Sancho IV of Castile), and others who had kept kings afloat with their loans and fiscal acumen, once they fell from favor or when their services were no longer needed (or when their wealth was needed even more) were executed or their fortunes confiscated. That was the fate of some of the most prominent Jews in Castile during the turbulent period from the 1270s to the 1391 pogroms. The kings of course murdered Christian noblemen as well, so there is no clear sense that Jews were the only target. There is, however, a crucial difference. High nobles could and did resist and, as we know, did so quite successfully in the fifteenth century. The Jews could seldom do so.

Violence against high-placed Jews and Jewish royal agents was paralleled by violence against lowly Jews (and Mudejars) at the local level. These antagonisms and violent responses to the presence of religious minorities within Christian Spain were fed from legislative benchmarks and pejorative literary representations. Berceo, perhaps the most significant literary figure of the mid-thirteenth century, represents Jews in one of his *Miracles of the Virgin* as re-enacting the killing of Christ. Jewish apostates, such as Abner of Burgos (known as Alfonso of Valladolid after his conversion to Christianity) conducted vitriolic polemics against his former co-religionists in his formidable treatise *The Wars of the Lord*. More of this was, sadly, coming.[20]

Even with the caveat that laws against religious minorities were seldom enforced or did not come into effect at all, or that literary sources also contain positive descriptions of Jews and, above all, Muslims, these sources served as signposts on the road to difference. Clearly neither the Cortes' or Corts' ordinances nor most of the important literary works, circulating as they did in manuscript form only to a small, learned elite, reached the people at the bottom or even the middling sorts. But such cultural artifacts – law and literature – set the tone for popular discourse and popular preaching. While the upper social groups were not particularly violent in their attacks against religious minorities – after all they profited greatly from them – they were not adverse to engaging in polemics against them. These ideas were transmitted to other social groups, mostly through the preaching of the Mendicants, and deployed as weapons by the middling sorts in their economic competition with Jews or to legitimize the subordination of Muslim rural laborers. What did these representations consist of?

The best known and most often quoted definition of the role and place of Jews in Christian society is found in Alfonso X's *Siete partidas*, the great legal compilation from the second half of the thirteenth century. At the court of Alfonso X (1252–84) of Castile and, to a lesser extent, at those of other Iberian kings in this period, Muslim, Jewish, and Christian scholars worked side by side in ambitious cultural programs. In fact, the court of Alfonso X the Wise has long stood as a model of *convivencia*. The Castilian king had an abiding interest in Arabic science and magic and promoted the work and scholarly cooperation of religious minorities. Jews, as we have seen, also played an important role in the fiscal affairs of the kingdom. Great Muslim lords accompanied the peripatetic royal courts, witnessed royal charters, and were often reliable and faithful allies in Castile's internal strife.

Jewish and Muslim music, artistic and architectural forms, agricultural practices such as irrigation and vertical watermills, craftsmanship in silk, iron, and leather work, words, types of food, forms of eating, dress, and other aspects of culture and material life were deeply woven into Spanish society. Nonetheless, when it came to defining the legal status of religious minorities, Alfonso X's legislative program was unforgiving.[21] In the *Siete partidas*, the great Roman-based legal code from the second half of the thirteenth century, the sections dealing with Jews and Muslims were particularly restrictive. *Partida* VII, title 24, while providing the usual bans on sexual intercourse with Christians or holding Christians as slaves, evokes some of the worst aspects of anti-Jewish rhetoric, even though tempered by the requirement of proof:

> And because we have heard it said that in some places Jews celebrated, and still celebrate Good Friday . . . stealing children and fastening them to crosses, and making images of wax and crucifying them, when they cannot obtain children, we order that hereafter . . . [if] anything like this is done and can be proved, all persons who were present when the act was committed shall be seized, arrested and brought before the king; and after the king ascertains that they are guilty, he shall cause them to be put to death in a disgraceful manner . . .[22]

Title 25 deals with Moors in only slightly kinder fashion. Although prohibitions on sexual intercourse remained, the thrust of the law was to foster the gradual conversion of Muslims to Christianity and to prevent Christian conversion to Islam. The constant reissuing of these legal measures tells us that they were not easily enforced but, nonetheless, something had changed for the worse.

This was obviously the case with the ordinances of the Provincial Council of Zamora in 1313. Following the spirit of the *Siete partidas*, and with a good number of bishops present, including the archbishop of Santiago of Compostela, the council passed a series of edicts which reflect the turn to more aggressive restrictions on Jews. Among the most salient of these were: the removal of Jews from royal service (a common petition in the Cortes); an end to relations and contacts between Christians and religious minorities; a ban on Christian servants or nannies; an order that Jews were to stay within their houses from Wednesday to Saturday of Holy Week and to close their doors and stay indoors throughout all of Good Friday; and laws that they were to carry an identifying signal, not eat with Christians, and other similarly restrictive measures – including returning to their humble condition synagogues which had by 1313 been improved and transformed into fashionable sites. These measures, which paralleled the legislative program of the Cortes, now gave religious sanction to a concerted policy of segregation and restriction.[23] As for the literary representations, they also escalated in virulence, reflecting the harsher tones of Jewish–Christian and Muslim–Christian polemics.

In the *Primera crónica general*, an official account of Castilian history commissioned by Alfonso X and very influential in the later chronicle tradition, the courage of the Visigoths – with whom Asturians and Castilians had established a fictitious historical link – is compared to that of the Moors. At the same time, the chronicle advances a dual historical explanation for the defeat and destruction of Visigothic power in the peninsula. The Muslims are represented – within the dichotomy Christians/Muslims, Goths/Moors – as inhuman and traitors. Their deeds are not those of noble knights. Spain has only fallen into the hands of this cruel and irrational foe because of the betrayal of the count Don Julián and because of Visigothic sins. Thus, the official history of Castile proceeds to contextualize the defeat by placing it on the same plane as the fall of Babylon, Carthage, Jerusalem, and Rome. Located in such exclusive company, the reader can now reflect upon the unpredictability of fortune, the workings of the Divine Will, and the historical links of self with an illustrious past.[24] In the *Poema de Fernán González*, written toward the middle of the thirteenth century in northern Castile, the Goths, guided by the Holy Spirit, settled in Spain and converted to Christianity. Their glorious rule over Iberia comes to an end, once again, because of Don Julián's treachery and their own sins, but here, as in the *Primera crónica general*, the Moors are represented in the same negative terms, including charges of cannibalism.[25]

Castile was not alone in this. James I, the great king of the Crown of Aragon, in his autobiography described the Muslims as "traitors ... ever seeking to do us harm," while Sancho IV in his book of advice to his son argued that "The Moor is nothing but a dog."[26] One should note that the French were also targets for these derisive comparisons.[27] There are other ways in which representations of the religious other served to define oneself. As indicated above, from the thirteenth-century onwards, the legislation of the Cortes sought to segregate Jews and Moors from the Christians by their clothing, hairstyle, and place of residence. Whether these ordinances were enforced or not, what is important here is that the negative representations of Muslims and, above all, Jews and conversos (or of some of the conversos) in the legislation of the Cortes, in the royal decrees, in local church synods, and in literary works, such as the influential Berceo's *Milagros de Nuestra Señora* and Juan Ruiz's *Libro de buen amor*, were intimately linked to the increasing violence against religious minorities.

While agreeing with Nirenberg that teleologies of persecution cannot be postulated and that the local context often determined the nature of the relationship between religious groups, it is clear that ways of formulating difference and engaging the "religious other" had grown exponentially and not for the better. In Andrés Bernáldez's *Historia de los Reyes Católicos* (a work written after the chronological terminus of this book), the ecclesiastical chronicler describes the attacks against the conversos and the work of the Inquisition. In the midst of his narrative, he inserts an exordium against Jews and conversos, providing a list of their alleged crimes. Not only Jews and heretical conversos transgressed against Christianity, but they smelled bad on top of that, with the smell of Jews. This pejorative representation is partially attributed to the food which Jews and conversos, in their perversity, ate (notice the distinctions made here between what one eats or doesn't). Above all, Bernáldez argued that their peculiar odor resulted from their lack of (or rejection of) baptism. The Jewish smell is a trope in Western medieval polemical literature, and one should not be surprised to find it in Castile. And Bernáldez adds a list of other charges: sexual misbehavior, rejection of rural life, laziness.[28]

***

After such a convoluted introduction we are now ready to see what happened to these relations in the late Middle Ages. Within the context of the rising articulation of difference and an economic downturn, violence against Jews and, after 1391, conversos (as well as, occasionally, against Muslims) became more frequent. Table 7.1 shows the widespread nature of violence throughout the peninsula and the increased frequency of these persecutory episodes. Several things may strike the reader in looking at this

Table 7.1   Attacks against Jews and Conversos, 1277–1474 (partial list)

Year	Place
1277	Pamplona (Navarre)
1285	Girona (Catalonia)
1295	Tierra de Campos (Castile)
1321	Tudela (Navarre)
1328	Tudela, Estella, Viana, Funes, etc. (Navarre)
1348	Morvedre (Valencia)
1355	Toledo (Castile). Civil war in Castile
1360	Nájera, Miranda de Ebro (Castile). Civil war
1385	Ribadavia (Galicia) English invasion
1391	Extensive pogroms throughout the peninsula: Seville, Cordoba, Montoro, Andújar, Ubeda, Baeza, Jaén, Huete, Villareal, Cuenca, Burgos, Toledo, Palencia (Castile), Valencia, Barcelona, Lérida, Teruel, Palma de Mallorca, Girona, and other places (Crown of Aragon)
1406	Cordoba (Castile)
1449	Attacks against conversos in Toledo and León
1459–64	Unrest in Burgos against conversos
1460s	Attacks against conversos in Jaén
1461	Attacks against Jews and French merchants in Medina del Campo (Castile)
1465	Conflicts between new and old Christians in Toledo and Seville
1467	Riots against conversos in Seville, Toledo, and Burgos
1468	Massacre of Jews in Sepúlveda (Castile)
1469	Attacks on Jewish tax collectors in Tolosa
1473	Massacre of conversos in Cordoba, Montoro, Bujalance, Adamar, La Rambla, Santaella, Ecija, Andújar, Ubeda, Baeza, Almodóvar del Campo, Jaén (southern Castile)
1474	Attacks on conversos in Segovia and Valladolid

Source: This is a modified and lightly expanded version of Table II (originally taken from Angus MacKay) in S. Freund and Teofilo F. Ruiz, "Jews, Conversos and the Inquisition in Spain, 1391–1492: The Ambiguities of History," in *Jewish–Christian Encounters over the Centuries: Symbiosis, Prejudice, Holocaust, Dialogue*, ed. M. Perry and F. Schweitzer (New York, 1994), 175.

table. The violence, though wide in its geographical scope, was not general. In many places, such as Avila, Jews, and, after 1391, conversos, were seldom troubled or persecuted. In others, such as Morvedre (Valencia), where Jews had held a lofty status in the wake of the Christian conquest of the town in the first half of the thirteenth century, Jewish success was reversed by devastating attacks in the mid-fourteenth century (coinciding with the plague and other structural problems). Yet by the fifteenth century, as Meyerson has shown, the community had recovered and prospered.

In Toledo, a city with a large Jewish population, the Jews sided with Peter I during the civil wars against his half-brother, Henry of Trastámara, arming themselves and sharing in the defense of the city walls against the usurper. When Peter was finally killed by his half-brother, the Jews of Toledo suffered the new king's wrath. Fined almost 900,000 *mrs.*, their goods and their bodies were sold to pay the fine.[29] These reprisals from the Crown came in 1369, but we know that a Jewish community endured in Toledo until 1391, since in 1385 the city's diocesan vicar passed sentence against the Jews requesting payment to the municipal authorities for the lambs Jews slaughtered at home. Here in the survival of the Jews of Toledo until the unprecedented violence of 1391 there is a salutary lesson showing the resilience of religious minorities in the face of adversity. Their ability to work within an increasingly repressive system, to survive persecution, and to maintain their communities was indeed one of the realities of these troubled relations. To a certain extent this was possible because kings and ecclesiastics, while squeezing them dry and sometimes acquiescing in persecution, also protected, or tried to protect, them from excessive violence.

Toward the late fourteenth century, however, the intensity of Mendicant preaching against the Jews rose dramatically. In the eastern kingdoms of the Crown of Aragon, Vincent Ferrer began his campaign to convert the Jews. (Note that the Jews were to be converted; no such serious effort was undertaken with regard to the Muslims until the early sixteenth century.) In this respect Ferrer's aims and preaching followed from a long tradition of peaceful attempts at conversion. Ramón Llull, the notable Catalan literary and mystical writer and passionate religious figure, had advocated learning Arabic as a way of facilitating the conversion of the Muslims. Formal disputations between Jews and Christians in the twelfth and thirteenth centuries (sponsored by Christians) sought to prove the superiority of Christianity and to make conversion a rational and unavoidable choice. Polemical writings, such as the already mentioned *Wars of the Lord*, sought also to hammer Jews for their stubborn adherence to their faith and their rejection of Christianity.

Ferrer's preaching, though not violent, nonetheless fed the passions of the population as he demanded that Jews choose between the Torah and the Cross, between synagogue and church. In a far more irascible key, the archdeacon of Ecija (a town near Seville) began his vitriolic attacks against the Jews, calling for a radical solution to their presence within Christian society. It is a reflection of the fluid nature of Spanish society that the Jewish *aljama* (community) of Seville protested against Ferrán Martínez de Ecija's calls to violence and applied to the king to put an end to his preaching. In 1388, with the archdeacon present at the royal court, Jewish representatives – showing previous royal privileges – asserted their exemption from ecclesiastical jurisdiction and reaffirmed their subservience to the Crown. They referred to three previous royal edicts (1378, 1382, and 1383) which forbade Ferrán Martínez's assertion that Christians could kill Jews with impunity, force their Muslim slaves to convert, and other such violations of the laws and customs of Castile.[30] The archdeacon responded by appealing to Jesus' injunction to his disciples to "Go and preach," by citing Old Testament passages showing untoward Jewish behavior, and by challenging the Crown itself on its stand in favor of religious minorities. Further, he stated that, if he could, he would raze to the ground all of the 23 synagogues still holding services in Seville, while alleging other Jewish actions contrary to the law, such as disrespect for the Host, cohabitation of Jews and Muslims with Christians, and other transgressive deeds.[31]

Ferrán Martínez's response provides a window into the extent of Seville's Jewish community, its prosperity, as well as the tenor of Jews' daily lives; it also reveals the level of heightened passions and the appeal which a close reading of the Gospels provided as a justification for violent attacks against Jews and Muslims. It did not matter that in 1389 the archbishop of Seville forbade the archdeacon to preach against the Jews, raised questions as to the archdeacon's orthodoxy, and commanded him to settle his litigation with the Jews under threat of excommunication. Ferrán Martínez continued his campaign. Two years later, in the midst of a troubled royal minority and widespread violence throughout Spain, a radical change took place in the manner in which Jews and Christians coexisted in Spain. The archdeacon of Ecija had now his opportunity.

1391

Scholars, while pointing to the importance of anti-Jewish violence in the history of late medieval Spain, have not been able to provide a satisfactory explanation for the widespread attacks against the Jews in 1391. From one end of the peninsula to the other, killing, looting, burning of synagogues, and the forced conversion of thousands of Jews brought great turmoil to the land. Although not every city experienced these events, the attacks were widespread enough to prompt strong royal responses. In some cities, such as Seville, the uncompromising and relentlessly provocative preaching of Ferrán Martínez and others tapped into long-standing anti-Jewish sentiments and provided the catalyst for the effective disappearance of the city's Jewish community. In Valencia and Barcelona pent-up social grievances seem to have fueled attacks against the Jews and then turned "religious strife" into a general attack on property and social inequality. As was to be expected, those at the top responded harshly to this breaching of the social order. Accounts from Valencia emphasized the terror created by attacks and insults, the killing of Jews, and, most of all, the robbing of Jewish property.[32]

Over the next five years, there were serious attempts to restore some of the property stolen, to carry out an inquest into the abuses perpetrated by Ferrán Martínez de Ecija against the Jews, and to prevent his razing synagogues to the ground. By then, however, it was too late. Many Jews had died. The loss of their property was considerable; the economic role of Jews within the kingdom was seriously diminished. Those Jews who remained were now firmly segregated from Christians by royal edicts. The most significant and irreversible outcome of the events of 1391, however, was conversion. Not all the conversions had been prompted by fear and violence. A year before the attacks in 1391, the very learned and much-respected rabbi of Burgos, Selomah ha-Levi, had converted to Christianity. After spending some time at the University of Paris studying theology, the New Christian, now known as Pablo de Santa María, returned to Burgos and was eventually elected as bishop of the city. His children (which he had the wisdom to father before becoming bishop) and relatives either entered the Church and rose to positions of great authority or became important advisers and/or intellectuals at Castile's royal court. Pablo de Santa María's conversion sent shock waves throughout the Jewish community and may have had an important role in the ease of conversions in 1391 and in the continuous flow of conversions in the decades that followed.

What would prompt someone of such standing and learning to convert? One of Selomah ha-Levi's brightest disciples, Yoshua Halorqui, raised this question before he also converted voluntarily, joining the Church under the name of Jerónimo de Santa Fe. The answers given by historians over the last few decades to explain the unusual number of converts have ranged from fear, self-interest, and desire for promotion within Christian society to the weakened faith of most upper-class Jews because of their predilection for Aristotelian and Averroist philosophy, and their awareness of Christianity's triumphs in the peninsula. The two latter explanations deserve some comment. Jews, as well as Christians (or at least those who were members of the intellectual elites), had been profoundly marked by the pervasive materialism of Aristotelian philosophy and some of its Arab commentators. In the case of the Jews (mostly the upper Jewish classes), their deep assimilation into Spain's social, economic, linguistic, and political structures forged a strong sense of Spanish identity. Assimilated in every other way, why not in religion, especially when Christian victories over Islam in Iberia and the Christians' obvious hegemony confirmed the power of Christianity over the other two religions? Conversions continued apace, especially after the Disputation of Tortosa, where Jerónimo de Santa Fe (the former Yoshua Halorqui) carried the Christian banner against his former co-religionists. Even though the outcome of the Disputation may have been inconclusive, the Christian announcement of victory triggered yet another wave of conversions in the 1410s. This time conversions took place without violence or open coercion.

The reader will notice that Muslims, or better yet Mudejars, have somewhat fallen out of the picture. There was as yet no great desire to convert them as a group. Although, as we have seen, individual Muslim slaves were sometimes forced to convert or did so, as Debra Blumenthal's research on Muslim slaves in Valencia shows, as a way to gain their freedom,[33] there was not a universal desire to convert all Mudejars to Christianity. The Mudejars' turn would come more than a century later. Jewish conversos, or New Christians as they were called, posed, however, a very different kind of problem. In reality after 1391 and 1412–13 (the Disputation of Tortosa) several distinct communities emerged. First, the Jews who remained faithful to their ancestral religion became very much diminished in number and in their economic roles. The great Jewish communities of Seville, Cordoba, Valencia, Jaén, Burgos, and other places had been forcefully erased. Jews, also because of the anarchy prevailing in early fifteenth-century Castile or because the peril of large cities everywhere in the peninsula, withdrew to small towns and sought the protection of local lords. This protection, and their low profile in these small towns and cities, provided a margin of safety. But by taking this path Jews forsook their influential roles in the economic life of the Spanish realms. Indeed, influential Jews and financiers could still be found at the royal court: Jews still functioned as royal agents and tax collectors, but many of their traditional functions had now been assumed by conversos.

The other radical change was that, battered by the violence, those who did not convert now embraced a more strict adherence to their faith. While in reality the relation between Jews and conversos was a very complex one, changing from place to place and depending on a variety of circumstances, Netanyahu has argued that by the mid-fifteenth century, almost two generations after the catastrophes of 1391 and 1412–13, Jewish rabbinical responsa literature shows that most Jewish religious leaders no longer thought of the conversos as Jews. This was not, however, always the case, and Gretchen

Starr-LeBeau's excellent book illustrates how itinerant Jewish merchants maintained close contacts with conversos in Guadalupe and kept some form of Jewish practice alive.[34] In Morvedre, as Mark Meyerson convincingly shows, the relationship between Jews and conversos was a close one as well. Although a very difficult question to answer, the real issue was: what did conversos or New Christians believe, and what were the consequences of their religious practices and the response of Old Christians to the influx of New Christians into their social milieu?

Conversos or New Christians

Conversion was a momentous event in medieval Christian Europe, and especially in Spain where a large number of Jews embraced, whether voluntarily or not, Christianity. We should not imagine that all conversions, or the conversos themselves, were alike. At the core of the difficulties troubling Spanish life for the next century were the social, economic, and religious variations found among conversos and the intolerance of most Old Christians toward some of these New Christians. If Jews formed a community, growing increasingly apart from former co-religionists, conversos fell into at least three distinct categories, even though these categories were themselves not immutable. Many of the influential, highly assimilated, and well-to-do Jews, who had already established close ties with members of the Christian elites, were able, upon conversion, to move easily into the ranks of the aristocracy or into high positions within the Spanish realms. Through marriage, royal service, and the like, they blended fairly seamlessly into the higher echelons of Spanish life. The family of Pablo de Santa María is a very good example, but it was not exceptional. The Caballería family in Aragon, together with the Santa Fe, Santángel, Villanueva, Maluenda, and Coscón families, rose to the highest ranks within the nobility, commercial activities, and intellectual life in the Crown of Aragon. Their counterparts in Castile – the Arias Dávila, the Santa Marías, fray Alonso de Espina (author of the most effective anti-Jewish and anti-converso treatise) – also rose to positions of great power and influence. For these conversos, moving with ease in the rarefied atmosphere of the Spanish royal courts, marrying into the best families – including the royal family of Aragon – having at their disposal immense fortunes and intellectual resources, the transition from one religion to another was, at least in its social and material aspects, not a difficult one. They were spared most of the resentment against conversos that dominated Spanish life from the mid-fifteenth century onwards, as they would also be spared most inquisitorial attention after

1484. After all, the Grand Inquisitor himself, the ill-famed Torquemada, was of converso origin.[35]

A second group of conversos had almost as much success. Former Jewish merchants and royal agents entered, upon conversion to Christianity, with a vengeance into the ranks of the Christian middling sorts. Municipal elites, canons in cathedral chapters, monks in important monasteries – such as that of Guadalupe – included large numbers of conversos or New Christians. So did the university-trained *letrados* (men of letters) who provided the backbone of the rising Spanish bureaucracies and the construction of new ways of ruling. Their success and visibility prompted harsh antagonism within Spanish towns (mostly in Castile), and table 7.1 shows the extent and frequency of these attacks. Although the actual violence was often directed at conversos of lower social standing, it reflected the rivalry of successful Old and New Christians for resources and political power. At stake, however, was far more than material standing. Old Christians, a term already laden with attempts at creating difference, sought to diminish the value of conversion, to raise doubts as to the New Christians' faith and orthodoxy, and to exclude them from plump ecclesiastical benefits and other profitable positions within Christian society. From pleas (and bribes) to the pope to learned communications to the royal court, Old and New Christians engaged in a lethal battle. The former sought to exclude the latter from important ecclesiastical offices; the latter wished to secure their rights as Christians. The tragic conclusion to this conflict lies beyond the chronological boundaries of this book; it was marked by ferocious inquisitorial activity against some of the conversos.

A third, and by far most numerous, group consisted of the descendants of less well-off and poor Jews: small shopkeepers, artisans, and laborers. Living in the same neighborhoods to which they had been somewhat segregated by rising anti-Semitism in earlier years, marrying endogamously, and maintaining an adherence to certain Jewish rituals even without sustained belief: not working on the Sabbath, reluctance to eat pork or cook with lard, lighting Sabbath candles, or taking baths on the eve of the Sabbath, these conversos became the preferred target for Christian mistrust of their faith. To complicate matters further, there is ample evidence that conversos at the bottom were often caught in urban internecine struggles, as was the case in Seville, the site of endless noble violence, or in Jaén, where noble opposition to Don Miguel Lucas de Iranzo was conflated with attacks against, and hatred of, conversos.

Historians have argued as to whether there was a racial – conversos remained Jews in spite of their adoption of Christianity not matter how sincere, which was Netanyahu's point – or religious – conversos were false

Christians and practiced Judaism in secret – element in the antagonism against Jews. It is hard to say what prompted such bitter hostility. Any single explanatory model is to be immediately suspected. Social filiation and economic standing played a significant role. Not all conversos suffered alike; some of them suffered not at all. The harshest polemics against Jews often came from conversos, and the list is impressive: from Abner of Burgos' (Alfonso of Valladolid's) *The Wars of the Lord* to Jerónimo de Santa Fe's *Azote de los hebreos* to the influential *Fortalitium fidei* or *Fortress of Faith* by fray Alonso de Espina, the list is long and bitter. At the same time, conversos engaged in a spirited defense of their ancestry, pedigree, and Christianity against some of the most vitriolic attacks against them.

What prompted the Spanish reaction to massive conversion and its eventual descent into the establishment of the Inquisition, the expulsion of the Jews, and eventually of the Muslims, is hard to say. By the fifteenth century most Jews and conversos had embraced their Spanish identity and were, in many respects, as committed to the different national projects then emerging in the peninsula as were their Old Christian counterparts. We must not forget that, even if Jews were expelled from Spain and many conversos died at the hands of the Inquisition or fled abroad to avoid its wrath, the large majority of conversos integrated into Christianity and became, in most cases, fully assimilated into Spanish society by the early modern period. Racial hatred and racial identification associated with religious beliefs – in the different modalities in which they existed in the Middle Ages – need to be located in specific chronological and historical contexts. They had waned somewhat by the early modern period, even though stereotypes and popular negative representations of Jews endured at the same time as many conversos were integrating into Spanish society.

For Mudejars and Muslims, however, the story was quite different. They seldom assimilated, or were not allowed to assimilate. These two different histories and trajectories bring vividly to our attention the difficulties of providing a monochrome explanation. The mix of social, economic, political, and religious factors yielded different results in different places at different times. What is clear, nonetheless, is that the fate of religious minorities was inexorably linked to the catastrophes of the late Middle Ages and to the responses of Iberian monarchs and people to these crises. Striking against Jews and Muslims, even though sometimes the kings, high nobles and ecclesiastical dignitaries sought to prevent or ameliorate these attacks, became the most facile way to direct popular anger and frustration about the enduring violence, social upheaval, and economic problems. In the end, Jews and Muslims became the most vulnerable and preferred targets. The end of religious plurality was close at hand.

Chapter 8

Culture and Society in an Age of Crisis

In the midst of enduring crises, the Spanish realms created novel and vibrant cultural forms. Although different forms of cultural production underwent a revival, literature led the way. Written in a diversity of languages – from Latin, Hebrew, and Arabic to Castilian, Galician, and Catalan – these works covered a vast range of literary genres and themes. Ranging from chronicles, erudite philosophical treatises, and commentaries on Classical texts to mystical works, satirical poetry, romances, and other literary forms, these works both reflected the reception of new ideas coming from Italy – the reception of Renaissance humanism and aesthetic concerns – and were autochthonous and highly creative works. Similar developments in painting, music, architecture, and other branches of the arts reshaped the Spanish realms' artistic landscape. Beyond that, many of these intellectual transformations, articulated as well through fashion, elaborate festivals, and royal entries, became deeply bound up with politics and were often placed at the service of contending factions in their cruel and endless struggles for power.

Literary references, artistic displays, and patronage became an integral part of the manner in which kings and nobles displayed their power for political ends throughout the fourteenth and most of the fifteenth centuries. Culture thus became part of elaborate hegemonic discourses and counter-discourses in courts and towns. These learned discourses touched, commingled with, affected, and were in turn affected by other cultural forms coming from below. While "popular culture" is an elusive category and difficult to pin down, the culture of those below sometimes emerged in festivals, above all in carnivals, or in expressions of popular piety and folklore. The circulation of culture between high and low is many respects an important component of this inquiry.

I therefore beg the reader's indulgence for attempting to avoid turning this chapter into an inventory of cultural landmarks. Rather, while highlighting some of the notable achievements of the period, I also wish to link cultural production to its social and political contexts and to see elite culture always in relation to popular culture. How was one affected by the other in ways which were peculiar to the Iberian peninsula? At the same time, and since there is not space here to embark on a cultural history of the Spains, my emphasis will be on some specific literary works and on festivities. In a single chapter it is impossible to do justice to other artistic genres. This does not mean that they were not important, or not as important as some of the literary examples deployed below. Architecture is just one instance in which social and political connections may have been far more crucial than they were in romances or lyrical works. The Alhambra in Granada or the Alcazar of Segovia are just two specific examples of the relationship between space and power; yet to look over the entire artistic history of the peninsula is a task for a study in itself.

It may be useful to reiterate that the formidable cultural developments of the fourteenth and fifteenth centuries, culminating in the dazzling achievements of court culture in the reign of the Catholic Monarchs and their Habsburg successors, took place in a period of severe crises. Not unlike the Italian Renaissance, the rich culture of late medieval France and England, or the impressive cultural displays of the Low Countries described so enchantingly by Huizinga in his *The Autumn of the Middle Ages*, Spain's cultural revival also took place in the midst of wars and violent social, economic, and political transformations. The Spanish realms also responded to the disasters of the age with a firm commitment to aesthetics and to turning the daily horrors of life into the beautiful.

One must begin by admitting that writing about culture in late medieval Spain presents very specific problems. Once again there is no such thing as a Spanish culture in this period. Regional manifestations, solidly anchored in local languages and particular literary traditions, make the history of Catalan culture, to give one example, as different from that of Castile as Castilian culture differed from that of France or England. All of them shared some common traits, as most of western European culture did, but they were not the same. The Crown of Aragon, because of its deep connections to Italy, was far more open to Renaissance influences than was Castile, though in Trastámara Spain and with frequent matrimonial alliances between the Spanish royal houses the flow of Renaissance culture easily reached every corner of the peninsula. Nonetheless, Alfonso V's court in Naples, crawling as it was with Catalan, Aragonese, and Valencian courtiers and men of letters, provided a site for direct and intimate contact with wider trends of Italian culture which was not always available to Castilians. Nothing, however, was as significant in marking difference as language.

Languages

By 1300 Spain was fragmented into well-defined linguistic communities. As outlined in chapter 1, Galicia in the northwest of the peninsula had its own language and cultural identity. Galician lyrical poetry reached its zenith in the twelfth century and parts of the thirteenth century. Alfonso X chose to use Galician when composing his fabled *Cantigas de Santa María*, a long collection of poems written in honor of the Virgin. But by the end of the thirteenth century Galician declined precipitously and played only a small role in succeeding centuries until its late nineteenth-century and present-day revival. The political shift marked by the rise of Castile in the peninsula's central and western regions and the ascent of Castilian as the language of business and, eventually, culture in the region marked the decline of Galician as an effective literary language in the late Middle Ages.

Hebrew, mostly a liturgical language, also showed remarkable vitality in the thirteenth century: the Zohar, written in Hebrew around 1285, is one of the high points of the Jewish mystical tradition, though Jewish literary figures wrote often, or sometimes exclusively, in Castilian. Interest in Hebrew in the eastern kingdoms, mostly as part of efforts to convert Jews, sometimes even spilled over to the Christian population, and Hebrew literary forms, under the impetus of large number of conversos, entered Castilian lyrical poetry in the late fourteenth and fifteenth centuries. Arabic also remained a vital vehicle for lyrical poetry, chronicles, and history in the kingdom of Granada, and the city itself was an important Muslim cultural center as described by Abd al Bāsit in his travel account for the years 1456–66. Ibn Zamrak (1333–93) wrote poetry in praise of the Nasrid rulers of the city, while Lisān al-Din ibn al-Khatib (1313–74) composed important works which mixed poetry and prose in a style known as *maqāma*. By 1300, however, the majority of the population of the Spains had little or no access to the languages of religious minorities or to their particular histories, and these literary traditions remained on the margins of broader movements throughout the peninsula. Catalan was another matter altogether.

The great achievements of Catalan culture endured throughout the entire late Middle Ages. Catalan literature ranged from lively chronicles, Muntaner's above all, to the works of Ramón Llull (in Latin and Catalan) and the enchanting chivalrous romances of the late fifteenth century. In many respects Catalan literature, architectural forms, and plastic arts represented a rich alternative to the rise of Castilian. But in their very dissimilar developments we have a vivid example of the connections between politics and culture. Castile's rise to prominence within the peninsula and within the Spanish monarchy in the early modern period – a political and cultural hegemony easily foreshadowed in the fifteenth century – delivered an almost fatal blow to Catalan aspirations. Once again, only in the nineteenth century (with a federal republic) and today in the Spain of autonomous regions has Catalan regained its rightful place among peninsular languages as a vital vehicle for aesthetic expression.

The play of languages and their future as either putative "instruments of empire," as Antonio de Nebrija the author of the first vernacular grammar published in Europe (a Castilian one) argued in the late fifteenth century, rested on the solid foundations of vernacular speech and writings emerging from below. Not only did the vernacular displace Latin, a long linguistic process that had its origins in the early Middle Ages, but it did so – in Castile above all – far earlier than in other parts of Europe as the language of material transactions and government. Castilian was a precocious language, and as some of its most significant literary works began to appear – *The Poem of the Cid* (ca. 1206) and the poetry of Berceo (around the mid-1200s) – Castilian also became the official language of the realm. As noted in chapter 1, in mid-thirteenth century Castile royal charters, the ordinances of the Cortes, the royally sponsored national histories, and every other form of official written communication between the Crown and its subjects, and between municipal councils and their dependent villages, was written in Castilian. Even in monasteries and cathedral chapters, which one may assume to have remained islands of Latinity, few if any documents were written in Latin. Throughout the land Castilian ruled. Since a formal notarial culture (by which I mean dynasties of notaries keeping their own registers) did not exist in Castile in 1300, the equivalent of notaries – the municipal and royal scribes – kept their records in the vernacular; when a well-established notarial class came into being in the fifteenth century, the language of wills, material transactions, and commercial ventures continued to be Castilian.

This stands in sharp contrast to the realms of the Crown of Aragon. There royal charters and other "official" documentation shifted between Latin and the vernacular (Catalan). The ordinances of the Corts were also redacted in Latin with some sections in Catalan. The formidable notarial records and culture which bound Catalonia to a wider western Mediterranean world were often drawn up in Latin. Some of the most influential works coming out of Spain and impacting late medieval culture – those of Arnau de Vilanova, Ramón Llull, and others – were often written in Latin. In the mid-fifteenth century, and one must remember that the distinguished humanist and philologist Lorenzo Valla worked at Alfonso V's court in Naples, the Aragonese kings of Naples were deeply influenced by the Renaissance emphasis on a return to Classical Latin forms.

In Catalonia the tension (but also the creativity engendered) between two linguistic cultures exploded forcefully into a brilliant collection of writers who could navigate with ease in both languages, providing, through their mastery of these two distinct linguistic mediums, a rich patina to their works. In Castile that creative tension became manifest in the learned works of writers such as Alfonso de Palencia, who could imitate Classical models while still delivering robust new works in the vernacular.[1] But Alfonso de Palencia was an exception rather than a model for other Castilian writers. Then there was the issue of imitation. Although some works, such as Juan de Mena's *Laberinto de fortuna* (*The Labyrinth of Fortune*), reached a nadir of pedantry in their search to imitate earlier masterpieces (in his case Dante's *Divine Comedy*), there was much in this period that was extraordinarily new, reflecting the cultural vitality of the Spanish realms.

Education and Cultural Resources

The precedents for the achievements of the Spanish late Middle Ages were manifold; the complex line connecting an earlier age with later developments provided a solid context for success. Adeline Rucquoi's article "Roads of Knowledge" describes the reciprocal character of cultural exchanges in an earlier period. Contrary to the general assumption that the cultural revival of the twelfth century radiated from centers of learning in northern Europe (mostly around the Ile de France) and came into the peninsula through visiting scholars, Cluniac and Cistercian monks, and pilgrims, Rucquoi points to the exportation of Arabic and Jewish culture to the north and to the numerous Spanish scholars who traveled abroad in search of new knowledge, but who also brought with them scholarly resources not available elsewhere in Europe.[2]

This give and take between distinct cultural worlds could reach intense levels in northern Catalonia. There, the Crown of Aragon was fully integrated, politically and culturally, into Occitanian civilization. Even after the French occupation of most parts of Languedoc and the end of Occitanian autonomy and linguistic independence in the thirteenth century, Catalan remained a vital force in the daily speech of most parts of southern France, as it does to this very day. In early fourteenth-century Perpignan, the capital of the fleeting kingdom of Majorca, material exchanges were rendered in Catalan. As Rebecca Winer has shown, Muslims, Jews, and Christians interacted in ways which were peculiar to the Iberian peninsula.[3] This last example, which departs considerably from the cultural focus intended in this chapter, nonetheless provides important evidence for the dynamic fashion in which diverse peninsular cultural modes and languages intruded into other areas such as politics and social relations.

Language and material transactions are not of course part of formal culture. Learned elites in the Spanish realms had benefited from a long educational tradition harking back to the Visigothic period. Though ecclesiastical learning in cathedral chapters and monasteries was badly impacted by the Muslim invasion, new and exciting forms of knowledge and lyrical poetry prospered under Muslim rule. Christians and Jews benefited equally from these developments and from the nurturing cultural climate – above all during the heyday of the Caliphate – created by the Muslim invasion. By the eleventh and twelfth centuries, as the tide of the Reconquest advanced south, new dioceses came into being or were restored. Each of them became a center of learning. A series of Church councils, held in Galicia and Castile in the eleventh century, ordered that cathedral chapters provide for the instruction of canons and that schools be created in parishes throughout the land.[4] There is abundant documentary evidence that attests to the vigor of local education.

An early university was founded in Palencia, following on the Bologna model. Dominic de Guzmán, the founder of the Mendicant order of Dominicans, received his education there together with other local and foreign scholars of renown. The studium at Palencia did not survive beyond the mid-thirteenth century, but around that time other universities rose throughout the peninsula. In the kingdom of Castile–León, Salamanca, Valladolid, Seville – the latter with a heavy emphasis on the teaching of Arabic – Toledo, and Murcia became centers of higher learning. In the Crown of Aragon the university of Montpellier (still an important center of learning) and Lérida became the locomotives for formal learning, although Barcelona, not a site for an early university, thrived in other significant cultural areas.[5]

By 1300 the peninsular realms, besides their own reservoir of particular knowledge – Arabic–Jewish–Christian scientific and philosophical learning, usually centered on the court – had become well connected to the new academic culture of the medieval West. If Spanish universities did not rank with the great "general studies" in Paris, Bologna, Orleans, and eventually Oxford, they nonetheless provided training centers for local ecclesiastics and a few adventurous outsiders. Complementing the universities, a series of cathedral schools and urban-based institutions focused on the study of the *trivium* (grammar, rhetoric, and logic), the foundations of the medieval seven liberal arts. Even lesser local schools provided well-structured learning environments. To be educated became an important aspect of daily life for the middling sorts, as well as for ecclesiastics and noblemen. In the small market town of Santa Coloma de Queralt in Tarragona's hinterland, Gregory Milton has unearthed an interesting and revealing fourteenth-century document in which one of the town's notaries, Bernart Boti, entered into an agreement with a teacher. Boti hired the latter to teach in a school (owned or endowed by Boti). The teacher and Boti were to share the tuition paid for by the students. This remarkable document opens a window onto and enhances our understanding of education in small Catalan towns in the late thirteenth century in particular and in the medieval West in general.[6] And there is no indication that this was an exceptional situation; rather, throughout the fourteenth century and in the midst of severe crises, local and regional centers of learning proliferated throughout Castile, Portugal, and the Crown of Aragon. Such developments, and the creation of a critical mass of young people capable of reading and writing with a somewhat formal knowledge of the *trivium* and, to a lesser extent, of the *quadrivium* (the other four subjects of the seven liberal arts: astronomy, arithmetic, music, and logic), provided the impetus for the expansion of universities. The critical period between 1300 and 1474 represents a watershed in the spread of universities in the peninsula, as it did in the rest of Europe. From Barcelona in the early years of the fifteenth century to Valencia, Girona, and Seville, plus the rise of Salamanca as an international center of learning, gave Spaniards "national" venues in which to study medicine, law, philosophy, and, especially at Salamanca, theology. Colleges to house and support students, both lay and ecclesiastical, were also founded throughout Spain.

At the universities the children of the middling sorts acquired new and necessary skills, and growing royal bureaucracies offered influential positions and rewards that served as incentives for the widening of education. Many pages have already been written about the role of the *letrados* (the university-trained bureaucrats who ran Castile in the late fifteenth century). They staffed the different offices in royal and local administrations and advanced royal agendas of order and power throughout the fifteenth century and, most forcefully, in the reign of the Catholic Monarchs. Of course, the *letrados* did not just spring into being in 1474. Throughout the waning years of the fourteenth century and the first half of the next century, the universities were training these "new men," a good number of them conversos. These *letrados*, in turn, reshaped the nature of governance in the Spanish realms and, in spite of the violence, continued to build royal authority. Yet we should not see the universities as inexorably linked to the emergence of royal power or to more "rational" forms of ruling. Learning occurred also outside the university, and it was manifest in different and distinct forms.

Learning and aesthetic manifestations also required access to books and to new ways of thinking. Cathedral chapters and monasteries were always the original depositories in Spain, as they were elsewhere in western Europe, of formidable libraries. Barcelona, Vic, Ripoll, La Seo d'Urgell, and other localities in Catalonia traced their holdings to the central Middle Ages, while Burgo de Osma, Toledo, Burgos, Oña, León, Santiago de Compostela, and other places fulfilled the same role in Castile. But by the fourteenth and fifteenth centuries, manuscripts – the central tools of learning – appear frequently in the extant documentation. Lowly ecclesiastics bequeathed books to their relatives or to their institutions in their wills. Books are also mentioned or cited in literary sources, chronicles, and philosophical treatises frequently enough for us to know that significant scholarly and literary resources were available to the learned communities in the Spains.[7] These books, some quite forgettable, others quite essential and influential, circulated widely. In some cases, the transmission of ideas and manuscript resources is quite remarkable, even flowing across confessional boundaries. The Zohar, the great kabbalah text, was written most probably in late thirteenth-century Castile by Moses of León, appeared in Catalonia shortly afterwards, and influenced some of Catalonia's most important thinkers before its transmission to Renaissance Italy and appearance in Pico della Mirandola's famous *Oration of the Dignity of Man*.[8] Knowledge always traveled both ways, in and out of the peninsula.

Libraries were not limited to ecclesiastical establishments. Royal courts were depositories of significant scholarly resources, so were the parallel courts of the high nobility. Iñigo López de Mendoza, the marquis of Santillana, one of the most active political actors of mid- and late fifteenth-century Castile and one of its greatest poets as well, has been rightly celebrated by his library's rich holdings.[9] He was not alone among the high-born aristocrats who collected books and art as assiduously as they entered into political conspiracies. Merchants in Barcelona, bound to special forms of piety, proudly owned books even if many of them were devotional manuals. Romances, of course, always exerted a great attraction and circulated widely among the nobility and middling sorts, or as widely as books could circulate before the printing revolution. After printing came to the Iberian peninsula, the flow of books (mostly romances) became a deluge. Spanish conquistadores carried them in their rucksacks to the New World.

All these things bring us face to face with the question of what was the nature of culture in late medieval Spain. Long ago Peter Russell, in a famous and much-debated article, raised the issue of the conflict between the pursuit of arms and that of letters. Departing from Pero Niño the count of Balbuena's well-known aversion to learning, Russell postulated a tension between the aristocratic ethos of arms and aristocrats' rejection of literacy. The reality was of course otherwise. Although the debate between arms and letters had a long and illustrious life, from the late fourteenth century to Cervantes' *Don Quixote*, where the arguments for and against are brilliantly reprised, the nature of Spanish learning and aesthetic sensibilities has to be located *outside* the dichotomy between arms and letters. It was precisely because the nobility and the middling sorts were educated, though often in ways which were very different from those of their ecclesiastical or university-trained counterparts, that Spanish culture in late fourteenth and fifteenth centuries was so pronouncedly aristocratic in nature. Indeed some of the most remarkable literary works of the period, above all, those of the mid-fifteenth century, were penned by aristocrats, often quite prominent at the royal court and benefiting from royal patronage. From Jorge Manrique's extraordinary poetry, to the marquis de Santillana's light and beautiful poems, to Ausias March's lyrical works, or the late medieval satirical and critical poetry, the authors were high-born noblemen, deeply engaged in the political turmoil of their age. Jorge Manrique, one of Castile's greatest poets, died at a fairly young age while besieging a castle during the civil wars in the early years of Isabella's reign. Others took similar active roles in Spain's perennial high political stakes. Below I provide impressionistic and brief mentions of some of the high points of literary production in the period between 1300 and 1469, as well as a typology of literary genres. Such an approach allows us to see the eclectic nature of Spanish literary culture and to draw sharp distinctions between the different peninsular kingdoms.

Poetry, Romances, and *Cancioneros*

Castile

In examining the poetic creations of fourteenth century and first half of the fifteenth, the reader may be struck by the deep shadow cast over Castilian literature by a small number of canonical works. The point of departure is the *Libro de buen amor* (*The Book of Good Love*), attributed to Juan Ruiz, archpriest of Hita and written most probably during the late 1330s. A long and complex work, the *Libro de buen amor* tells the story of a seemingly lecherous ecclesiastic, of his loves and travels back and forth over the mountain passes north of Madrid (the geographical border between Old and New Castile) in search of adventures. The *Libro de buen amor* mixes jocular and lecherous accounts with sound Christian admonitions. It includes a delicious description of the battle between Carnality and Lent, providing a remarkable window into the culinary resources of fourteenth-century Castile and the sharp contrast between carnivalesque excess consumption of a pre-Lent world and the austerity of the sacred time leading to the passion, death, and resurrection of Christ. In its pages, Juan Ruiz incorporates stories circulating throughout western Europe, along the lines of what Boccaccio and Chaucer would do decades later.[10]

In many respects, the *Libro de buen amor* compares to the *Decameron* and the *Canterbury Tales* in its fluid and joyful celebration of carnality, the human body, and its underlying (and not contradictory) reflective Christian purpose. It entertains and titillates while drawing moral examples and admonitions. Although Juan Ruiz's book looks back to poetical traditions of the thirteenth century and, most of all, to Berceo's use of the vernacular and poetical structure, it, nonetheless, marks a watershed in Castilian literature. It powerfully shows the stylistic and thematic range of the vernacular and the versatility of clerical culture in weaving together so many different strands. At the same time, the *Libro de buen amor* stands in sharp contrast to other contemporary works, as for example Don Sentob (a rabbi) de Carrión's subtle and insightful *Proverbios morales* (*Moral Proverbs*). Sentob's poetry combines a close examination of human values and an austerity of expression which is rendered, paradoxically, with elegant metaphors and lyrical dexterity.[11]

Notice must also be taken of Don Pero López de Ayala's (1332–1407) *Rimado de palacio*. A royal official in the court of Henry II, the Trastámara usurper, and chronicler of the reigns of Peter I and Henry II, a large part of our negative appraisal of the Peter the Cruel's rule has been shaped by López de Ayala's partisan descriptions. Moving among the highest circles in the land, a witness to, and participant in, the turbulent world of the second half of the fourteenth century, López de Ayala was also a poet of considerable range and effectiveness. Without Juan Ruiz's wit or Sentob's reflectiveness, López de Ayala wrote numerous poems late in life covering a vast range of themes and styles. From a satirical condemnation of the vices and deeds of his social milieu to religious poetry and lyrical expression, the *Rimado de palacio* (*Palace Rhymes*) – as the collected poetry is known, reflecting the courtly provenance of the poet – reveals the contradictions of late medieval life and the juxtaposition of moral examples and admonitions with obscene stories. What for us today seems contradictory was for medieval men and women part and parcel of their daily experience.[12]

In López de Ayala, as had been the case with Juan Ruiz and Sentob of Carrión's poetry, the personal account – sketches of a literary autobiography – frequently mixes with sharp observations of the world around and criticism of contemporaries and the Church. And here as well, although still fairly faithful to the *cuaderna vía* (a poetical form predominant in Berceo's work and consisting of strophes of four rhyming lines of fourteen syllables each), López de Ayala and others who followed him deployed other rhyming schemes and poetic forms, heralding a veritable revolution in the manner in which feelings were to be expressed in the future. In many respects this served as a suitable and necessary counterpoint to the enduring political conflicts. The Castilian and Aragonese courts became sites for the development of new cultural forms. In both royal courts, nobles and royal officials wrote lyrical poetry which unlike the *cuaderna vía* (of ecclesiastical provenance) reflected "courtly and cultured" (*cortesana y culta*) values of a small elite at the top. Collected in extensive compilations of poems, the so-called *cancioneros* (from *canción* or song), this courtly poetry showed an exaggerated proclivity to allegorical representations, sentimental expression, and often contradictory perspectives on life, love, and politics. All these diverse emotions and observations were rendered in a highly refined and cultivated language. Although some of the authors included in the *cancioneros* were better known and far more prolific than others – Carvajales (or Carvajal), Francisco Imperial, Villasandino, Rodríguez Padrón stand out – the two large compilations that follow chronologically from López de Ayala's *Rimado de palacio*, the *Cancionero de Baena* and the *Cancionero de Stúñiga* are, on the whole, important landmarks in Castilian lyrical poetry.[13]

From Villasandino to Macias to Imperial (whose poems are found in the *Cancionero of Baena*), these poets blossomed in the heated political atmosphere of John II's court, as well as in those of John II's favorite Alvaro de Luna and his political rivals. Patronage of poets and artists, and an admiration for erudition, manners, and courtly behavior, was far more than a refined artifice. As will be seen in the case of Suero de Quiñones or in the example of romance writers of the fifteenth century, the lyrical greenhouse environment of the court also yielded improbable forms of behavior. The same noblemen who could engage in the basest of conspiracies and political betrayals could also swoon and cry while listening to or reading lyrical works or sentimental romances. A point worth making here is the international reach and vigor of Castilian in this period. The victory of Castilian as the dominant language in the peninsula was immensely helped by the Trastámara hegemony in the Spanish realms. At the same time, the language was also able to provide a suitable vehicle for new sentiments and ideas. Francisco Imperial, the son of a Genoese merchant settled in Seville, is a very good example. While freely borrowing from the Italian poetical tradition and incorporating its poetical forms into Castilian poetry, his themes and language were deeply grounded in his new homeland.[14] Holding the same lofty position as the *Cancionero de Baena*, the *Cancionero de Stúñiga* was compiled toward the mid-fifteenth century at Alfonso V's court in Naples.

Gathering lyrical poetry – mostly by Carvajal and in Castilian – it also included other literary genres of a more popular nature. We tend to forget that in mid-fifteenth-century Naples, a city where an elaborate revival of Latin was coming to its high point, the language of sentimental expression was Castilian. But of course Castilian and Aragonese–Catalan poets also borrowed heavily from the fertile ground of Renaissance learning.

The flip side(s) of the courtly and learned lyrical tradition in late medieval Castile had five very distinct forms. One was erudite and restricted to those in full possession of high culture. Juan de Mena's highly symbolic and pedantic work, above all his *Laberinto de fortuna*, represents the best example of this genre. The second can be characterized by the *serranillas*, the light, ironic, and pleasing verse, best exemplified by Iñigo López de Mendoza's *Serranillas*. The third consists of the compositions known collectively as the *romancero* (a collection of poetical romances). The fourth includes the satirical and protest poetry of mid-fifteenth-century Castile which has already been glossed in chapter 2; finally, we have the stunning and evocative poetry of Jorge Manrique which, in many respects, stand on its own. Juan de Mena (1411–56) was also a member of John II's court, one of the foremost Latinists in Castile, and one of the king's scribes. His claim to fame rests mostly on the *Laberinto de fortuna*, a long allegorical poem (297 strophes) about the ephemeral nature of human life and the uncertainty of fortune. The poem focuses on themes quite common in late medieval Europe – most prominently the mutability of fortune – and it was highly imitative of Dante's *Divine Comedy* and of Dante's poetical and symbolic structure (as Francisco Imperial and most of the poets of the period were) but without Dante's brilliancy. Themes such as that of fame, which also resonated in Manrique's poetry, and direct references to political events during John II's reign made the *Laberinto de fortuna* the literary landmark of the period for contemporaries, even though many modern critics do not share this high estimation.[15]

The *serranillas*, above all those of Don Iñigo López de Mendoza, marquis of Santillana (1398–1458), often relate the amorous encounters of young and pretty peasant mountain women with high nobles as they traveled across the mountain passes of Castile's rough topography. There is already in them elements of the pastoral novel and poetry of a later age and the juxtaposition of an idealized countryside to a corrupted court. That the marquis of Santillana, a very learned aristocrat, owner of one of the most remarkable libraries in Castile, and a major (and selfish) player in the political turmoil of John II and Henry IV's reigns, should have produced such enchanting verses is fairly representative of the complex nature of late medieval noble society. It echoes Huizinga's description of the "autumn of the Middle Ages."

Writing between old medieval traditions and new Renaissance forms, in the midst of crises, and with growing marginalization of religious minorities, a great lord and master of extensive holdings in northern Spain could compose such poetry as the few stanzas included below:

> Moça tan fermosa
> non vi en la frontera
> como una vaquera
> de la Finojosa
> Faziendo la vía
> del Calatraveño
> a Sancta María,
> vencido del sueño,
> por tierra fragosa
> perdí la carrera,
> do vi la vaquera
> de la Finojosa.
> En un verde prado
> de rosas e flores,
> guardando ganado
> con otros pastores,
> la vi tan graciosa
> que apenas creyera
> que fuese vaquera
> de la Finojosa.

> [I have never seen on the frontier such a lovely
> young woman as the one from Finojosa who tended the cattle
> From Calatrava as I took my way
> At Holy Mary's shrine to kneel and pray,
> And sleep upon my eyelids heavy lay,
> There where the ground was very rough and wild,
> I lost my path and met a peasant child:
> From Finojosa, with the herds around her,
> There in the fields I found her.
> Upon a meadow green with tender grass,
> With other rustic cowherds, lad and lass,
> So sweet a thing to see I watched her pass:
> My eyes could scarce believe her what they found her,
> There with the herds around her.][16]

Although the translation above is quite faulty and unyielding (confusing a young woman for a girl, obscuring the heavily sexual implications of the poem in later stanzas), the Castilian of the *serranillas* is new and fresh.

The serranillas, very much like the *romanceros* (compilations of romances), brought together a rich oral tradition which, in the case of the romances, evoked the many encounters between Muslims and Christians, providing a rich and nuanced counterpart to the refined poetry of the court. The *romancero* drew its inspiration from historical or semi-historical sources. Romances established a link between the medieval romance tradition and the Golden Age. Some of the late medieval romances became quite popular in the early modern period. That of *Gaiferos y Melisendra* resonated, as performed by a puppeteer, in the pages of Don Quixote.[17]

Beyond the *Romancero*

On the eve of Isabella and Ferdinand's reign, Castilian poets produced some of the most significant literary works of the late Middle Ages. Although some of these works date from a few years after the chronological terminus of this book, they emerged from the cultural context of the early and mid-fifteenth century. Some of them, such as Alfonso Martínez de Toledo, archpriest of Talavera's *Corbacho* (*Reproach of Worldly Love*) was written earlier than the mid-century (in the 1430s). It juxtaposes erudite pronouncements with popular misogyny. Others, such as Diego de San Pedro's iconic *Cárcel de amor* (*Prison of Love*) was not published until 1492, but it was written in the 1460s. *Cárcel de amor* became one of the most popular books of the late Middle Ages and a model for later writers. It tells the sorrowful story of a knight who dies by his own hands upon finding that his beloved does not return his love. The popularity of the book and of its imitators point to the enduring power of certain tropes in Castilian literature and to the fact that the cultural renewal taking place at the court of the Catholic Monarchs was solidly grounded in an earlier period.[18] There is not space to mention other works of note here, but I cannot move on without some brief reference to Jorge Manrique's poetry.

Writing about Jorge Manrique and, above all, about his extraordinarily beautiful and moving poem, *Coplas por la muerte de su padre* (*Ode on the Death of his Father*), is not an easy task. Manrique's work has received close scrutiny from generations of literary critics. Not being one, my reading of Manrique is shaped both by my interest as a historian in how his work offers a window into the mentality of the period, and by my own personal reaction to the wealth of references, ideas, and sensibilities populating his poem. Born around 1440 and dying in 1479 while serving the Catholic Monarchs at the siege of a noble enemy, Manrique, whose poem was written shortly after the death of his father Don Rodrigo Manrique, Master of the

Order of Santiago, achieved heights not previously reached by Castilian poets of his age. Borrowing liberally from themes common to the late fifteenth century and prominent in the waning literary traditions of most western European countries (but not Italy), Manrique engages in a long disquisition on the ephemeral nature of life and courtly display, reminding rich and poor that they are equal before death:

> Nuestras vidas son los ríos
> que van a dar a la mar,
> que es el morir:
> allí van los señoríos
> derechos a se acabar
> y consumir;
> allí los ríos caudales,
> allí los otros medianos
> y más chicos
> allegados son iguales,
> los que biven por las manos
> y los ricos

> [Our lives are rivers gliding free
> To that unfathomed, boundless sea,
> the silent grave:
> Thither all earthly pomp and boast
> Roll to be swallowed up and lost
> In one dark wave
> Thither the mighty torrents stray,
> Thither the brook pursues its way,
> And tinkling rill.
> There are all equal. Side by side,
> The poor man and the son of pride
> Lie calm and still.][19]

Manrique emphasizes faith as a bulwark against fleeting time and inexorable death. Yet the poem is an ode to the importance of fame and remembrance, to the just life spent in the protection of the weak, of being loyal to one's friends and fierce to one's enemies. Left behind are the ashes, the remnants, of sumptuous feasts – the ode cites the great feasts of 1428 and the arrogance of the Infantes of Aragon now dead and gone – the excesses which, like rivers flowing to the ocean, flow to that inexorable end which is death. If a whole literary tradition can be said to have a natural conclusion and to be representative of the disorders and creative tensions of an age, then that honor and burden belong to Jorge Manrique. His poem is deeply grounded in Castile's turbulent century of crises and in late medieval nostalgia and angst for a world slowly but unfailingly vanishing. It is as good an ending as anyone could hope for.

Poetry in the Literature of the Crown of Aragon

As was the case with the Castilian language, Catalan acquired characteristics resembling the modern form from the eleventh century onward. Closely linked to the languages of southern France (Occitania), Catalan was distinct from Castilian and the outcome of a separate linguistic evolution. Catalan poetry begins in earnest with troubadour poetry – a genre widespread throughout Occitania – toward the twelfth century. Without reaching the heights found in the lively troubadour tradition of Provence, the Languedoc, and Eleanor of Aquitaine's court, Catalan troubadours (*jonglars*) produced notable works, such as Guerau de Cabrera's *L' ensegnyament de joglar* (which could be roughly translated as *The Instruction of the Troubadour*, ca. 1160). Yet Catalan had not become a fully suitable vehicle for lyrical poetry and, to give just one example, the talented Ramón Llull (1233–1316) chose to write his poetical works in Provençal, a much more supple and poetic language.

Llull's poetry, above all his *Disconhort* (*Discomfort*), which was written late in life, is, together with his 1299 *Cant de Ramón* (*The Song of Ramón*), autobiographical and mystical in nature. Yet Llull, as was the case with many other Catalan literary figures, was also well connected with the court and with the everyday affairs of the kingdom, and thus open to the courtly and lyrical influences of the age. Another poet of note who began to show the possibilities of Catalan as a poetical language was Bernat Metge (ca. 1346–1413). His masterpiece, *Lo somni* (*The Dream*, 1399), suffers from excessive dependence on a whole array of Classical (Cicero, Boethius, and others) and modern (Boccaccio, Petrarch) worthies, which, while leaving little room for originality, provided a good measure of Catalonia's cultural resources and aesthetic interests even during a very difficult social, economic, and political period.[20]

Perhaps the most distinguished and influential Catalan poet (who wrote exclusively in Catalan) was Ausiàs March (1397–1459). March was a nobleman active in Alfonso V's early Mediterranean campaigns. Retiring to his lands in the mid-1420s, March was briefly married to Joanot Martorell's sister (Joanot was the author of the popular *Tirant lo Blanc*), and formed part of an expansive Catalan literary circle. Work and themes were widely shared among authors, and in some cases, as in this particular one, joint intellectual and aesthetic interests also translated into familial relations. Deeply grounded in the courtly tradition, March's poetry provides an exploration of what love is – in all of its spiritual and physical aspects – that transcends early courtly traditions. But his reflections on love are deeply bound up with reflections on death and the inexorable link between love and death. It is, above all, the personal element, the autobiographical references, that make these poems so moving. In them he journeys from human love to the death of his beloved to the love of God in a pilgrimage not unlike – and most probably inspired by – that of Dante in his *Divine Comedy*.[21]

Catalan and Castilian Chronicles, Religious Writings, and Romances

As vital as lyrical poetry proved to be in this period, prose – which I consider here as a single topic overcoming linguistic differences – showed a remarkable vitality and creativity. While poetry was deeply bound up with the language in which it was written and does not translate easily, a whole range of prose works, from chronicles to romances, represented new ways of thinking across regional and linguistic boundaries. Writing and reading depended also on several significant factors – all of them in flux in the late Middle Ages. Royal patronage of culture, so central to the intellectual achievements of Alfonso X and James I's courts,[22] continued unimpeded over the next century and a half. Whether at the court of John II or even Henry IV of Castile, weak kings presiding over brilliant courts, or Alfonso V of Aragon's dazzling cultural world in Naples, these sites for cultural production, though often filled with ideological and political purpose, flourished in the period under study. But courts could not be sufficient to sustain cultural change and growth. As noted earlier, a growing interest in reading made the demand for books – still in manuscript form but soon to be available in print (in the very late fifteenth century) – quite high. Barcelona's middling sorts and lower nobility read, as we have seen earlier, assiduously, as did their counterparts in Burgos, Cuenca, Seville, Valencia, and Valladolid.

Chronicles

Chronicles, which in Castile were royally sponsored throughout the fourteenth century, had a long ancestry dating back to the early Middle Ages. By the mid-thirteenth century in both Castile and the Crown of Aragon important shifts in how chronicles were written took place. Most significant of all was the shift to the vernacular, a change intimately tied to the formulation of "national" histories. Alfonso X's *Primera crónica general* and James I's *Libre dels feyts* are very different types of chronicles – the first with pretensions to a universal history while the second was purportedly autobiographical – but both were linked by their purpose (to enhance royal authority and prestige) and by being written in the vernacular: the former in Castilian and the latter in Catalan. Both chronicles had an impact beyond their century of composition, as they were read and imitated by later writers.[23]

In the case of Castile, the *Primera crónica general* and the chronicles of individual kings that followed in the second half of the thirteenth century would be continued throughout the rest of the Middle Ages by officially sponsored royal chroniclers. Besides setting down an almost day-to-day account of important events in the kingdom, royal perambulations through the realm, political events, natural phenomena, and, from time to time, references to international events, the chronicles served as useful weapons to rewrite history. Walter Benjamin's statement that history is written by the victors is easily illustrated by the manner in which the history of specific kings, Peter I and Henry IV above all, were ideologically bent to serve the aims of usurpers.

Not only did the chronicles grow in length, becoming not just longer but far more detailed during the transition from the fourteenth to the fifteenth centuries, but they also shifted their attention to ceremonies and festivities that exalted royal power. Castile was also remarkable in a negative sense, for it did not foster private chronicles until the mid-1400s, the *Hechos del condestable Don Miguel Lucas de Iranzo* being among the first.[24] When we turn to Catalonia, the first-person account of James I, translated from Catalan into Latin in 1313, provides a narrative structure the main thrust of which is the self-glorification of the king, while testifying to the providential support of the king's "deeds" (*feyts*). James I's chronicle, however, quickly gives way to a very different type of narrative: those of Desclot (late thirteenth century) and the great chronicle of Ramón Muntaner. While Desclot's chronicle (composed in Catalan) was written while in close contact with the Aragonese–Catalan court and has a strong tendency to exalt the Aragonese kings and people and their enterprises within and without the Crown of Aragon's realms, Muntaner (1265–1336), whom we have already met as one of the Valencian envoys to the crowning of Alfonso IV in 1327, tells the story not only of kings but of the Aragonese–Catalan people's bold deeds in the wider Mediterranean. An eyewitness to and participant in the campaigns in Sicily and the Levant, Muntaner's chronicle exudes a sense of patriotism (as does Desclot's), linking praise for the ruling house with a fervid embracing of the uniqueness of the Aragonese–Catalan people and their destiny in the turbulent world of the western Mediterranean. In the same vein, Peter III, the Ceremonious, a king fastidious about protocol if ever there was one, wrote a chronicle or history of his own times (from 1319 to 1382). It contains brilliant sketches of some of the important figures of the age and thoughtful reflections on the changes sweeping his realm. Unlike the Castilian royal chronicles, the Aragonese–Catalan ones, even when of royal provenance, present a far more complex portrait of late medieval society.[25] Lyrical poetry, chronicles, and other literary genres were not, however, the only representatives of the great cultural transformation of the fourteenth and fifteenth centuries.

Religion and Philosophy

A counterpart to chronicles and lyrical poetry were the devotional, theological, and philosophical treatises produced voluminously in this period. While theological and philosophical discussions tended to be in Latin, connecting learned men in Castile and the Crown of Aragon with ongoing debates on these topics north of the Pyrenees, there were works, often in the vernacular and often only of local interest, that differed from these Europe-wide manifestations of elite culture. The distinction I draw here, one mentioned earlier but worth glossing again, between Latin and the vernacular is an important one. Those writing in Latin, someone for example like the Valencian Arnau de Vilanova (1237–1311), wrote in both Latin and Catalan. His Latin treatises, in which he displayed an extensive knowledge of Arabic and Jewish thought, received far more attention outside the Crown of Aragon than they did south of the Pyrenees. Yet his short Catalan works, emphasizing millenarian ideas and radical Franciscan piety, had only a narrow impact on his peninsular contemporaries.[26] One could also point to the example of Ramón Llull. One of the most interesting figures in Catalan (and Spanish) literature – Martín de Riquer wrote that one should "underline the greatness and genius of the great Majorcan writer, who eclipsed all those who had written before him"[27] – Llull was one of those proto-Renaissance men whose works ranged widely over different scholarly and literary genres. A nobleman by birth, close to the centers of power at the court of James II, king of Majorca, a husband and father, Llull experienced a mystical conversion in the early 1260s. Entering the Franciscan Order, he traveled extensively to great pilgrimage sites and throughout the lands on the shores of the western Mediterranean. He wrote numerous works (in Latin and Catalan), ranging from mystical and devotional texts to theological debates to poetry, elaborate philosophical treatises, and stunning literary works. In 1276 Pope John XXI authorized him to build a monastery (named Miramar) in Majorca. There the teaching of Arabic was to be a main activity. And Llull, following in St. Francis' footsteps, advanced the bold idea that the peaceful and rational conversion of Muslims was far better than slaughtering them in the battlefield.[28]

Llull's prose works in Catalan – the first time in which the language had been deployed for a specific creative enterprise and not just for translations, chronicles, or material transactions – are significant and accomplished. They range from autobiographical sketches to the impressive *Blanquerna* (or *Romanç d'Evast e Blanquerna*) and his *Libre de Fèlix* (or *Libre de Meravelles*). Underlying his vernacular works is an aristocratic sense of the importance of knighthood – most evident in his *Libre de l'orde de cavalleria* (*Book of the Order of Chivalry*) and his concern with the Christian instruction of knights as *milites Christi* (soldiers of Christ). In *Blanquerna*, perhaps Llull's most significant work and one that is still popular today (I remember the great pleasure of reading it and writing a paper on Llull in a graduate seminar almost 35 years ago), the author creates what is probably the first proto-novel in the peninsula. The book tells the story of Blanquerna's parents, his birth and upbringing, his embracing of a religious life, and his rapid ascent through the ecclesiastical ranks from monk to pope until, relinquishing the throne of St. Peter, Blanquerna becomes a hermit, leading the world to a kind of Christian utopian paradise. As Cervantes would do in his *Don Quixote*, Llull in *Blanquerna* includes stories within the main story, most notably his great mystical work, *Llibre d'amic et amat* (*Book of the Lover and the Beloved*). Written in either the late 1270s or early 1280s, *Blanquerna*'s plot foreshadows the later renunciation of Pope Celestine V in 1305 and his failed attempts to return to his life as a hermit.[29] Though Llull wrote a good number of his most influential works before 1300, they shaped, especially *Blanquerna* and his other Catalan prose works, especially his work on knighthood (translated into English and French soon after its composition), most Catalan literary production in the next two centuries, above all the outburst of chivalrous romances in the fifteenth century.

Castile

When we turn to Castile's political and religious works, we can alternate between the well-known works by university-trained legal and theological scholars and obscure cultural productions. Although the latter often had little impact beyond their immediate circle, they nonetheless also provide important insights into Castilian and Spanish society in this period. Of the former the Infante Don Juan Manuel's vast opus marks an important stage in Castilian literature. Born in the early 1280s, a member of the royal family, and one of the most disruptive magnates of the troubled first half of the fourteenth century, Don Juan Manuel throughout his long life (he died in 1349) had equal enthusiasm for political intrigue and literary pursuits. His *Libro del Conde Lucanor*, which was written before Boccaccio's *Decameron* and to which it may be compared (though it lacks Boccaccio's range), tells a series of unconnected stories. Some of them serve as moral examples along the general lines of that well-known medieval genre, exempla literature. Others present secular and salacious themes with the usual moral admonition. Together with his *Libro de los estados*, a survey of medieval social structures and politics, or his old-fashioned *Libro del caballero y el escudero* (a dialog on knighthood, religion, and human life), Don Juan Manuel's works highlight the seemingly contradictory temperament and behavior of Spanish magnates. Deep and heartfelt spiritual and cultural concerns paralleled an active political life, endless ambition, and selfishness. Aesthetic preoccupations and a reflected life of reading and writing were not at all incompatible with a life in the battlefield or endless political intrigues.[30]

In a different vein altogether are Fernán Pérez de Guzmán's (1375–ca. 1460) series of individual biographies known as *Generaciones y semblanzas*. A true landmark in Castilian literature, Pérez de Guzmán's work dissects Castilian society and its problems, while providing probing sketches of Castile's main political protagonists in the early fifteenth century. In the same biographical mode, Gutierre Díaz de Games' *El Victorial* tells the story of an adventurous Castilian nobleman, Don Pero Niño, count of Balbuena: his childhood, his deeds in military campaigns in the Canary Islands and the western Mediterranean, and his later life and travels, while weaving in fictional details and heartfelt reflections on chivalry and the place of knights in Christian society.[31]

Although other significant prose works appeared in the crowded cultural Castilian landscape – we are barely scratching the surface of a wide sea of literary works – I would like to turn briefly to a far less well known composition. I particularly want to do this as it allows one to open a window on a theme sorely missing from this account – the spiritual and religious life of the peninsula. Although religion cannot be the main focus of discussion in a book that is essentially a political narrative in the context of the late medieval crisis and institutional transformation, religion was nonetheless an important component of Spaniards' mental landscape. The diverse human and material manifestations of religious observation and belief (forms of worship, moral prescriptions, religious festivals, and the like) constitute after all a significant aspect of the social and cultural history of the peninsula. Even in examining literary production one is struck by the constant juxtaposition of secular and religious themes. But what about works produced not for literary effect but to circulate only among a limited number of ecclesiastics and for pastoral purposes? What do they tell us about society as a whole?

In a synod held in the diocese of Segovia in 1325, the bishop of the city of Segovia, Don Pedro de Cuéllar, ordered the writing of a guide for the proper education of Segovia's clerics, informing them of the nature of the sacraments, about sin, and about the regulations for ecclesiastical conduct. Edited and published with a superb introduction by José Luis Martín, Antonio Linage Conde, and their research team at the University of Salamanca, *El catecismo de Pedro de Cuéllar (1325)* provides an insightful perspective into the different religious currents agitating one of Spain's middling dioceses and, by implication, into most of Spain's churches.[32]

The most salient aspect of the guide is that it is written in the vernacular (Castilian). Latin intrudes but little in the text and, when it does, it appears in the most elementary prescriptive fashion. The Latin phrases that are incorporated are along the lines of: "This is what you need to say when you baptize someone," or are basic and crucial incantations, such as those included in the ceremony of baptism: *Ego te baptizo [sic] in nomine Genitoris et Nati et Flaminis.*[33] Since this type of guidance is peppered throughout most of the book, one cannot but entertain the suspicion that most local priests (the intended audience of this manual) were quite deficient in their Latin and in the required formulas for the ritual of baptism, for other sacraments, and for the mass.

In a section on the consecration of the Host, the text reflects priestly and popular opinion as to what happens before, during, and after transubstantiation (the ritual during mass that transforms bread and wine into the flesh and blood of Christ). Beyond showing the growing importance of the Corpus Christi in Castilian devotional practices, the manual emphasizes that the sacrament should not be performed with either vinegar (*agraz*), wine mixed with honey, or, most surprising of all, with bacon (what in the world was going on in the Castilian liturgy that bacon is mentioned in this context?).[34] The injunction to all Christians to take communion at least once a year is accompanied by very clear directions as to what to do if any consecrated wine is spilt (the priest should lick it up) or if an insect or a spider falls into the chalice and comes into contact with the consecrated wine (burn the wine and the spider separately).[35] Here we see the numberless occurrences and practical matters of daily life and the bishop's concern with his motley and highly suspect crew of priests, canons, and congregation of the faithful. References to the enduring rivalry with monastic orders, and keen concerns about ecclesiastical income and adherence to the proper enactment of the liturgy and sacraments show the character of religious practices at the local level and the wide gulf that existed between the lofty pronouncements of Church councils or papal edicts and the reality on the ground.

Far more revealing are dispositions aimed at regulating ecclesiastical behavior, above all sexual behavior, or rather misbehavior. We know from Peter Linehan's brilliant works of Castilian clerical sexual transgressions in the thirteenth century and the many efforts, often failed, to address priestly and monastic sexual excesses.[36] Pedro de Cuéllar's instructions in 1325 do not offer any evidence that matters had improved since those glossed by Linehan in the late thirteenth century. Rather, most of the clergy (certainly those addressed in this manual) seem to be as ignorant and as prone to misconduct as those of a previous age. The clear admonitions in Cuéllar's guide against violation of the vow of chastity or the keeping of concubines (an accepted fact throughout the Iberian peninsula in the form of the *barragana* or ecclesiastical concubine) provide us with a guide to ecclesiastical behavior in the period. Clerics were forbidden to live with nuns or monks or to visit monasteries too frequently.[37] The bishop's injunctions also discuss ways of identifying clerical fornicators, placing the issue within the question of how "public" ecclesiastical sexual misconduct may have been, that is, how much the "public" knew.[38] Sanctions against such behavior were often financial. They could have involved either the loss of a benefice or the removal from office altogether. Yet, in a revealing section of his guide, Pedro de Cuéllar's manual gives leeway to ecclesiastical authorities to either waive or reduce the penalties for sexual misconduct because "such a vice [breaking the vows of chastity] is very common and men fall into this sin easily and far more often than other sins."[39]

Accepting that keeping concubines and being a notorious fornicator is the norm for priest, the text lists other forms of misbehavior, from drinking and eating too much (to the point of habitual drunkenness), missing the singing of the canonical hours, and absenteeism from ecclesiastical duties (seemingly a very common occurrence), to not keeping the ecclesiastically mandated tonsure or style of haircut (and thus passing as a layman), or lacking gravity in one's walk, speech, and demeanor.[40] Far more to the point, clerics should not dress in certain colors, use spurs, rings, or silk, attend the wedding and baptismal feasts of their children or grandchildren, carry arms, or gamble.[41] Although we know that clerical conduct throughout most of western Europe left a great deal to be desired, Pedro de Cuéllar's catechism provides a first-hand entry into clerical mores and the nature of popular religion. What one is led to suspect is that the mass was often performed in irregular fashion, that priests, canons, and regular clergy often engaged in illicit acts, that their Latin was atrocious or non-existent, and that simple formulaic phrases that were necessary for the correct performance of some of the central sacraments of the Church – baptism, communion, and marriage – needed to be included in his guide because the bishop could not trust his priest to know how to perform these rituals correctly.

These lapses, or what may appear as bad habitual behavior by the clergy, do not detract from the enduring presence of religion in every facet of Spanish daily life. Although few local saints walked the roads of Spain in this period, religion, as I argued earlier, pervaded every aspect of Spanish society. Yet there were different ways of thinking about or defining religion. In a much-quoted sentence, Cervantes' Don Quixote states that "religion is knight-errantry." In festivals, romances, and knight-errantry, religious aspirations were transformed into performances and ways of being that, while serving specific ideological purposes, conflated diverse cultural forms with the pursuit of salvation and the divine.

Religion, Romance, and Knight-Errantry

Here as we come close to our conclusion, we may wish to consider the proliferation of romances (written in the different peninsular vernacular languages) in fifteenth-century Spain, and the close links between this literary form (the romance) and the elaborate cycles of festivities (most of all the royal entry). As cultural artifacts, festivals played a growing and significant role in the peninsula's political life. Chronicles, from the mid-fourteenth century onward, paid greater attention to celebrations, describing them in luxurious detail and glossing explicitly their varied symbolic and ideological meanings. I have already noted some of the links between performance and politics in earlier chapters. One example was Alfonso IV's crowning as reported by Muntaner, or the fabled feasts of 1428 and Miguel Lucas de Iranzo's carnivalesque celebrations in 1460s Jaén (see chapters 4, 5, and 6). What I wish to do here, by presenting a few specific additional examples, is to connect the politics of the period to literature and performance, and to show how what people read was then enacted in real life. At the same time, and in many instances, real deeds served as models for literary works. As important, however, is to explain what all these variegated performances, knightly fantasies, and literary artifices meant within the changing political world of fifteenth-century Spain. And how did these festivals articulate values and function as responses to the late medieval crises on the eve of the marriage between Isabella and Ferdinand in 1469?

Festivals, royal entries, and performance

In a deservedly famous book, *Art and Power: Renaissance Festivals 1450–1650*, Sir Roy Strong describes the rich texture of performances in late medieval and early modern Europe and their inextricable relation to politics and power.[42] Following on from the paradigmatic treatment of festivals and their role in Renaissance culture and life found in Jacob Burckhardt's *The Civilization of the Renaissance in Italy*, in Huizinga, and others, Strong and other scholars have presented a complex portrait of festivals and of their role in late medieval and early modern Europe. Unfortunately their references to Spain are either scant or non-existent. The Iberian realms participated fully in the performative culture of the late Middle Ages, but these activities are not reflected in the historiography. What was, then, the nature of this culture and what does it tell us about Spain?

Festivals and performances (and the two terms can often be used interchangeably) were an integral part of daily life in the peninsula. From the calendrical celebrations of the great Church holidays – Christmas, the Epiphany, Easter, St. John's Day, and other significant liturgical landmarks – to the non-calendrical festivities, such as the coming of a king into a city for the first time, coronations, royal births, a royal or princely visit, and other such events, the year was filled with well-organized festivals. A whole array of activities was carefully planned for each of these occasions, and the chronicles never failed to note the festivities associated with holidays or to wax lyrical while glossing both calendrical and non-calendrical festivities.

All of these celebrations had a basic script with the usual variations demanded by specific political circumstances and geographical location. After all, the power and impact of festivals, both as political tools and cultural artifacts, resided precisely in their reiterative character. They were, at the same time, familiar and unfamiliar: unfamiliar because of some of the motifs present were too arcane or culturally distant to be known by the popular audience; familiar because almost every festival included jousting, *tableaux vivants*, theatrical skits, parades of the mighty, processions, masses, carnivalesque aspects, banquets for those on top, and generous and extravagant distributions of food for those below. All festivals referred to each other, creating a bonding sense of meaning and memory. In the celebrations of 1428 Valladolid, a feast dominated by the presence of two kings and the Infante Henry (the Infante of Aragon), a fantastic artificial castle was built at the cost of 50,000 florins (an extraordinary expense), while courtly references were displayed in the vestments and performances of the main participants. *Pas d'armes*, public dancing by the royal and princely participants, and banquets filled an entire month of lavish displays and celebrations.[43]

Similarly, in the princely entry of Ferdinand of Antequera (soon after to become king of the Crown of Aragon) into Seville in 1410, or that of Henry IV into Jaén in the 1460s, powerful messages were conveyed, either because the performances did happen entirely as described by the chroniclers (which is to be doubted) or because the accounts tended to embellish the actual events for political and aesthetic purposes. An example worth noting and quoting extensively is the entry of Alfonso V into Naples. We already know how very hard Alfonso had struggled to gain control of the kingdom of Naples. When victory finally arrived, it was marked by an elaborate royal entry. It may be useful to quote from Burckhardt's account of the event:

> Alfonso the Great, on his entrance into Naples (1443), declined the wreath of laurel . . . For the rest, Alfonso's procession, which passed by a breach in the wall through the city to the cathedral, was a strange mixture of antique, allegorical, and purely comic elements. The car, drawn by four white horses, on which he sat enthroned, was lofty and covered with gilding; twenty patricians carried the poles of the canopy of cloth of gold which shaded his head. The part of the procession which the Florentines then present in Naples had undertaken was composed of elegant young cavaliers, skillfully brandishing their lances, of a chariot with the figure of Fortune, and of seven Virtues on horseback . . . Sixty Florentines, all in purple and scarlet, closed this splendid display . . . Then a band of Catalans advanced on foot, with lay figures of horses fastened on to them before and behind, and engaged in mock combat with a body of Turks [one must imagine pretend Turks], as though in derision of Florentine sentimentalism. Last of all came a gigantic tower, the door guarded by an angel with a drawn sword; on it stood four Virtues, who each addressed the king with a song.[44]

The obvious attempts in all these celebrations to buttress power, to teach, to entertain, or simply to engage in fanciful display do not need to be explicated in detail here. Royal entries or festivals provided a commingling of social orders, sites for dialog and reiteration of social hierarchies. The colors and fabrics wore by those on top – and described with fastidious detail by the chroniclers – served as clear reminders of the social gulf separating those on top from those below. When the citizens of Jaén came out to meet Henry IV, king of Castile, at a preordained distance from the city gate, in a well-ordered and hierarchically organized procession, country and urban spaces came together at that liminal point – two and a half leagues from the city walls – that marked the boundaries of urban jurisdiction over the surrounding countryside. City officials used the royal entry to also make a statement about civic power and to reiterate Jaén's rule over its unruly hinterland. Likewise, when Burgos' municipal officials, all dressed up in scarlet, marched out of the city to receive the Infanta Doña Blanca who had come to Castile for her ill-fated marriage to the Infante Henry, the urban oligarchs were engaging in a two-pronged negotiation: with the Crown, from which they expected privileges (mostly tax exemptions), and simultaneously with the people of the city, from whom they expected an acknowledgment of the council's power and of the citizens' obedience.

But what about the cultural signs deployed at these festivals and in the circulation of culture between different levels of society? Most festivals, although following a traditional script, also introduced new cultural themes. As such, celebrations served as ways of transmitting and popularizing specific aspects of elite culture. For the late Middle Ages, this was mostly focused on the obsessive concerns with chivalrous motifs. Thus no festivity ever lacked elaborate performances aimed at highlighting knightly valor and prowess. At the feats of May 1428 in Valladolid, the kings of Castile, Navarre, the Infante Henry (the Infante of Aragon), Alvaro de Luna, and other high-ranking members of the Castilian and Aragonese nobilities broke many lances and displayed their military skills in extravagant fashion. The chronicler took great delight in enumerating them and providing lavish remainders to the readers of the king's martial abilities. This of course was fiction since John II of Castile was hardly skilled at anything. In the prelude to the entrance of the Infanta Doña Blanca into Briviesca, 50 knights dressed in white fought fiercely with 50 knights dressed in red. Once they were suitably covered with blood to impress the Infanta and onlookers, they all proceeded to an enclosed meadow where bear-baiting and a hunt were performed for the Infanta while her retinue gazed at this bizarre spectacle from a well-decorated stage.[45]

All these displays of knightly excellence were performed in public to throngs of spectators. They poured into the towns or countryside to delight in fictitious warfare.[46] As had been the case in Valladolid or as was the case at other festive events throughout the Iberian peninsula, these celebrations were liberally sprinkled with allusions – in the garments, plotting, and *tableaux vivants* – to courtly romances. The festivals were essentially coded with references to contemporary literary works, twelfth-century romances (mostly the inexhaustible treasure-trove of Arthurian legends), and mythology. In Valladolid, a woman dressed as the goddess Fortune (think of Alfonso V's entry into Naples almost 20 years later and of Juan de Mena's *Laberinto de fortuna*) presided over a large wheel, reminding noble and humble spectators about the mutability of one's destiny.

How much of these copious literary references were understood by those below is difficult to discern. Clearly a great part of elite culture, above all that having to do with courtly themes, had strong echoes in the popular imagination and impressed those below by the sheer imagery of its splendor and warring elements. While some of the references – John II of Castile wearing a diadem of butterflies as he appeared in one of the jousts (symbolizing the resurrection of his power) – may have been lost on most of the citizens of Valladolid and those from the surrounding villages attending the festival, it was pretty and unusual and drew their gaze to the figure of the king. This would have been reinforced at the next event, following shortly afterwards, when the king reappeared dressed in green as king of the woods (it was May) with a bear and a lion in chains – how thrilling and entertaining it must have been for the people of medieval Valladolid to see a lion – or when John II, dressed as God the Father and surrounded by twelve of his knights garbed as the Apostles, showed up for the final event in the festive cycle. The significant point here is that there was a continuous flow of cultural messages between elite and popular culture (although such categories as elite and popular should rightly be questioned). Perhaps what we should do here is to see these performances as an endless juxtaposition of different cultural traditions within a broad frame of cultural references. In these exchanges and borrowings, new and more effective ways of ruling were forged.[47] And this took place in the twilight years of the Middle Ages, as rulers faced enormous fiscal and political challenges.

This ebb and flow was not limited to knightly themes. During Henry IV's entry into Jaén, as the king followed the royal entry's traditional route through the city, he gazed on a performance of the play of the three Magi. The chronicler's mention of this event is the first extant reference to the play in Castilian literature. Together with *tableaux vivants*, representing scenes from literary works or well-known mythological stories, these "public" performances also brought elements of a written culture to those who did not read or would not (or could not) own a manuscript. In imitative patterns, those below also engaged in mock-combat. Whether a battle of eggs between the constable Miguel Lucas de Iranzo and his men playfully besieged in a tower by the people of Jaén, or a duel with pumpkins or dead chickens (food fights were quite common) in 1460s Jaén and elsewhere, these are ongoing references to how elite forms and lifestyles circulated (in carnivalesque forms) throughout the general population.[48]

Elite courtly displays were also accompanied by extensive and lavish distributions of food. The people came out to see these festivals because of the great entertainment value they provided. Sometimes they were even forced to do so, as Jews, Muslims, and guild members were forced, under the penalty of a fine, to attend Corpus Christi processions. But they also came because these great events provided much-needed relief from hunger or from the tedious nature of their daily diet. As the chroniclers are prompt to remind us, the food and the wine were of a quality seldom enjoyed by those below.

In many respects celebrations enacted political agendas, provided salutary lessons to the people at large as to the correct ordering of society, and reiterated the nature of power: whether royal, princely, or municipal. At the same time festivals served important social and economic functions. By recirculating income in the form of lavish banquets, they emphasized the largesse of those on top while providing a delectable escape from the humble fare of every day. In the *Hechos del condestable Don Miguel Lucas de Iranzo* the description of food is only second in importance to the description of the constable's clothing. In the princely entry of the Infanta Doña Blanca to Briviesca we are told in great detail about the abundance of wine and tasty food.

But it was not only about clothing and food, the great markers of social difference in the Middle Ages and today. It was also about space. What festivals and royal entries did was to delimit spaces, which became closely associated with rituals of power. Sometimes this secular appropriation of space intruded into traditional understandings of sacred space. For example, coronations in the Crown of Aragon, royal knightings, and vigils over arms in Castile intruded forcefully into ecclesiastical spaces and bent them to political purposes. Royal entries, as I have already noted, followed a well-prescribed circuit. It is no coincidence that this would often be the route of the Corpus Christi processions. Places for the great tournaments were not selected randomly but carefully chosen to heighten the significance of the event – the main square of the town, the square in front of the cathedral. These sites often alternated between secular festivals and displays, executions, and inquisitorial *autos-da-fé*. On the issue of how to display power, secular and older ecclesiastical scripts overlapped to the benefit of both. Under the impetus of the importance of place, those planning festivals sought to sacralize these urban spaces and to give their performances greater validity through their obvious association with them.

Although much later than the chronological terminus of this book, Charles V's (Charles I in Spain) royal entry into Barcelona in 1519 is symbolic of the relationship between power (or in this case the hope and expectation of power) and place. After all Charles' rule over his Spanish realms was tenuous indeed in 1519, and Barcelona was always a wasp's nest of political troubles and resistance to outside authority. The circuit of his ceremonial procession through the city linked Barcelona's traditional medieval ritual spaces with the centers of secular government, concluding with his final stop at the cathedral.[49] The role that political symbolism played in these royal entries, especially in a place such as Barcelona, reminds us forcefully that these performances were not always successful. The give and take between different protagonists – king, nobility, urban oligarchs, and the like – did not always yield the desired outcome. But in many respects, these events provided a unique opportunity to project a representation (or diverse representations) of royal power directly to those below without the mediation of royal agents or local elites. Although everything is, at the end, about politics, cultural artifacts and cultural performances, besides playing a well-defined role in the political conflicts of the age, also reflected the values of a narrow elite at the top and aesthetic concerns which were quite often divorced from political reality. It is to them that we now turn.

Courtly Romances

The fifteenth century witnessed the composition, and enactment of, elaborate courtly romances. A culture of chivalry, of romance, of devotion to the lady thrived in the Iberian royal courts, as it did elsewhere in the medieval West. But these highly aestheticized forms also had a vigorous life in the streets of Barcelona, Valencia, Seville, and other great Spanish commercial centers. The most popular literary genre was not the reflective poetry of someone like Jorge Manrique or the erudite compositions of Juan de Mena or Metge. The most popular and influential works were the tales of knights-errant and their deeds. More than a generation after the heyday of these books of chivalry, Bernal Díaz del Castillo evoked *Amadís of Gaul* (one of the late fifteenth century's bestsellers) in his account of the Castilians' reactions to their first sight of the fabled Techtnochitlan. More than a century later, Cervantes sought to debunk their enduring popularity by ironically writing what is the most famous of all books about knights-errant. Yet the most remarkable thing about the genre was that real-life examples were as numerous and far more bizarre than the literary accounts. Remember that many of those selfish and cruel noblemen who tormented the peninsular realms through their inexhaustible greed and ferocious wars read these romances and sought to live their lives in imitation of them.

A few examples will prove the point. In the early 1430s, Suero de Quiñones, one of the noblemen in Alvaro de Luna's retinue, frequented the royal court wearing an iron collar on his neck, a sign of his being a prisoner of Love. Suero asked John II for permission to hold a *pas d'armes* along the pilgrimage road to Compostela. He planned to hold the *pas* until, by breaking 300 lances in honor of his unnamed lady, he would be freed from his captivity. Accompanied by some of his friends, attendants, and a notary who was to (and did) record every detail of the event, Suero de

Quiñones and his entourage settled on a narrow bridge across the river Órbigo in the outskirts of León to hold his *pas d'armes* or *paso honroso*. I have stood with students on the bridge (which still stands in all its medieval glory) right on the spot where Suero and his friends challenged to combat every noble pilgrim on his way to the tomb of the Apostle James, and wondered about the implausibility of the whole enterprise. Those refusing to fight had to surrender a token – a spur, the glove of their lady – as a sign of their obligation to meet in combat in the near future. Those foolish enough to take on the challenge were provided with a horse, weapons, and armor if they lacked them. One could visualize what a nuisance the whole affair must have been for early fifteenth-century travelers, and how very bizarre such behavior would appear to us today. The whole affair, lasting almost a month – from July 10 to August 9, 1434, that is, at the height of the pilgrimage season – would have continued for far longer had it not been for the intervention of four Valencian knights-errant. Upset at the impediments placed on the peaceful pilgrims' progress, they came to the bridge at Órbigo and offered to break all the remaining lances, forcing Suero and his friends to decamp. This they did in convincing fashion, beating Suero and his men into a pulp until they had to withdraw from the field, after breaking just over half of the promised lances, to tend to their wounds. And Suero's was only the most notable among many such *pas d'armes* held throughout Iberia in the fifteenth century. What are we to make of all of this?

In his idiosyncratic yet delightful book, *Caballeros andantes españoles* (*Spanish Knights-Errant*) Martín de Riquer provides us with an enchanting romp through the world of Iberian and foreign knights-errant at the waning of the medieval world. Spanish knights traveled abroad in search of adventures, exciting (and dangerous) jousts, and the fulfillment of their calling. Foreign knights from every corner of Europe received a lavish welcome at the Spanish courts, as they engaged in fictitious combat. In this respect, the actual real life and chivalrous deeds of Jacques de Lalaigny, a knight at the court of Philip the Good, the duke of Burgundy, were turned into a half-fictionalized romance, the *Livre des faits de Jacques de Lalaigny*. It served as a model for further chivalrous adventures. Echoes of this appear in Castile with Gutierre Díaz de Games' *El Victorial* which, as has been noted above, tells of Pero Niño count of Buelna's deeds but which also offers, besides a hagiographically laden biography, a spirited defense of the superiority of knighthood and knights.

The flow between reality and fiction is most evident in *Tirant Lo Blanch*, one of the most popular books of chivalry in late fifteenth-century Spain and one of the inspirations for Don Quixote in his hopeless quest. It is written by Johanot Martorell (b. ca. 1413; d. 1468), a knight involved in real-life adventures, who traveled to England to challenge his rival Johan de Monpalau (who seems to have dishonored Martorell's sister), to a duel to the death. His adventures and those of his fictional protagonist (Tirant) intertwined life experiences with artistic artifice. Or what are we to make of Miguel d'Oris, a Catalan knight who, on August 20, 1400, while in Paris challenged all English knights to single combat until, by doing so, he was freed from his oath and love's prison? And until his preposterous vow was fulfilled (which it obviously never was) he walked around with a *punzón* (similar to an ice pick) piercing his leg. Similarly, Bernat de Coscón, another of those indomitable and ingenious Catalan knights, walked through the streets of Barcelona on the feast-day of St. Sebastian with his leg also pierced by a knife, not to be removed until he had fought on foot and on horseback.[50]

These bizarre deeds and challenges were announced in posters throughout the city, themselves a form of literary expression and as such an articulation of the chivalrous culture of the age. But what did all these things mean? Contemporary with the Barcelona merchant who read devotional literature and kept small shrines at home,[51] the culture of these knights blended seamlessly into the brilliant but nostalgic atmosphere of the royal courts. These celebrations, displays, and lifestyles, whether feasts, Corpus Christi processions, the more elusive (but also highly scripted) carnivals, or individual combats and *pas d'armes* occurred in the context of the endless internecine struggle between Crown and noble factions. Yet, as Spain reached the end of the Middle Ages and the growing centralization of the Catholic Monarchs, these celebrations and exuberant noble behavior took place within the boundaries of royal authority. Suero de Quiñones requested permission from his king to hold the *passo honrosso*. Knights wrote and published the accounts of their deeds. Court festivals served as the ideal sites for memorable duels and jousts. The apparent freedom and anarchic quality of these events and individual knightly deeds was highly illusory. All these festive enterprises had been inscribed into new forms of government and authority. Diverse and dazzling as these cultural artifacts were, they had become part of new ways of thinking about political relations within the realm and of a future that loomed closer and closer after the marriage of Ferdinand and Isabella in 1469.

Chapter 9

Epilogue

Toward the Reign of the Catholic Monarchs, 1469–1474

In the wake of Ferdinand and Isabella's much-romanticized and even mythologized wedding on October 19, 1469, the young couple faced fierce opposition from France, Portugal, the still ruling, though much weakened, king of Castile, Henry IV (Isabella's half-brother), and from a vigorous coalition of high noblemen and cities. The months preceding the actual marriage had been fraught with the usual shifting alliances, betrayals, and turbulent politics common to late medieval Castile. Before Isabella and Ferdinand had exchanged vows, Henry IV had made elaborate plans to secure Portuguese support by proposing a marriage between Isabella and Afonso, the much older Portuguese king. Failing that, the Castilian king was ready to replace Isabella with his own daughter, Joanna, who, although rightly suspected by many to be illegitimate, still had significant claims to the throne. While Henry IV was plotting matrimonial alliances and the magnate house of the Villenas was hoping to snatch the young princess for its own ends, Isabella and her advisers, among them initially and most prominently, Archbishop Carrillo of Toledo, had exacted an agreement from the Aragonese king John II and his son Ferdinand (by then already the acknowledged heir to the Crown of Aragon, and king of Sicily), at Cervera on March 5, 1469. The accord, which gave notice of Isabella's desire to claim the throne for herself, completely assuaged Castilians' fear of Aragonese meddling and attempts to control the realm.

The marriage, of course, brought immediate clarity to the situation. Isabella was not yet queen, but the issue of who was to rule Castile was now to be settled between 1469 and Henry II's eventual death, which occurred either late in the evening of December 11, 1474, or the following morning. Who of the contending parties was to be in the best position to claim Castile?

Was it to be Isabella and her new husband Ferdinand, or was it to be Joanna and the magnate families and Portuguese king backing her candidacy? The intervening years between the marriage of the two heirs to Castile and Aragon and Isabella's eventual ascent to the throne late in 1474 witnessed a flurry of activity in both camps. Here Ferdinand's cunning (and Aragonese resources and family connections) and Isabella's resolute determination to rule without interference proved invaluable. But in 1470 it was not yet clear who would have the upper hand at the end. The couple's efforts to secure Henry IV's blessing for their union – as you may remember from chapter 5, according to the Pact of Guisando Isabella was not to marry without Henry's permission – proved unsuccessful. Their early allies wavered. Even John II, king of the Crown of Aragon, beset by open rebellion in Catalonia and by a serious French threat, could not, or did not wish to, provide much-needed support. Nonetheless, between 1470 and mid-December 1474 the young couple adroitly managed their scant resources, made alliances with great noble families, and gained enough urban support to place themselves in a strong position when Henry IV's death finally came.

The first successes were found in the north – from the Basque region and from nobles and towns in Old Castile. The south and the great noble houses in Andalusia and Murcia, most of all the always hostile Villena family, would have to be won over by compromise in the next few years or harshly defeated in the long civil war that followed Henry's death. But in the intervening years before Isabella claimed the throne for herself the struggle was mostly a political one, consisting of the building of strong alliances and gathering as many resources and supporters as possible. Isabella and Ferdinand's strategy to achieve these ends can be summarized briefly. First, the great noble houses of Haro and Treviño defeated Henry IV's supporters in the Basque region and went over to Isabella's side. This provided a secure base in the rearguard of Isabella's center of operations in Old Castile, freeing her hand for action in other regions of the realm. The Haros' and Treviños' willingness to declare their obeisance to the young princess also taught other great noble families about the advantages of joining Isabella's party. Second, Ferdinand's diplomatic skills secured an alliance with Charles the Bold, the Burgundian ruler, offsetting Louis XI of France's support for Henry. France was thus effectively removed as a threat to a Spain ruled by Isabella and Ferdinand, as it had been removed from the matrimonial sweepstakes. Third, towns in Old Castile, such as Sepúlveda and eventually even Segovia, Henry's favorite city, joined Isabella's side. That the princess and self-declared heiress to Castile claimed to be a strong defender of municipal liberties did not harm her cause either. Urban support would prove essential to Isabella; far more significant, growing urban backing of Isabella granted legitimacy, through the Cortes, to her claims, as well as substantial subsidies and military contingents. Fourth, Henry II, though never fully accepting Ferdinand and Isabella's marriage, was, nonetheless, disengaged enough from the conflict and sufficiently courteous to her sister during a parlay in Segovia in 1473 to create doubts among Isabella's enemies as to the king's ultimate allegiance. Fifth, some of the most important families in Old Castile – the Enríquez (Ferdinand's mother was an Enríquez), the Mendozas, the Manriques, and other magnate lineages lined up solidly behind Isabella's claims. With growing urban acceptance and magnate backing, Isabella and Ferdinand had put together a formidable coalition, capable of claiming and wresting power from their enemies.[1]

When Henry IV died outside Madrid in December 1474, Ferdinand was in Aragon and Isabella was in Segovia. Learning of her half-brother's death (she was probably given the news late in the evening of December 12), Isabella took bold steps to claim the throne and to insure Castilian autonomy and sovereignty free from Aragonese interference. Andrés Bernáldez, one of the chroniclers of the Catholic Monarchs' reign, tells us, in laconic language, the sequence of events:

> [upon hearing the news] the Princess Doña Isabel covered herself with mourning clothes and cried, as it was to be done, for her brother the king, and she went to the church of St. Michael, and there also went the banners of the king Don Enrique [Henry], and those of the city of Segovia, covered in black mourning and carried low, and after doing all the ceremonies [and prayers] of mourning, masses, and obsequies, they [the people of Segovia] built a stage and they [the magnates and people of Segovia] raised Doña Isabel queen of Castile and León. Then the *mayordomo* [the king's steward] Cabrera gave the newly named queen the keys to the fortresses [*alcazares*] in the city, the staff of justice, and the treasures of her brother, whose *mayordomo* he was . . .[2]

Hernando del Pulgar, a far more reliable chronicler than Bernáldez, describes the raising of the banners of Castile to the traditional cry of "Castile, Castile for the king Don Ferdinand and for the queen Doña Isabella, his wife and *owner of these kingdoms.*" This was followed by other acclamations throughout many cities in northern Castile and by processions of nobles coming to Segovia to kiss Isabella's hand in obeisance.[3]

The emphasis in the above quote is mine, because it reiterates John Edwards' description of Isabella's self-proclamation as queen as a "coup." At Segovia – and Alfonso de Cartagena's description of the procession through the city with the newly elected queen marching behind the sword of justice held high by its point justifies the idea of Isabella's rushing to claim power – Isabella did not wait for Ferdinand to claim her rights over Castile and to assert the full extent of her authority. It took the Catholic Monarchs some time to achieve a compromise between Castilian and Aragonese interests and to achieve an efficient working relationship and shared responsibility. Isabella gave much in terms of titles and honors, but little in terms of real authority over Castile. It took them a few years (essentially until 1480) to fully restore order to Castile, to tame its selfish nobility and restless cities, to reform the kingdom's economy, religious life, and culture, and to reignite the long struggle against Granada. But this they did with a sure hand, adding to the administrative and institutional edifice that had been slowly built over a century and a half of crises.

***

A World of Crises and Renewal, 1300–1474

When our story began in 1300 the kingdom of Castile tilted perilously on a knife edge. A royal minority threatened the integrity of the realm. Royal administrative structures and an incipient bureaucracy had not yet been formalized. The Castilian and Catalan languages, beyond some notable landmarks (*The Poem of the Cid*, the work of Berceo, royal chronicles, and the like), had not yet become an organic part of Iberian life. Looming on the horizon were even more severe threats to the stability of the realm. In the Crown of Aragon how to settle the new Mediterranean conquests was still to be fully decided. The rising kingdom of Majorca and Sicily presented peculiar problems to the count-kings of the Realms of Aragon. Relations between Crown and Corts had not been fully formalized. Even though by 1300 territorial frontiers began to be defined, the lines separating one realm from another were not yet fully fixed. Aragonese–Catalan culture, far more precocious than that of Castile, was not yet ready for its impressive display in the next 150 years. In both realms festivals did not receive the attention from chroniclers that they would in later years. By 1474 everything had changed. The structures of governance and ruling were fully in place, even though they did not always work as well as expected. A sense of identity, grounded in legal, linguistic, and festive tradition, had been fully developed. Borders between both polities were clearly delimited.

But as we near the end of the story I do not wish to leave the reader with the impression that the Catholic Monarchs' far-reaching reforms were inevitable or that, in some teleological fashion, all of Spanish history, its politics and culture, moved inexorably to centralization and greater royal control. Although I have tried to show how some of Ferdinand and

Isabella's policies and the dazzling cultural achievements of their age were grounded in the previous century and emerged from the attempts to respond to the late medieval crisis, my intention has certainly not been to present a facile linear account of the development of the Spanish polities in the fourteenth and fifteenth centuries. In the midst of innumerable and seemingly insurmountable crises, Castilians, Aragonese, Catalans, and Valencians strove valiantly to make sense of the world they had found. They sought, more often than not unsuccessfully, to buttress their respective societies against the disorder and malaise of the age. Solutions differed from one kingdom to the other, but their aims were usually similar. Kings, though often weak and facing perennial challenges from unruly and selfish nobles in Castile, or from jealous defenders of ancient privileges and liberties in the Crown of Aragon, nonetheless promoted bureaucratic structures that underpinned the reforms of the late fifteenth century and the territorial expansion and cultural achievements of the Golden Age. The Spains did not treat their kings well, but, in the end, Spaniards could not do without their kings.

In the midst of crisis, bold Aragonese and Catalan sailors, merchants, and soldiers projected the Crown of Aragon into the wider Mediterranean world, laying the foundations for centuries of Spanish presence in Italy. At the same time, Castilians ventured into the Atlantic, establishing their rule over the Canary Islands, the most important launching point for later Atlantic ventures. At Antequera and elsewhere, the frontier with Granada was advanced, foreshadowing the campaigns of the 1480s against the last Muslim stronghold in the peninsula.

Culture thrived in the intrigue-laden atmosphere of the Spanish courts. New literary genres came into being in the century and a half after 1300. Fashion changed, as did protocol at court. By the end of the fourteenth century the calendar was changed to bring Spain into step with the rest of the West. Fantastic performances marked the transformation of the Spanish realms; the Corpus Christi processions, which by the early modern period would subsume all types of celebrations, began to gain greater importance in this period, linking religion and kingly power, politics and spirituality, in a neat and well-scripted package.

In many respects, the late Middle Ages laid the foundations for the substantial achievements of the Catholic Monarchs and the Spanish empire of the sixteenth century, but the age needs to be seen independently of what followed. The achievements of those centuries were produced by men and women in the diverse Spanish realms for their own profit and delight. They were not to prepare, in some Whiggish historiographical fashion, a far-away future. For contemporaries the times seemed often to wax evil indeed – plague, wars, civil strife, the persecution and forceful conversion of Jews, and disputed successions. The satirical and critical poetry of the age bemoaned the cruelty and violence of those above against those below, the stupidity and meekness of the poor and peasants. The General Dance of Death served as a reminder of the onslaught of the plague, while other poets, Jorge Manrique most notable among them, reminded their readers of the ephemeral quality of life on this earth, of the importance of memory, honor, and fame. These messages were, after all, not so discordant. They were different tunes, polyphonic voices singing strange and almost unrecognizable chants in a world that, through the unceasing labor and suffering of its inhabitants, propelled Spain into a new age.

Notes

Chapter 1

1 F. Javier Pereda Llarena, ed., *Documentación de la catedral de Burgos (1294–1316)*, in *Fuentes medievales castellano-leonesas*, vol. XVII (Burgos, 1984), 84–5.

2 For the history of the Iberian realms in the Middle Ages up to the thirteenth century the old, but still most thorough, account is that of Luis García de Valdeavellano, *Historia de España*, I, 2nd edn (Madrid, 1955). It unfortunately ends in 1212. In English, two general accounts of worth are Angus MacKay, *Spain in the Middle Ages: From Frontier to Empire, 1000–1500* (New York, 1977), and Joseph F. O'Callaghan, *A History of Medieval Spain* (Ithaca, NY, 1975). For the Crown of Aragon specifically see Thomas N. Bisson, *The Medieval Crown of Aragon: A Short History* (Oxford, 1986). The present Blackwell series, of which this volume covers one specific segment, will provide a detailed account of Spain's history in the Middle Ages.

3 See John H. Elliott, *Imperial Spain, 1469–1716* (New York, 1964), 1–3: "A dry, barren, impoverished land: 10 per cent of its soil bare rock; 35 per cent poor and unproductive; 45 per cent moderately fertile; 10 per cent rich." Fernand Braudel, *The Mediterranean and the Mediterranean World in the Age of Philip II*, trans. Siän Reynolds, 2 vols (New York, 1972), I. 25–354.

4 See Carlos Barros, *Mentalidad justiciera de los Irmandiños, siglo XV* (Madrid, 1990), and my *Spanish Society, 1400–1600* (London, 2001), 190–3.

5 José García Mercadal, ed., *Viajes de extranjeros por España y Portugal*, repr. in 6 vols (Salamanca, 1999), I. 277.

6 *Liber Sanct Jacobi* or the alleged relation by Americ Picaud in García Mercadal, *Viajes de extranjeros*, I. 159 *et passim*.

7 See *Primera crónica general: Estoria de España que mando a componer Alfonso el Sabio y se continuaba . . .* , ed. Ramón Menéndez Pidal, 2 vols (Madrid, 1956), I. 311 *et passim*; *Poema de Fernán González*, ed. John Lihani (East Lansing, 1991), 5–6, 22, *et passim*.

8   See Paul Freedman, *The Origins of Peasant Servitude in Medieval Catalonia* (Cambridge, 1991). I will refer to this book repeatedly in coming chapters for it raises significant points as to the social and economic evolution of Catalonia in the late Middle Ages.

9   *Desde Estella a Sevilla: Cuentas de un viaje (1352)*, ed. María Desamparados Sánchez Villar (Valencia, 1962).

10   For this entire section on the geographical diversity of the Spains I depend heavily on Ruth Way, *A Geography of Spain and Portugal* (London, 1962), and on my own work in my *Crisis and Continuity: Land and Town in Late Medieval Castile* (Philadelphia, 1994), ch. 1, and *Spanish Society*, ch. 1.

11   For the Reconquest, the emergence of crusading ideals in Spain and their transformation over time see Abilio Barbero and Marcelo Vigil, *Sobre lor orígenes sociales de la Reconquista* (Barcelona, 1974); Derek Lomax, *The Reconquest of Spain* (London, 1978); Joseph F. O'Callaghan, *Reconquest and Crusade in Medieval Spain* (Philadelphia, 2003).

12   See O'Callaghan, *Reconquest and Crusade*.

13   This discussion of changes in the system of values, the emergence of new economic forms, and the construction of new models of charity and attitudes toward the poor is a summary of my *From Heaven to Earth: The Reordering of Castilian Society, 1150–1350* (Princeton, 2004). See specifically chs 1 through 5.

14   For a more detailed discussion of linguistic changes see my *From Heaven to Earth*, 12–36 *et passim*.

15   This discussion of Castilian developments in the thirteenth century summarizes some of the arguments in my *Crisis and Continuity*, 287–324. See also my *The City and the Realm: Burgos and Castile, 1080–1492* (Aldershot, 1992), chs 7 and 8.

Chapter 2

1   See my *Crisis and Continuity: Land and Town in Late Medieval Castile* (Philadelphia, 1994), chs 10 and 11.

2   Thomas N. Bisson. *The Medieval Crown of Aragon: A Short History* (Oxford, 1986), 136.

3   See my *Crisis and Continuity*, 308, and also *Colección documental de Alfonso XI. Diplomas conservados en el archivo histórico nacional sección de clero. Pergaminos*, ed. Esther González Crespo (Madrid, 1985), 53, 59, 60–1.

4   *Crisis and Continuity*, 309 *et passim*.

5   José Angel García de Cortázar, *Historia de España Alfaguara II: La época medieval* (Madrid, 1973), 206.

6   Bisson, *The Medieval Crown of Aragon*, 165.

7   *Crisis and Continuity*, chs 4, 5, 10, and 11.

8   On the *Fuero viejo* see Alfonso García Gallo, *Manual de historia del derecho español*, 2 vols, 4th edn (Madrid, 1971), I. 396–7. On the attempts to impose

wage and price controls see Bisson, *The Medieval Crown of Aragon*, 166, 171–2, and *Cortes de los antiguos reinos de León y Castilla*, 5 vols (Madrid, 1861–3), II. 75–144 (1351).

9 See *Cortes de León y Castilla*, I. 64–85 (1268) *et passim*.

10 Making sense of the monetary history of fifteenth-century Spain, and Castile in particular is an almost thankless job. Angus MacKay's great book on the subject is one of the most careful and insightful treatments of this difficult topic. See his *Money, Prices and Politics in Fifteenth-Century Castile* (London, 1981). See also Jaume Vicens Vives, ed., *Historia de España y America: Social y económica* (1st pub. 1957; Barcelona, 1972), II. 96–7.

11 See Joseph R. Strayer, *The Reign of Philip the Fair* (Princeton, 1980). The reign ended in turmoil with the nobility in arms because of the king's fiscal demands.

12 Luis García de Valdeavellano, *Curso de historia de las instituciones españolas: De los orígenes al final de la edad media* (Madrid, 1968), 608. Also on the *alcabala* see ch. 6.

13 Bisson, *The Medieval Crown of Aragon*, 172.

14 For violence in general see my *Spanish Society, 1400–1600* (London, 2001), chs 7 and 8. For Ribafrecha see p. 170.

15 *Cortes de León y Castilla*, I. 147–8, 152.

16 Ibid. I. 177.

17 See Thomas N. Bisson, *Tormented Voices: Power, Crisis, and Humanity in Rural Catalonia, 1140–1200* (Cambridge, MA, 1998), and also his article, "The Feudal Revolution," *Past & Present*, 42 (1994), 6–42, and comments and reply in *Past & Present*, 152 (1996) and 155 (1997).

18 *Poesia crítica y satírica del siglo XV*, ed. Julio Rodríguez Puértolas (Madrid, 1981), 95–7.

19 Ibid. 127–47, 217–32.

20 See his *El libro de los estados*, ed. and introd. Ian Macpherson and Robert Brian Tate (Madrid, 1991).

21 See Paul Freedman, *The Origins of Peasant Servitude in Medieval Catalonia* (Cambridge, 1991), 214–23, and his *Images of the Medieval Peasant* (Stanford, 1999).

22 *Crónica del rey Don Fernando IV* (Biblioteca de Autores Españoles, vol. LXVI; Madrid, 1953), 119: "E este año fue en toda la tierra muy grand fambre; e los omes moriénse por las plazas e por las calles de fambre, e fue tan grande la mortadad en la gente, que bien cuidaran que muriera el cuarto de toda la gente de la tierra; e tan grande era la fambre, que comían los omes pan de grama, e nunca en tiempo del mundo vio ombre tan gran fambre ni tan gran mortadad." See also César González Mínguez, *Fernando IV de Castilla (1295–1312): La guerra civil y el predominio de la nobleza* (Victoria, 1976), 111.

23 See Julio Valdeón Baruque's pioneer articles, "Aspectos de la crisis castellana en la primera mitad del siglo XIV," *Hispania*, 111 (1969), 5–24, and "La crisis del siglo XIV en Castilla: Revisión del problema," *Revista de la Universidad de Madrid*, 79 (1972), 161–84.

24   See Julio Valdeón Baruque, *Los conflictos sociales en el Reino de Castilla en los siglos XIV y XV* (Madrid, 1975).
25   See Mark D. Meyerson, *Jews in an Iberian Frontier Kingdom: Society, Economy, and Politics in Morvedre, 1248–1391* (Leiden, 2004).
26   Freedman, *The Origins of Peasant Servitude*, 211.

Chapter 3

1   For the reign of Ferdinand IV see Antonio Benavides, *Memorias de Fernando IV de Castilla*, 2 vols (Madrid, 1860). The second volume includes a good number of the documents covering his reign. See also *Crónica del rey Fernando IV* (Biblioteca de Autores Españoles, vol. LXVI; Madrid, 1953). See César González Mínguez, *Fernando IV de Castilla (1295–1312): La guerra civil y el predominio de la nobleza* (Vitoria, 1976), from which I borrow a great deal of the following discussion, and also his popular biography of the king *Fernando IV (1295–1312)* (Palencia, 1995) and his study of political developments during Ferdinand's reign *Contribución al estudio de las hermandades en el reinado de Fernando IV de Castilla* (Vitoria, 1974). For the events leading to Sancho IV's rebellion against his father see Joseph F. O'Callaghan, *The Learned King: The Reign of Alfonso X of Castile* (Philadelphia, 1993), 234–69. For Sancho IV's reign see Mercedes Gaibrois de Ballesteros, *Historia del reinado de Sancho IV de Castilla*, 3 vols (Madrid, 1922–8).
2   See Peter Linehan, *Spain 1157–1312* (Blackwell, forthcoming).
3   See *Cortes de los antiguos reinos de León y Castilla*, 5 vols (Madrid, 1861–3), I. 130–3; González Mínguez, *Fernando IV de Castilla y la guerra civil*, 33–40.
4   On María de Molina (a new biography is needed) see Mercedes Gaibrois de Ballesteros' hagiographical *María de Molina tres veces reina* (Madrid, 1967).
5   González Mínguez, *Fernando IV de Castilla y la guerra civil*, 119.
6   Ibid. 121–72; *Crónica de Fernando IV*, 129–37.
7   On Alfonso XI see the many articles written by Salvador de Moxó, who before his untimely death was planning a biography and a study of Alfonso's reign. See also *Colección documental de Alfonso XI. Diplomas reales conservados en el archivo histórico nacional. Sección de clero, pergaminos*, ed. Esther González Crespo (Madrid, 1985), which provides a partial edition of the large number of documents extant for the reign, and *Crónica de Alfonso XI* (Biblioteca de Autores Españoles, vol. LXVI; Madrid, 1953); *Poema de Alfonso XI*, in *Poetas castellanos anteriores al siglo XV* (Biblioteca de Autores Españoles, vol. LVII; Madrid, 1966).
8   Joseph F. O'Callaghan, *A History of Medieval Spain* (Ithaca, NY, 1975), 414.
9   *Colección documental de Alfonso XI*, 40–1 (1313), 41–2 (1314), 45–6 (1314), *et passim*.
10   Ibid. 54.
11   Ibid. 74.

12   *Cortes de León y Castilla,* I. 265ff. For the identity of Burgalese representatives to the *hermandad* of 1315 meeting see my "The Transformation of the Castilian Municipalities: The Case of Burgos, 1248–1350," *Past & Present,* 77 (1977), 3–33.

13   *Crónica de Alfonso XI,* 198, 203, and 263.

14   Ibid. 350–92.

15   For the thirteenth-century history of the Crown of Aragon and the Sicilian affair see Thomas N. Bisson, *The Medieval Crown of Aragon: A Short History* (Oxford, 1986), 58–72, 86–94. See also O'Callaghan, *A History of Medieval Spain,* 383–91, 394–6; Jocelyn N. Hillgarth, *The Problem of a Catalan Mediterranean Empire 1229–1327* (London, 1975). Here and in the following pages I also borrow liberally from Hillgarth's *The Spanish Kingdoms, 1250–1516,* 2 vols (Oxford, 1976–8).

16   See Bisson, *The Medieval Crown of Aragon,* 94–100; O'Callaghan, *A History of Medieval Spain,* 398–401, 404–6. On James II see note 15; Antonio Arribas, *La conquista de Cerdeña por Jaime II de Aragón* (Barcelona, 1952); Josep-David Garrido I Valls, *La conquesta del sud Valencia ì Múrcia per Jaume II* (Barcelona, 2002).

17   Bisson, *The Medieval Crown of Aragon,* 100–3, O'Callaghan, *A History of Medieval Spain,* 407–11. See also *Cortes de los antiguos reinos de Aragón y de Valencia y principado de Cataluña* (Madrid, 1896), vol. I, pt 2, 291–317, Corts of 1333. For the reign of Alfonso IV see Francisco Roca Traver, *Alfonso II el Benigno, rey de Valencia* (Valencia, 2003), and Jesús E. Martínez Ferrando and S. Sobrequés, *Els descendents de Pere el Gran: Alfons el Franc, Jaume II, Alfons el Benigne* (Barcelona, 1954).

18   Bisson, *The Medieval Crown of Aragon,* 104–17; O'Callaghan, *A History of Medieval Spain,* 414–19. On Peter IV (Peter III in Catalonia) see Rafael Tasis i Marca, *La vida del rei En Pere III* (Barcelona, 1954); and his *Chronicle,* 2 vols, trans. Mary Hillgarth, ed. J. N. Hillgarth (Toronto, 1980).

Chapter 4

1   *Cortes de los antiguos reinos de Aragón, y de Valencia y principado de Cataluña* (Madrid, 1896), vol. I, pt 2, 366–7.

2   See ch. 6 for Peter IV's requests for funds to the Catalonian Corts meeting in Girona and Barcelona in 1358.

3   For this entire period see Thomas N. Bisson, *The Medieval Crown of Aragon: A Short History* (Oxford, 1986), 120–32; Joseph F. O'Callaghan, *A History of Medieval Spain* (Ithaca, NY, 1975), 534–42; and Philippe Wolff, "The 1391 Pogrom in Spain: Social Crisis or Not?", *Past & Present,* 50 (1971), 4–18. There is no full biography of John I. See Joaquín Gimeno Casalduero, *La imagen del monarca en la Castilla del siglo XIV: Pedro el Cruel, Enrique II y Juan I* (Madrid, 1972); Eliseo Vidal Beltrán, *Valencia en la época de Juan I* (Valencia, 1974).

4   I will have a bit more to say about the role of consort queens in the Crown of Aragon, and I have already discussed the signal role of María de Molina in defending the Crown during the turbulent regencies of her son and grandson. For Aragon see Theresa Earenfight, "Absent Kings: Queens as Political Partners in the Medieval Crown of Aragon," in *Queenship and Political Power in Early Modern Spain*, ed. Theresa Earenfight (Aldershot, 2005), 33–51.

5   Bisson, *The Medieval Crown of Aragon*, 131. There are no full biographies or studies of Martin I's reign. See Alberto Boscolo, *La politica italiana di Martino il Vecchio re d'Aragona* (Padua, 1962), and María Teresa Ferrer I Mallol, "L'infant Martí I un projecto d'intervenció en la guerra de Portugal (1381)," in *La Corona de Aragón en el siglo XV* (Valencia, 1973), 205–33.

6   See John H. Elliott, *Imperial Spain 1469–1715* (New York, 1964), 316–54, and his magisterial *The Count-Duke of Olivares: The Statesman in an Age of Decline* (New Haven, 1986), 553–99.

7   There is no full-fledged biography of Peter I, the Cruel. The closest is Luis V. Díaz Martín, *Itinerario de Pedro I de Castilla* (Valladolid, 1975). See also Pedro López de Ayala's partisan (against Peter) chronicle, *Crónica del rey don Pedro* (Biblioteca de Autores Españoles, vol. LXVI; Madrid, 1953). Here and in what follows in this and next chapter I am guided by the very detailed and thorough political narrative found in Luis Suárez Fernández, *Nobleza y monarquía: Puntos de vista sobre la historia política castellana del siglo XV*, 2nd edn (Madrid, 1975): see pp. 9–97 for the above discussion and the early Trastámaras.

8   O'Callaghan, *A History of Medieval Spain*, 419–24; *Crónica del rey don Pedro*, 500–25.

9   *Crónica del rey don Pedro*, 525ff. O'Callaghan, *A History of Medieval Spain*, 424–7.

10   On Henry of Trastámara see Julio Valdeón, *Enrique II de Castilla: La guerra civil y la consolidación del régimen (1366–1371)* (Valladolid, 1966); *Crónica del rey don Enrique, segundo de Castilla* (Biblioteca de Autores Españoles, vol. LXVIII; Madrid, 1953); O'Callaghan, *A History of Medieval Spain*, 523–8.

11   Suárez Fernández, *Nobleza y monarquía*, 21–34.

12   On the short rule of John I of Castile see Luis Suárez Fernández, *Juan I, rey de Castilla (1379–1390)*, 2nd edn (Madrid, 1978). See also documents for his reign (mostly the area of Murcia) in *Documentos de Juan I*, ed. José Manuel Díez Martínez, Amparo Bejarano Rubio, and Angel Luis Molina Molina (Murcia, 2001).

13   A full study of the reign of Henry III, a pivotal reign in the history of late medieval Castile, is still needed. See *Crónica del rey don Enrique, tercero de Castilla é de León* (Biblioteca de Autores Españoles, vol. LXVIII; Madrid, 1953). See also Luis Suárez Fernández, *Estudios sobre el regimen monarquico de Enrique III de Castilla* (a series of articles that appeared in *Hispania*, 47–8; Madrid, 1954); Gonzalo Torrente Ballester, *Minoridad de Don Enrique III el Doliente* (Madrid, 1947).

Chapter 5

1   See ch. 7 and also Jaume Vicens Vives, ed., *Historia de España y America: Social y económica* (1st pub. 1957; Barcelona, 1972), II. 237–312.

2   On the reign of John II and for most of the political history of the fifteenth century see Luis Suárez Fernández, *Nobleza y monarquía: Puntos de vista sobre la historia política castellana del siglo XV*, 2nd edn (Valladolid, 1975), 101–221; *Crónica del serenísimo príncipe Don Juan, segundo de este nombre en Castilla y León* (Biblioteca de Autores Españoles, vol. LXVIII; Madrid, 1953). See also *Crónica del halconero de Juan II* (Madrid, 1946); Pedro A. Porras Arboledas, *Juan II, 1406–1454* (Palencia, 1995).

3   There is a full study of Alvaro de Luna by Nicholas G. Round, *The Greatest Man Uncrowned: A Study of the Fall of Don Alvaro de Luna* (London, 1986). See also *Crónica de don Álvaro de Luna, condestable de Castilla, Maestro de Santiago*, ed. Juan de Mata Carriazo (Madrid, 1940).

4   I have already explored this cycle of festivals in some detail in my "Festivités, couleurs et symboles du pouvoir en Castille au XVe siècle: Les Célébrations de mai 1428," *Annales ESC*, 3 (1991), 521–46, and in more general way in my "Fiestas, torneos, y símbolos de realeza en la Castilla del siglo XV," in *Realidad e imágenes de poder: España a fines de la edad media* (Valladolid, 1988), 249–66.

5   Suárez Fernández, *Nobleza y monarquía*, 135.

6   For this period see ibid. 141–79.

7   *Crónica del serenísimo príncipe Don Juan*, 682–3.

8   For the reign of Henry IV of Castile see William D. Phillips, *Enrique IV and the Crisis of Fifteenth-Century Castile, 1425–1480* (Cambridge, MA, 1978); J. Calvo Poyano, *Enrique IV el impotente y el final de una época* (Barcelona, 1993); and Suárez Fernández, *Nobleza y monarquía*, 181–222.

9   See my "L'Image du pouvoir à travers les sceaux de la monarchie Castillane," in *Genèse médiévale de l'etat moderne* (Valladolid, 1987), 217–27.

10   For this narrative see *Crónica del rey Don Enrique el Cuarto de este nombre* (Biblioteca de Autores Españoles, vol. LXVIII; Madrid, 1953), 99–222; Suárez Fernández, *Nobleza y monarquía*, 181–222. For the *farsa* of Avila see Angus MacKay, "Ritual and Propaganda in Fifteenth Century Castile," *Past & Present*, 107 (1985), 3–43.

11   Suárez Fernández, *Nobleza y monarquía*, 225–6.

12   John Edwards, *The Spain of the Catholic Monarchs 1474–1520* (Oxford, 2000), 1–37.

13   On Ferdinand I and the Compromise of Caspe see Thomas N. Bisson, *The Medieval Crown of Aragon: A Short History* (Oxford, 1986), 133–9.

14   Ibid. 141.

15   Ibid.

16   Ibid. 144. For Alfonso's rule over Naples and the Aragonese–Catalan ventures in the western Mediterranean in this period see Alan Ryder, *The Kingdom of Naples under Alfonso the Magnanimous* (Oxford, 1976).

17   I am aware of the sketchy quality of this assessment. For the long and complex reign of Alfonso V see Bisson, *The Medieval Crown of Aragon*, 140–7; Jocelyn N. Hillgarth, *The Spanish Kingdoms, 1250–1516*, 2 vols (Oxford, 1976–8), II. 215–99. See also Alan Ryder, *Alfonso the Magnanimous: King of Aragón, Naples and Sicily, 1396–1458* (Oxford, 1990), and Ryder, *The Kingdom of Naples*.

18   On the history of Navarre see José María Lacarra, *Historia política del reino de Navarra: Desde sus orígenes hasta su incorporación a Castilla*, 3 vols (Pamplona, 1973), vol. III.

19   Bisson, *The Medieval Crown of Aragon*, 147.

20   For John II's life and reign see Jaume Vicens Vives, *Juan II de Aragón (1398–1479): Monarquía y revolución en la España del siglo XV* (Barcelona, 1953); Bisson, *The Medieval Crown of Aragon*, 147–53.

Chapter 6

1   On this see Joseph R. Strayer, *On the Medieval Origins of the Modern State* (Princeton, 1970) and bibliography therein. There is a new edition (Princeton, 2005) with a preface by William C. Jordan.

2   On the rise of bureaucracies in Castile see my *From Heaven to Earth: The Reordering of Castilian Society, 1150–1350* (Princeton, 2004), ch. 7.

3   Luis García de Valdeavellano, *Curso de historia de las instituciones españolas: De los orígenes al final de la edad media* (Madrid, 1968).

4   *Cortes de los antiguos reinos de León y Castilla*, 5 vols (Madrid, 1861–3), I. 188–202.

5   García de Valdeavellano, *Curso de historia de las instituciones españolas*, 485–6.

6   Rita Costa Gomes, *The Making of a Court Society: Kings and Nobles in Late Medieval Portugal* (Cambridge, 2003), 56–290. For the accounts of 1293–4, published in volume 3 of Mercedes Gaibrois de Ballesteros, *Historia del reinado de Sancho IV de Castilla*, 3 vols (Madrid, 1922–8), see my forthcoming "Textile Consumption in Late Medieval Spain."

7   Alfonso García Gallo, *Manual de historia del derecho español*, 2 vols, 4th edn (Madrid, 1971), I. 400–1. For other Spanish realms where older legal traditions were quite successful in resisting the innovations of the late Middle Ages see pp. 91–2.

8   On the lieutenancy and the rule of María of Castile see the forthcoming book by Theresa Earenfight, *Partners in Politics: The Aragonese Monarchy of María of Castile and Alfonso V, 1416–1458*, from which I derive most of the information for this paragraph and for my comments in the introduction to this chapter.

9   *Libro becerro de las behetrías*, ed. Gonzalo Martínez Díez, 3 vols (León, 1981).

10   For the relation between Crown and Cortes in Castile see my "Oligarchy and Royal Power: The Castilian Cortes and the Castilian Crisis 1248–1350," *Parliaments, Estates and Representation*, 2/2 (Dec. 1982), 95–101, and also Joseph F. O'Callaghan, *The Cortes of Castile-León, 1188–1350* (Philadelphia, 1989), 152–92.

11   See my "The Transformation of the Castilian Municipalities: The Case of Burgos, 1248–1350," *Past & Present*, 77 (1977), 3–33.

12   *Cortes de León y Castilla*, I. 236–7.

13   John H. Elliott, *Imperial Spain, 1469–1716* (New York, 1964), 81.

14   *Cortes de León y Castilla*, I. 169, 184–5, *et passim*.

15   Ibid. I. 500–1.

16   Ibid. II. 524.

17   *Cortes de los antiguos reinos de Aragón, Valencia y Principado de Cataluña* (Madrid, 1896), vol. I, pt 2, 505–739.

18   See Peter Linehan, *The Spanish Church and the Papacy in the Thirteenth Century* (Cambridge, 1971), 101–87.

19   Burgos paid around 33,000 *mrs.* a year in *moneda forera* and a similar amount (30,000 *mrs.*) in *fonsadera*. Archivo Municipal de Burgos, clasif. 2935 (3-August-1284).

20   J. Amador de los Ríos, *Historia social, política, y religiosa de los judíos de España y Portugal* (1st pub. 1875–6; repr. Madrid, 1973), 915–31.

21   Ibid. 996–1003.

22   *Cortes de León y Castilla*, I. 198–202.

23   The bibliography on these subjects is vast indeed. Here I refer only to the influential work of Ernst Kantorowicz and, most importantly, to his *The King's Two Bodies: A Study in Mediaeval Political Theology* (Princeton, 1957); Marc Bloch, *The Royal Touch: Sacred Monarchy and Scrofula in England and France*, trans. J. E. Anderson (London, 1973); see also Strayer, *On the Medieval Origins*, and bibliography therein.

24   On the crowning of Aragonese kings see Bonifacio Palacios Martín, *La coronación de los reyes de Aragón, 1204–1410: Aportación al estudio de las estructuras medievales* (Valencia, 1975); Percy Schramm, *Las insignias de la realeza en la Edad Media española*, trans. L. Vázquez de Parga (Madrid, 1960).

25   Thomas N. Bisson, *The Medieval Crown of Aragon: A Short History* (Oxford, 1986), 86–7.

26   Ramón Muntaner, *Crónica*, introd. Joan Fuster, trans. J. F. Vidal Jové (Madrid, 1970); the entire description occupies pp. 610–29.

27   See Angus MacKay, "Signs Deciphered: The Language of Court Displays in Late Medieval Spain," in *Kings and Kingship in Medieval Europe*, ed. A. Duggan (London, 1993), 287–304.

28   See my "Unsacred Monarchy: The Kings of Castile in the Late Middle Ages," in *Rites of Power: Symbolism, Ritual & Politics Since the Middle Ages*, ed. Sean Wilentz (Philadelphia, 1985), 109–10.

29   Peter Linehan, *History and the Historians of Medieval Spain* (Oxford, 1993), 593–5 *et passim*.

30   See José Manuel Nieto Soria, *Fundamentos ideológicos del poder real en Castilla (siglos XIII–XVI)* (Madrid, 1988), and Linehan's critique in *History and the Historians of Medieval Spain*, 428–30, 586, *et passim*.

31   See my *From Heaven to Earth*, ch. 7.

32   On these topics see my *Spanish Society, 1400–1600* (London, 2001), ch. 9.
33   For Henry IV's entry into Jaén and other such festivities see my "Elite and Popular Culture in Late Fifteenth-Century Castilian Festivals: The Case of Jaén," in *City and Spectacle in Medieval Europe*, ed. B. A. Hanawalt and K. L. Reyerson (Minneapolis, 1994), 296–318.
34   Ibid. 304–5.

Chapter 7

1   See my *From Heaven to Earth: The Reordering of Castilian Society, 1150–1350* (Princeton, 2004), ch. 1.
2   Jonathan Ray, *The Sephardic Frontier: The Reconquista and the Jewish Community in Medieval Iberia* (Ithaca, NY, 2005).
3   See Mark D. Meyerson, *Jews in an Iberian Frontier Kingdom: Society, Economy, and Politics in Morvedre, 1248–1391* (Leiden, 2004), and his sequel to this work, *A Jewish Renaissance in Fifteenth-Century Spain* (Princeton, 2005).
4   See David Nirenberg, *Communities of Violence: Persecution of Minorities in the Middle Ages* (Princeton, 1996).
5   Teofilo F. Ruiz, *Crisis and Continuity: Land and Town in Late Medieval Castile* (Philadelphia, 1994), 272–80.
6   Ibid. 281–2 and references therein.
7   Antonio Ubieto Arteta, *Ciclos económicos en la Edad Media española* (Valencia, 1969).
8   José María Monsalvo Antón, *Teoría y evolución de un conflicto social: El antisemitismo en la Corona de Castilla en la baja edad media* (Madrid, 1985).
9   Gregory B. Milton, "Commerce and Community in a Medieval Town: Santa Coloma de Queralt, AD 1276–1313," Ph.D. dissertation, University of California at Los Angeles, 2004.
10   There are innumerable works on Muslim society in Iberia. An excellent and most accessible description of Islamic Spain can be found in Richard Fletcher, *Moorish Spain* (New York, 1992).
11   See my *Crisis and Continuity*, 272–82; "Trading with the 'Other': Economic Exchanges Between Jews, Muslims, and Christians in Late Medieval Castile," in *Essays in Honour of Angus MacKay* (London, 2002), 63–78; "Judíos y cristianos en el ámbito urbano bajomedieval: Avila y Burgos, 1200–1350," in *Xudeos e conversos na historia: Actas do Congreso Internacional de Judíos y Conversos en la Historia*, 2 vols (Santiago de Compostela, 1994), II. 69–93.
12   See Nirenberg, *Communities of Violence*.
13   Archivo histórico nacional. Clero, carpeta 355, no. 5 (12-X-1330).
14   See Milton, "Commerce and Community in a Medieval Town," and Nirenberg, *Communities of Violence*.
15   *Crisis and Continuity*, 278–9.
16   *Spanish Society, 1400–1600* (London, 2001), ch. 4.
17   Nirenberg, *Communities of Violence*, 127–65 *et passim*.

18 *Cortes de León y Castilla*, I. 144, 284–5, 312, 334, 378–9, 418–19, 421–2, 464–5, 486, 598–9, 613, II. 38–9.

19 Ibid. I. 60, 80–1, 114, 127, 195, 227–30, 280–2, 285, 352–6, II. 39, *et passim*.

20 For this discussion see Yitzhak Baer, *A History of the Jews in Christian Spain*, 2 vols (Philadelphia, 1961), vol. I.

21 Parts of this and the following paragraphs have been adapted from a forthcoming article, "The Limits of Convivencia," in *A People's History of Christianity*.

22 *Las Siete Partidas*, ed. Robert I. Burns, SJ, trans. S. P. Scott, 5 vols (Philadelphia, 2001), vol. V, 1433–4.

23 J. Amador de los Ríos, *Historia social, política, y religiosa de los judíos de España y Portugal* (1st pub. 1875–6; repr. Madrid, 1973), 935–8.

24 *Primera crónica general: Estoria de España que mando a componer Alfonso el Sabio y se continuaba...*, ed. Ramón Menéndez Pidal, 2 vols (Madrid, 1956), I. 310–13.

25 *Poema de Fernán González*, ed. John Lihani (East Lansing, 1991), 15 *et passim*. Spain the gentle was then destroyed / unbelieving people were lords / poor Christians had a very bad life / never had Christians come to such a difficult pass / they [the Muslims] made stables in the churches / on the altars engaged in fierce follies / stole the treasures from the sacristies / the Christians cried day and night / Some said and attest that they saw [the Muslims] cook / cook and roast to eat ... / kill the mothers and the children in their arms / everyone went around mad with fear" (my translation).

26 As cited in Fletcher, *Moorish Spain*, 135.

27 See my "Representation: Castilian, los castellanos y el nuevo mundo," in *Historia a debate: Medieval* (Santiago de Compostela, 1995), 73–7. Portions of this discussion closely follow my earlier piece on these topics.

28 Andrés Bernáldez, *Historia de los Reyes Católicos* (Biblioteca de Autores Españoles, vol. LXX; Madrid, 1953), 599–600.

29 Document edited in Amador de los Ríos, *Historia*, 940.

30 Documents edited ibid. 945–9.

31 Document edited ibid. 949–52.

32 See Philippe Wolff, "The 1391 Pogrom in Spain: Social Crisis or Not?", *Past & Present*, 50 (1971), 4–18. Documents edited in Amador de los Ríos, *Historia*, 953ff.

33 See the forthcoming excellent book by Debra Blumenthal, *Enemies and Familiars: Muslim, Eastern and Black Africans Slaves in Late Medieval Valencia* (Cornell University Press).

34 See Benzion Netanyahu, *The Marranos of Spain: From the Late Fourteenth to the Early Sixteenth Century* (New York, 1966); Gretchen Starr-LeBeau, *In the Shadows of the Virgin: Religious Identity, Inquisition, and Political Authority in Guadalupe, Spain* (Princeton, 2004).

35 See S. Freund and T. F. Ruiz, "Jews, Conversos, and the Inquisition in Spain, 1391–1492: The Ambiguities of History," in *Jewish–Christian Encounters over the Centuries: Symbiosis, Prejudice, Holocaust, Dialogue*, ed. M. Perry and F. M. Schweitzer (New York, 1994), 169–95.

Chapter 8

1   References will be provided below for most of the themes explored in this discussion. For Alfonso de Palencia see his "Tratado de la perfección militar," in *Dos tratados de Alfonso de Palencia* (Madrid, 1978).

2   Adeline Rucquoi, "Las rutas del saber: España en el siglo XII," *Cuadernos de historia de España*, 75 (1998–9), 41–58.

3   See Rebecca L. Winer, *Women, Wealth, and Community in Perpignan, c. 1250–1300: Christians, Jews, and Enslaved Muslims in a Medieval Mediterranean Town* (Aldershot, 2006).

4   Most of this section follows closely Adeline Rucquoi's brilliant synthesis of education in medieval Iberia. See her "Education et société dans la péninsule ibérique médiévale," *Histoire de l'education*, 69 (Jan. 1996), 13.

5   Ibid. 16.

6   Gregory Milton, "Commerce, Crisis and Society in a Medieval Village: Santa Coloma de Queralt, AD 1276–1313," Ph.D. dissertation. University of California at Los Angeles, 2004.

7   John Dagenais and Adeline Rucquoi have been independently gathering references on mentions of books in medieval documents and other sources. The ongoing lists are impressive indeed and show the availability of books throughout the peninsula.

8   See Gershom Scholem et al., *Kabbalistes chrétiens* (Paris, 1979), and his *Kabbalah* (New York, 1978) and *Major Trends in Jewish Mysticism* (New York, 1954), where he engages in a historiographical debate on the authorship of the Zohar. See also François Secret, *Les Kabbalistes chrétiens de la Renaissance* (Paris, 1964).

9   See Isabel Beceiro and Ricardo Córdoba de la Llave, *Parentesco, poder y mentalidad de la nobleza castellana, siglos XII–XV* (Madrid, 1990); Helen Nader, *The Mendoza Family in the Spanish Renaissance, 1350 to 1550* (New Brunswick, NJ, 1979).

10 There are many different editions and translations of the *Libro de buen amor*, as well as numberless studies of the works in all the major European languages. For a recent edition see Juan Ruiz, *Libro de buen amor*, ed. Alberto Blecua (Madrid, 1992).

11 See an edition of his *Proverbios morales* in *Poetas castellanos anteriores al siglo XV* (Biblioteca de Autores Españoles, vol. LVII; Madrid, 1966), 331–72.

12 See Pero López de Ayala, *Rimado de palacio*, ed. Germán Orduna (Madrid, 1987). This Castalia edition includes a substantial study of the poet and his work.

13 For the *cancioneros* see *Poesía de cancionero*, ed. Alvaro Alonso (Madrid, 1986). Like most of the Cátedra and Castalia editions (the two textual editions cited in this chapter), they include extensive discussions of the works and authors. This particular volume has samples from a wide variety of poets from Imperial to Macías.

14 Portions of this chapter are drawn from a collection of general histories of Castilian (and Spanish) medieval literature and from critical introductions to texts mentioned throughout the chapter and cited in other endnotes.

Among the most notable and/or recent contributions one should list: Alain D. Deyermond, *La edad media*, 10th edn (Barcelona, 1984); *Historia de la literatura española*, 2 vols (Madrid, 1990) – the first volume covers the Middle Ages; Jesús Menéndez Peláez, ed., *Historia de la literatura española*, 4 vols (Madrid, 2005) – the first volume covers the Middle Ages; and the well-known Angel Valbuena Prat, *Historia de la literatura española*, 4 vols, 8th edn (Barcelona, 1968). See also Otis H. Green, *Spain and the Western Tradition: The Castilian Mind in Literature from El Cid to Calderón*, 4 vols (Madison, WI, 1968).

15   See Juan de Mena, *Laberinto de fortuna*, ed. John G. Cummings (Madrid, 1984). Cummings' introduction (pp. 11–46) is an excellent guide to Mena's work and the period.

16   In *Ten Centuries of Spanish Poetry*, ed. Eleanor L. Turnbull (Baltimore, 1955), 22–3; the first line is my own translation; the rest of the translation is by John Pierrepont Rice.

17   On the *romancero* and romances in general see *Historia y crítica de la literatura española: Edad Media*, ed. Alan Deyermond (Barcelona, 1980), 255–94; Ramón Menéndez Pidal, *Romancero hispánico (hispano-portugués, americano y sefardí)*, 2 vols (Madrid, 1953).

18   Alfonso Martínez de Toledo, *Arcipreste de Talavera o Corbacho*, ed. Michael Gerli, 4th edn (Madrid, 1992); see pp. 15–58 for an introduction to the author and his work. See also Diego de San Pedro, *Cárcel de amor: Arnalte y Lucenda. Sermón*, ed. J. F. Ruiz Casanova (Madrid, 1995), 11–60, for a study of San Pedro's life and work.

19   Jorge Manrique, "Coplas por la muerte de su padre," in *Ten Centuries of Spanish Poetry*, ed. Eleanor L. Turnbull (Baltimore, 1955), 48–50.

20   Giovanni M. Bertini, *La poesia di Raimondo Llull* (1934); *Nova edició de les obres de Ramón Llull* (Palma de Mallorca, 1990–2003), vols I, II, and VI published of a projected six. For Bernat Metge there is a recent translation of *Lo somni* with a critical study. See *The Dream of Bernat Metge*, trans., with an introd. and notes, Richard Vernier (Aldershot, 2002). For this and succeeding sections on Catalan literature I have borrowed liberally from Arthur Terry, *A Literary History of Spain: Catalan Literature* (New York, 1972); Ferrán Gadea, *Literatura Catalana medieval* (Barcelona, 1986), and mostly from Martín de Riquer, *Història de la literatura catalana* (Barcelona, 1964).

21   On Ausiàs March see his *Poesies*, ed. Pere Bohigas; 2nd, rev., edn Amadeu-J. Soberanas and Noemi Espinas (Barcelona, 2000); *Ausiàs March: Selected Poems*, ed. and trans. Arthur Terry (Edinburgh, 1976).

22   See the collection of articles on the topics found in Robert I. Burns, ed., *The Worlds of Alfonso the Learned and James the Conqueror: Intellect and Force in the Middle Ages* (Princeton, 1985).

23   See *Primera crónica general: Estoria de España que mando a componer Alfonso el Sabio y se continuaba . . .*, ed. Ramón Menéndez Pidal, 2 vols (Madrid, 1956).

24   For Castilian royal chronicles see *Crónicas de los reyes de Castilla*, 3 vols (Biblioteca de Autores Españoles, vols LXVI, LXVIII and LXX; Madrid, 1953). They include the chronicles of Alfonso X, Sancho IV, Ferdinand IV, Alfonso

XI, Peter I (vol. I); Henry II (Trastámara), John I, Henry III, the very extensive chronicle of John II (vol. II); and Henry IV, Ferdinand and Isabella (vol. III), plus assorted additional materials in vols II and III. For Don Miguel Lucas de Iranzo see Juan Mata Carriazo, ed., *Hechos del condestable Don Miguel Lucas de Iranzo: Crónica del siglo XV* (Madrid, 1940).

25   For Aragonese–Catalan chronicles translated into English see *The Chronicle of James I, King of Aragon*, ed. J. Forster, 2 vols (London, 1883); Bernat Desclot, *Chronicle of the Reign of Peter III of Aragon*, trans. L. Critchlow, 2 vols (Princeton, 1928–34); Ramón Muntaner, *The Chronicle of Muntaner*, trans. H. Goodenough, 2 vols (London, 1920–1). See also *Chronique catalane de Pierre IV d'Aragon*, ed. A, Pagès (Toulouse, 1941); *Crònica general de Pere III el Cerimoniós*, ed. A. J. Soberanas Lleó (Barcelona, 1961).

26   On Arnau de Vilanova's vernacular works see F. Santi, *Arnau de Vilanova: L'opera spirituale* (Valencia, 1987).

27   Martín de Riquer, *Història de la literatura catalana*, I. 204.

28   Llull's works are extensive indeed and his writings have been translated into many languages. There are also numerous works about his life and activities. See for example Jocelyn N. Hillgarth, *Ramón Llull and Lullism in Fourteenth-Century France* (Oxford, 1971), and also the published volumes of *Nova edició de les obres de Ramón Llull*. A partial translation can be found in *Selected Works of Ramón Llull (1232–1316)*, ed. A. Bonner, 2 vols (Princeton, 1985).

29   See the English translation of Llull's *Blanquerna* by E. A. Peers (London, 1988). Among other writers of note that should be mentioned, even if only in the notes, are Francesc Eiximenis – see his *Regiment de la cosa pública* (Mexico, 1947), and his *Dotze llibre del Crestià* (Girona, 1986–7) – and the already mentioned Metge – see *Obras de Bernat Metge*, ed. M. Riquer (Barcelona, 1959).

30   The literature on Don Juan Manuel is extensive indeed, as are the translations of his work. See "La prosa en los siglos XIII–XIV: Don Juan Manuel," in *Historia y crítica de la literatura española: Edad Media*, ed. A. Deyermond (Barcelona, 1980), 197–201; Don Juan Manuel, *Obras completas*, ed. J. M. Blecua, 2 vols (Madrid, 1983).

31   See Fernán Pérez de Guzmán, *Generaciones y semblanzas* (Biblioteca de Autores Españoles, vol. LXVIII; Madrid, 1953). Note that the extensive chronicle of John II of Castile, which precedes *Generaciones* in the same edition, was also authored by Pérez de Guzmán. For *El Victorial* see *El Victorial: Crónica de Pero Niño, conde de Balbuena. Por su alférez Gutierre Díaz de Games*, ed. J. M. Carriazo Mata (Madrid, 1940). There is an excellent 1928 English abridgement and translation by J. Evans.

32   José-Luis Martín and Antonio Linage Conde, *Religion y sociedad medieval: El catecismo de Pedro de Cuéllar (1325)* (Salamanca, 1987).

33   Ibid. 188.

34   Ibid. 207–8.

35   Ibid.

36   See Peter N. Linehan, *The Spanish Church and the Papacy in the Thirteenth Century* (Cambridge, 1971), and his *The Ladies of Zamora* (Manchester, 1997).

37 *El catecismo de Pedro de Cuéllar*, 237.

38 Ibid. 238.

39 Ibid.

40 Ibid. 240.

41 Ibid. 240–1.

42 Roy Strong, *Art and Power: Renaissance Festivals 1450–1650* (Woodbridge, Suffolk, 1984).

43 I have already referred to this festival in previous pages. For a summary of festivals in Iberia in this period see my *Spanish Society, 1400–1600* (London, 2001), chs 5 and 6.

44 Jacob Burckhardt, *The Civilization of the Renaissance in Italy* (repr. New York, 2002), 291–2.

45 See my *Spanish Society*, chs 5 and 6.

46 For an example of the public participation in French duels and other festive events see Eric Jager, *The Last Duel: A True Story of Crime, Scandal, and Trial by Combat in Medieval France* (New York, 2004).

47 See my attempts at explicating the feast of 1428 in my article "Festivités, couleurs et symboles du pouvoir en Castille au XVe siècle: Les Célébrations de mai 1428," *Annales ESC*, 3 (1991), 521–46.

48 For Jaén see my "Elite and Popular Culture in Late Fifteenth-Century Castilian Festivals: The Case of Jaén," in *City and Spectacle in Medieval Europe*, ed. B. A. Hanawalt and K. L. Reyerson (Minneapolis, 1994), 296–318.

49 For Charles V's entry see A. Duran and J. Sanabre, *Llibre de les solemnitats de Barcelona*, 2 vols (Barcelona, 1930–47), I. 103–6. The reference is found in James S. Amelang, Xavier Gil, and Gary W. McDonogh's wonderful guide, *Doze passajedes per la història de Barcelona: Guia* (Barcelona, 1992), 59–61.

50 See Martín de Riquer, *Caballeros andantes españoles* (Madrid, 1967), 123 *et passim*.

51 Jaume Aurell I Cardona and Alfons Puigarnau, *La cultura del mercader en la Barcelona del siglo XV* (Barcelona, 1998).

Chapter 9

1 For a careful and thorough description of the period between 1469 and 1474 see John Edwards, *The Spain of the Catholic Monarchs 1474–1520* (Oxford, 2000), 1–22; Luis Suárez Fernández, *Nobleza y monarquía: Puntos de vista sobre la historia política castellana del siglo XV* (Madrid, 1975), 225–50.

2 The citation is a free translation from Andrés Bernáldez, *Historia de los Reyes Católicos Don Fernando y Doña Isabel* (Biblioteca de Autores Españoles, vol. LXX; Madrid, 1953), 576.

3 Hernando del Pulgar, *Crónica de los señores Reyes Católicos Don Fernando y Doña Isabel de Castilla y Aragón* (Biblioteca de Autores Españoles, vol. LXX; Madrid, 1953), 253.

Bibliographical Essay

More than two decades ago, I recollect attending a conference in Madrid where a most distinguished and senior scholar of late medieval Spanish history (whose name, in Cervantine fashion, I "cannot quite recall") argued that the key to all of Spanish history was to be found in the fifteenth century. I do not know if he was right or not, but if that is so, the history of late medieval Spain is still only partially known and the key has not been yet found. Unlike other periods in Spanish history, as for example the thirteenth century or the reign of the Catholic Monarchs, the history of the fourteenth and most of the fifteenth centuries is still to be fully written. And it is not as if the sources for that history were lacking.

From the 1360s onwards the number of documents that are still extant grows exponentially. Chronicles become longer and longer and far more detailed than anything written in the previous centuries. The amount and variety of literary works are remarkable when compared to earlier periods. The complexities of politics and institutional developments experienced also increased substantially. Yet the historiography has somewhat lagged behind. Although great strides have been made in the last three decades, a great deal remains to be done. Paradoxically, part of the problem lies in the abundance of material. The number of extant documents becomes overwhelming and difficult for any individual scholar to master on his or her own. Another significant difficulty is paleographical. Documents in the Iberian peninsula, which were written in a clear and easy-to-read French hand until around the mid-fourteenth century, become very difficult to decipher when the script turned into a florid and convoluted style shortly after the Black Death. Below I have attempted to provide an entry into this history. Although I have emphasized works in English, it is impossible to understand the history of Spain between 1300 and 1469 without access to the monographic literature in Castilian, Catalan, and/or French.

Sources

Few of the sources for this period are available in translation. Olivia Remie Constable's edited volume, *Medieval Iberia: Readings from Christian, Jewish and Muslim Sources* (Philadelphia, 1997) offers a wide-ranging (but short) sampling of the available documentation. Except for translations of literary works, there is little else available in English from the vast number of sources extant for the period. Among notable collections in the original languages or in translation for the kingdom of Castile one should mention José García Mercadal, ed., *Viajes de extranjeros por España y Portugal*, repr. in 6 vols (Salamanca, 1999), which has engaging and useful descriptions of the Spanish realms and its people as seen by foreign visitors. Those of the late fourteenth century are particularly rich in social, economic, and ethnographic detail. The incomplete and abandoned collection of Castilian sources found in *Fuentes medievales castellano-leonesas*, 25 vols of a projected 100 (Burgos, 1983–) includes a good number of volumes with documents up to 1400. A similar and far more ambitious and successful effort is the *Fuentes documentales medievales del Pais Vasco*. Started in 1982, the collection is rapidly approaching 100 volumes and published documents reach into the early modern period. Although it focuses exclusively on a discrete area of the peninsula (the Basque country but including Navarre), it is a major editorial effort. A short description of the travel of some Navarrese merchants through Castile in the mid-fourteenth century, *Desde Estella a Sevilla: Cuentas de un viaje (1352)*, ed. María Desamparados Sánchez Villar (Valencia, 1962), provides a wealth of information about diet, travel, and roads. The published ordinances of the Castilian Cortes is one of the great sources for our knowledge of Castilian legislation. The first two volumes of *Cortes de los antiguos reinos de León y Castilla*, 5 vols (Madrid, 1861–3) cover the entire period under study, while all the relevant legislation for both peninsular kingdoms can be found in *Los códigos españoles concordados y anotados*, 12 vols (Madrid, 1847–51). For the reign of Alfonso XI, a partial list of his reign's most significant documents have been edited and published in *Colección documental de Alfonso XI: Diplomas conservados en el archivo histórico nacional sección de clero. Pergaminos*, ed. Esther González Crespo (Madrid, 1985). Alfonso García Gallo, *Manual de historia del derecho español*, 4th edn, 2 vols (Madrid, 1971), includes significant excerpts from legal codes, even though it is presented in a rather confusing fashion. The *Crónicas de los Reyes de Castilla*, 3 vols (Biblioteca de Autores Españoles, vols LXVI, LXVIII, LXX; Madrid, 1953), include the chronicles of all the Castilian kings for the period under study. They represent one of the most valuable sources for the understanding of the period. In addition Juan Mata Carriazo, ed., *Hechos del condestable Don Miguel Lucas de Iranzo: Crónica del siglo XV* (Madrid, 1940), and *Poesia crítica y satírica del siglo XV*, ed. Julio Rodríguez Puértolas (Madrid, 1981), give us an entry into the turbulent political life of the period and, in the case of the former, into its festive life.

For the Crown of Aragon the very extensive and thorough rendering of the debates and decisions of its Cortes is found in the first two volumes of the *Cortes de los antiguos reinos de Aragón y de Valencia y principado de Cataluña*, 25 vols (Madrid, 1896–1919). Also of importance are the chronicles of Muntaner and Desclot, as well as the chronicles of individual kings of the Crown of Aragon (see below and chapters 3 through 5). See also Heinrich Finke, *Acta Aragonensia. Quellen zur deutschen, italeinischen, französischen, spanischen Kirchen und Kulturgeschichte aus der diplomatischen Korrespondenz Jaymes II*, 3 vols (Berlin, 1903–33) and José Coroleu, *Los dietarios de la generalidad de Cataluña* (Barcelona, 1889).

Chapter 1

For the history of the Iberian realms in the Middle Ages until the end of the thirteenth century the old but still most thorough and insightful account is that of Luis García de Valdeavellano, *Historia de España*, I, 2nd edn (Madrid, 1955). It unfortunately ends in 1212. In English, three general accounts of worth are Angus MacKay, *Spain in the Middle Ages: From Frontier to Empire, 1000–1500* (New York, 1977); Joseph O'Callaghan, *A History of Medieval Spain* (Ithaca, NY, 1975), and J. N. Hillgarth, *The Spanish Kingdoms, 1250–1516*, 2 vols (Oxford, 1976–8). In Spanish the now old but luminous work by José Angel García de Cortázar, *Historia de España Alfaguara II: La época medieval* (Madrid, 1973) and Ramón Menéndez Pidal, ed., *Historia de España*, vol. XIV: *España cristiana: Crisis de la reconquista* (Madrid, 1966); vol. XV: *Los Trastámaras de Castilla y Aragón en el siglo XV* (Madrid, 1964). For the Crown of Aragon see Thomas N. Bisson's *The Medieval Crown of Aragon: A Short History* (Oxford, 1986), which I think is the best one-volume rendering in English of the history of the Crown of Aragon. The present Blackwell series, of which this volume covers one specific segment, will provide a detailed account of Spain's history in the Middle Ages. For the peninsular geography and its peculiar topography see Ruth Way, *A Geography of Spain and Portugal* (London, 1962), as well as my own work in *Crisis and Continuity: Land and Town in Late Medieval Castile* (Philadelphia, 1994), ch. 1, and my *Spanish Society, 1400–1600* (London,

2001), ch. 1. For the Reconquest, the emergence of crusading ideals in Spain, and their transformation over time, see Abilio Barbero and Marcelo Vigil, *Sobre los orígenes sociales de la Reconquista* (Barcelona, 1974); Derek Lomax, *The Reconquest of Spain* (London, 1978); and Joseph F. O'Callaghan, *Reconquest and Crusade in Medieval Spain* (Philadelphia, 2003).

Chapter 2

For the crises of late medieval Iberia see my *Crisis and Continuity. Land and Town in Late Medieval Castile* (Philadelphia, 1994), chs 10 and 11. See also Angus Mackay's remarkable study of the relations between fluctuating currency, politics, and social history in his *Money, Prices and Politics in Fifteenth-Century Castile* (London, 1981). Although volume II does not rise to the forward-looking quality of volume III in its coverage of social history see Jaume Vicens Vives, ed., *Historia de España y America: Social y económica* (1st pub. 1957; Barcelona, 1972), vol. II. Julio Valdeón Baruque's pioneer articles, "Aspectos de la crisis castellana en la primera mitad del siglo XIV," *Hispania*, 111 (1969), 5–24 and "La crisis del siglo XIV en Castilla: revisión del problema," *Revista de la Universidad de Madrid*, 79 (1972), brought the entire issue of the late medieval crises in Castile to the forefront of historical research. At the same time his *Los conflictos sociales en el Reino de Castilla en los siglos XIV y XV* (Madrid, 1975) also pioneered the study of social conflicts in the peninsula, while Paul Freedman, *The Origins of Peasant Servitude in Medieval Catalonia* (Cambridge, 1991), provides a brilliant reading of the origins of the *remenças* and the social conflicts that plagued the Crown of Aragon in the late fifteenth century.

Chapters 3, 4, and 5

The political history of the 169 years between 1300 and the marriage of Ferdinand and Isabella is still to be written in detail. A narrative of these events can be found in the comprehensive histories listed in the bibliography for chapter 1. In addition, Luis Suárez Fernández's *Nobleza y monarquía: Puntos de vista sobre la historia política castellana del siglo XV*, 2nd edn (Valladolid, 1975) provides a careful description of political events in Castile. Examining the history of individual kings, one needs to depend on the original sources and on recent monographs. Nonetheless, there are no full-fledged studies of individual reigns along the lines of what we have for the reigns of Alfonso X of Castile, James I of the Crown of Aragon, or the Catholic Monarchs. See the old study with additional documents and chronicle of Ferdinand IV in Antonio Benavides, *Memorias de Fernando IV de Castilla*, 2 vols (Madrid, 1860). In addition, César González Mínguez, *Fernando IV de Castilla (1295–1312): La guerra civil y el predominio de la nobleza* (Vitoria, 1976), his popular biography of the king *Fernando IV (1295–1312)* (Palencia, 1995), and his study of political developments during Ferdinand's reign *Contribución al estudio de las hermandades en el reinado de Fernando IV de Castilla* (Vitoria, 1974), offer the most thorough examinations of any Castilian king in the period under study. For Sancho IV's reign – which served as a prelude to that of Ferdinand IV and to a great deal of the trouble that followed see Mercedes Gaibrois de Ballesteros, *Historia del reinado de Sancho IV de Castilla*, 3 vols (Madrid, 1922–8), and her hagiographical *María de Molina tres veces reina* (Madrid, 1967).

For the reign of Alfonso XI there is little except for the chronicle (see above the list of sources for the narrative of individual kings or *Crónica de Alfonso XI*), the published documentation, and a series of monographic articles. One of the most important reigns in the Spanish late medieval period, it still awaits a monographic study. His Trastámara heirs have been more fortunate. See Julio Valdeón Baruque, *Pedro I, el Cruel, y Enrique de Trastámara: La primera guerra civil española* (Madrid, 2002), and his earlier and pioneer work on Henry II of Castile, *Enrique II de Castilla: La guerra civil y la consolidación del régimen, 1366–1371* (Valladolid, 1966). Luis Suárez Fernández, whose work on the Castilian Trastámaras is unsurpassed, has written the standard work on the short reign of John I in his *Juan I, rey de Castilla* (Madrid, 1956), while Peter E. Russell has examined in detail the issue of conflicts over succession in his *English Intervention in Spain and Portugal in the Time of Edward III and Richard II* (Oxford, 1955). On the short but important reign of Henry III, Luis Suárez Fernández's *Estudios sobre el regimen monarquico de Enrique III de Castilla* appeared as a series of articles in *Hispania* (47–8) before being collected and published (Madrid, 1954), and the older book by Gonzalo Torrente Ballester, *Minoridad de Don Enrique III el Doliente* (Madrid, 1947), needs to be revised and expanded in light of new knowledge. In fact, these books' dates of publication are grim reminders of how much still needs to be done in the field. There is additional interest in Ferdinand of Antequera, from the older study by Inez Isabel Macdonald, *Don Fernando de Antequera* (Oxford, 1948), to a collection of insightful articles written by Angus Mackay and found (under a misleading title) in Jacob Torfing, ed., *Politics, Regulation, and the Modern Welfare State* (New York, 1998).

On the long and unproductive reign of John II see a recent biography of the king by Pedro A. Porras Arboledas, *Juan II, 1406–1454* (Palencia, 1995), and a formidable study of his favorite by Nicholas G. Round, *The Greatest Man Uncrowned: A Study of the Fall of Don Alvaro de Luna* (London, 1986). See also *Crónica de don Álvaro de Luna, condestable de Castilla, Maestro de Santiago*, ed. Juan de Mata Carriazo (Madrid, 1940). On John II's successor see one of the first and best studies of Henry IV's reign in English by William D. Phillips, *Enrique IV and the Crisis of Fifteenth-Century Castile, 1425– 1480* (Cambridge, MA, 1978), as well as the more recent work of J. Calvo Poyano, *Enrique IV el impotente y el final de una época* (Barcelona, 1993). For the *farsa* of Avila see Angus Mackay's careful reading of the event in his "Ritual and Propaganda in Fifteenth Century Castile," *Past & Present*, 107 (1985), 3–43.

When we turn to the Crown of Aragon, individual studies are not necessarily more abundant, though some of them are far more thorough and based upon a far more extensive deployment of the documentary evidence. A great deal of the history of the Crown of Aragon is wound up in Mediterranean affairs so that histories of the western Mediterranean are important. See Antonio Arribas, *La conquista de Cerdeña por Jaime II de Aragón* (Barcelona, 1952), which complements Josep-David Garrido I Valls, *La conquesta del sud Valencia i Múrcia per Jaume II* (Barcelona, 2002). Francisco Roca Traver, *Alfonso II el Benigno, rey de Valencia* (Valencia, 2003), provides a formidable entry into Alfonso II's rule, while Jesús E. Martínez Ferrando and S. Sobrequés, *Els descendents de Pere el Gran: Alfons el Franc, Jaume II, Alfons el Benigne* (Barcelona, 1954) is older but does superbly for the Aragonese kings what Suárez Fernández did for the Trastámaras. Rafael Tasis i Marca, *La vida del rei En Pere III* (Barcelona, 1954), follows the chronicle closely, and the latter is available in English in *Chronicle*, trans. Mary Hillgarth, ed. J. N. Hillgarth, 2 vols (Toronto, 1980). Alan Ryder, *The Kingdom of Naples under Alfonso the Magnanimous* (Oxford, 1976), and his *Alfonso the Magnanimous: King of Aragón, Naples and Sicily, 1396–1458* (Oxford, 1990), are formidable studies of Alfonso V's Mediterranean policies and his rule over Naples, while the great Jaume Vicens Vives' study of John II's reign is a masterpiece: *Juan II de Aragón (1398–1479): Monarquía y revolución en la España del siglo XV* (Barcelona, 1953).

Chapter 6

In chapter 6 we turn to institutional developments. The best guide to these is the incomparable work by Luis García de Valdeavellano, *Curso de historia de las instituciones españolas: De los orígenes al final de la Edad Media* (Madrid, 1968). In addition Joseph F. O'Callaghan, *The Cortes of Castile-León*

1188–1350 (Philadelphia, 1989), gives us entry into the workings of the Cortes, while Miguel Angel Ladero Quesada, in his "La Genèse de l'état dans les royaumes hispaniques médiévaux (1250–1450)," in *Le Premier Age de l'état en Espagne, 1450–1700,* ed. Christian Hermann (Paris, 1989), 9–65, offers a most useful synthesis of institutional developments in the peninsular kingdoms. Pere Molas Ribalta, in his "Les Royaumes de la couronne d'Aragon," in *Le Premier Age de l'état,* 113–45, provides a similar service for the realms of the Crown of Aragon though focused on a later period.

For a discussion of sacrality or its absence in the Iberian realms see Bonifacio Palacios Martín, *La coronación de los reyes de Aragón, 1204–1410: Aportación al estudio de las estructuras medievales* (Valencia, 1975), while the old but still useful book by Percy Schramm, *Las insignias de la realeza en la Edad Media española,* trans. L. Vázquez de Parga (Madrid, 1960), is still worth reading. Angus Mackay, "Signs Deciphered: The Language of Court Displays in Late Medieval Spain," in *Kings and Kingship in Medieval Europe,* ed. A. Duggan (London, 1993), 287–304, and T. F. Ruiz, "Unsacred Monarchy: The Kings of Castile in the Late Middle Ages," in *Rites of Power: Symbolism, Ritual and Politics Since the Middle Ages,* ed. Sean Wilentz (Philadelphia, 1985), provide different perceptions of royal power in Castile. Peter Linehan, in his magisterial *History and the Historians of Medieval Spain* (Oxford, 1993), covers a myriad of different topics, but some are closely related to the issue of the absence of coronation and anointment in Castile. Finally José Manuel Nieto Soria, in *Fundamentos ideológicos del poder real en Castilla (siglos XIII–XVI)* (Madrid, 1988), and also in many of his articles, provides a critique of my own position on the subject as presented in "Unsacred Monarchy." For festivals see the bibliography for chapter 8.

Chapter 7

The history of Jews and Muslims and their interaction with Christians has received a plethora of studies and growing attention over the last 20 years. Many of these new books are quite remarkable. One of the most comprehensive general histories of the Jews is Yitzhak Baer, *A History of the Jews in Christian Spain,* 2 vols (Philadelphia, 1961). Richard Fletcher, *Moorish Spain* (New York, 1992), provides a lively entry into the complex history of Islam in the peninsula. The reader may wish to look as well at L. P. Harvey, *Islamic Spain, 1250–1500* (Chicago, 1990), which focuses mostly on the period covered by this book. In Spanish, Antonio Ubieto Arteta, *Ciclos económicos en la Edad Media española* (Valencia, 1969), deserves a reading because of his emphasis on the social and economic reasons (as opposed to religious motivations) for Christian–Jewish antagonisms. José María Monsalvo Antón, *Teoría y evolución de un conflicto social: El antisemitismo en la Corona de Castilla en la baja edad media* (Madrid, 1985), is a superb book providing a sober and intelligent look at anti-Jewish feelings in Castile. The old but still formidable book by J. Amador de los Ríos, *Historia social, política y religiosa de los judíos de España y Portugal* (repr. Madrid, 1973), contains a good number of the documents cited in this chapter.

Of the new books published over the last ten years or so there are many dealing with aspects of this topic, see Jonathan Ray, *The Sephardic Frontier: The Reconquista and the Jewish Community in Medieval Iberia* (Ithaca, NY, 2005); Mark D. Meyerson, *Jews in an Iberian Frontier Kingdom: Society, Economy, and Politics in Morvedre, 1248–1391* (Leiden, 2004), and his sequel to this work, *A Jewish Renaissance in Fifteenth-Century Spain* (Princeton, 2005). Meyerson provides a very close examination of the Jewish community of Morvedre, overthrowing a good number of stereotypes and misconceptions about Jewish–Christian relations in the period. His first book, *The Muslims of Valencia in the Age of Fernando and Isabel: Between Coexistence and Crusade* (Berkeley, 1991), although focusing on the reign of the Catholic Monarchs, is an excellent discussion of the place of Muslims in Christian society. David Nirenberg, *Communities of Violence: Persecution of Minorities in the Middle Ages* (Princeton, 1996), is rightly one of the most influential works on the intertwined histories of Christians, Muslims, and Jews in Iberia written in the last 20 years. Conceptually and in terms of its archival evidence this book should be required reading for anyone interested in the topic. My articles, "Trading with the 'Other': Economic Exchanges Between Jews, Muslims, and Christians in Late Medieval Castile," in *Essays in Honour of Angus MacKay* (London, 2002), 63–78, and "Judíos y cristianos en el ámbito urbano bajomedieval: Avila y Burgos, 1200–1350," in *Xudeos e conversos na historia: Actas do Congreso Internacional de Judíos y Conversos en la Historia*, 2 vols (Santiago de Compostela, 1994), II. 69–93, deal with social and economic aspects of Jewish life in Castile. Philippe Wolff, "The 1391 Pogrom in Spain: Social Crisis or Not?", *Past & Present*, 50 (1971), 4–18, provides an early and flawed reading of what 1391 meant. There are two forthcoming works, one by Benjamin Gampel and the other by David Nirenberg, which I hope will illuminate the controversial and not yet well explained issue of 1391. Benzion Netanyahu, *The Marranos of Spain: From the Late Fourteenth to the Early Sixteenth Century* (New York, 1966), is part of a bitter polemic on the nature and status of conversos (with Baer), while Gretchen Starr-LeBeau, *In the Shadows of the Virgin: Religious Identity, Inquisition, and Political Authority in Guadalupe, Spain* (Princeton, 2004), offers new evidence on the ambivalent status of Jewish conversos. A short piece by S. Freund and T. F. Ruiz, "Jews, Conversos, and the Inquisition in Spain, 1391–1492: The Ambiguities of History," in *Jewish–Christian Encounters Over the Centuries: Symbiosis, Prejudice, Holocaust, Dialogue*, ed. M. Perry and F. M. Schweitzer (New York, 1994), 169–95, summarizes the bitter debates on this subject and provides bibliographical suggestions.

Chapters 8 and 9

Unlike the reign of Alfonso X (1252–84) or the Golden Age, late medieval culture before the reign of the Catholic Monarchs has not received substantial scholarly attention. The collection of articles found in José María Soto Rábanos, ed., *Pensamiento medieval hispano: Homenaje a Horacio Santiago Otero*, 2 vols (Madrid, 1998), is a good beginning and reflective of recent scholarship. Adeline Rucquoi, "Las rutas del saber: España en el siglo XII," *Cuadernos de historia de España*, 75 (1998–9), 41–58, shifts the discussion away from Spain as a receptor of a new knowledge, but her emphasis is on an earlier period. Her "Education et société dans la péninsule ibérique médiévale," *Histoire de l'education*, 69 (Jan. 1996), on the other hand, offers a synthetic long view of the development of culture in the peninsula. A series of comprehensive studies of medieval literature includes lengthy narratives of peninsular authors and their works. Among the best are Alain D. Deyermond, *La edad media*, 10th edn (Barcelona, 1984), and his *Historia de la literatura española*, 2 vols (Madrid, 1990; the first volume covers the Middle Ages). Of great interest is the more recent *Historia de la literatura española*, ed. Jesús Menéndez Peláez, 4 vols (Madrid, 2005; the first volume covers the Middle Ages); and the well-known Angel Valbuena Prat, *Historia de la literatura española*, 8th edn, 4 vols (Barcelona, 1968). See also Otis H. Green, *Spain and the Western Tradition: The Castilian Mind in Literature from El Cid to Calderón*, 4 vols (Madison, WI, 1968).

On libraries and the relationship between learning and aristocratic ethos see Isabel Beceiro and Ricardo Córdoba de la Llave, *Parentesco, poder y mentalidad de la nobleza castellana, siglos XII–XV* (Madrid, 1990), and Helen Nader, *The Mendoza Family in the Spanish Renaissance, 1350 to 1550* (New Brunswick, NJ, 1979). The texts published by either Clásicos Castalia or Cátedra Letras Hispánicas (both excellent publishing houses) not only include the best critical editions available of medieval literary texts but also offer introductions which are formidable studies of the individual authors. Both editorial houses should be commended for their willingness to engage the best scholars available (even if they are not Spaniards) to edit specific texts. Among some of the most interesting discussions – and I have leaned considerably on these short studies for these two chapters – are Juan Ruiz, *Libro de buen amor*, ed. Alberto Blecua (Madrid, 1992); Pero López de Ayala, *Rimado de palacio*, ed. Germán Orduna (Madrid, 1987); Juan de Mena, *Laberinto de fortuna*, ed. John G. Cummings (Madrid, 1984); Alfonso Martínez de Toledo, *Arcipreste de Talavera o Corbacho*, ed. Michael Gerli, 4th edn (Madrid, 1992); and Diego de San Pedro, *Cárcel de amor. Arnalte y Lucenda. Sermón*, ed. J. F. Ruiz Casanova (Madrid, 1995).

Beyond the editions of Cátedra and Castalia, there are the older (and often faulty) versions found in *Poetas castellanos anteriores al siglo XV* (Biblioteca de Autores Españoles, vol. LVII; Madrid, 1966). The scholarly interest in Don Juan Manuel and his works is extensive indeed, as are the translations of his books and essays. See "La prosa en los siglos XIII–XIV: Don Juan Manuel," in *Historia y crítica de la literatura española: Edad Media*, ed. A. Deyermond (Barcelona, 1980), 197–201; Don Juan Manuel, *Obras completas*, ed. J. M. Blecua, 2 vols (Madrid, 1983). On *Generaciones y semblanzas* see Fernán Pérez de Guzmán, *Generaciones y semblanzas* (Biblioteca de Autores Españoles, vol. LXVIII; Madrid, 1953). Please note that the extensive chronicle of John II of Castile, which precedes *Generaciones* in the same edition, was also authored by Pérez de Guzmán. For *El Victorial* see *El Victorial. Crónica de Pero Niño, conde de Balbuena. Por su alférez Gutierre Díaz de Games*, ed. J. M. Carriazo Mata (Madrid, 1940). There is an excellent 1928 English abridgment and translation by J. Evans.

Both Castalia and Cátedra tend to emphasize Castilian works. For Catalan literature I have borrowed liberally from Arthur Terry, *A Literary History of Spain: Catalan Literature* (New York, 1972); Ferrán Gadea, *Literatura catalana medieval* (Barcelona, 1986), and, mostly, from Martín de Riquer, *Història de la literatura catalana* (Barcelona, 1964). For individual examples of Catalan literature see the following. For Bernat Metge there is a recent translation of *Lo somni* with a critical study: see *The Dream of Bernat Metge*, trans. with introd. and notes by Richard Vernier (Aldershot, 2002); his complete works can be found in *Obras de Bernat Metge*, ed. M. Riquer (Barcelona, 1959). For the great Ausiàs March see his *Poesies*, ed. Pere Bohigas; 2nd, rev., edn ed. Amadeu-J. Soberanas and Noemi Espinas (Barcelona, 2000). There is an English translation in *Ausiàs March: Selected Poems*, ed. and trans. Arthur Terry (Edinburgh, 1976). Ramón Llull's works are extensive indeed and his writings have been translated into many languages. There are also numerous works about his life and activities. See for example Jocelyn N. Hillgarth, *Ramón Llull and Lullism in Fourteenth-Century France* (Oxford, 1971), and *Nova edició de les obres de Ramón*

Llull (Palma de Mallorca, 1990–2003), vols I, II, and VI have already been published. A partial translation can be found in *Selected Works of Ramón Llull (1232–1316)*, ed. A. Bonner, 2 vols (Princeton, 1985). See an English translation of *Blanquerna* in Ramón Llull, *Blanquerna*, trans, E. A. Peers (London, 1988). See also Giovanni M. Bertini, *La poesia di Raimondo Llull* (1934). Francesc Eiximenis' important work, *Regiment de la cosa pública* (Mexico, 1947), and his *Dotze llibre del Crestià* (Girona, 1986–7).

For Aragonese–Catalan chronicles which, unlike Castilian chronicles, have been translated into English see *The Chonicle of James I, King of Aragon*, ed. J. Forster, 2 vols (London, 1883); Bernat Desclot, *Chronicle of the Reign of Peter III of Aragon*, trans. L. Critchlow, 2 vols (Princeton, 1928–34); and Ramón Muntaner, *The Chronicle of Muntaner*, trans. H. Goodenough, 2 vols (London, 1920–1). In the original version see *Chronique catalane de Pierre IV d'Aragon*, ed. A. Pagès (Toulouse, 1941), and *Crònica general de Pere III el Cerimoniós*, ed. A. J. Soberanas Lleó (Barcelona, 1961). On the *Romancero* and romances in general see *Historia y crítica de la literatura española: Edad Media*, ed. Alan Deyermond (Barcelona, 1980), 255–94; Ramón Menéndez Pidal, *Romancero hispánico (hispano-portugués, americano y sefardí)*, 2 vols (Madrid, 1953).

Finally on festivals, knights errant, and performative culture see the delightful book by Martín de Riquer, *Caballeros andantes españoles* (Madrid, 1967). Miguel Angel Ladero Quesada has published a survey of festive performances in late medieval Spain: M. A. Ladero Quesada et al., *Las fiestas medievales* (Canary Islands, 1994). See also my two articles on the subject, "Festivités, couleurs et symboles du pouvoir en Castille au XV siècle: Les Célébrations du mai 1428," *Annales ESC*, 3 (1991), 521–46, and "Elite and Popular Culture in Late Fifteenth-Century Castilian Festivals: The Case of Jaén," in *City and Spectacle in Medieval Europe*, ed. B. A. Hanawalt and K. L. Reyerson (Minneapolis, 1994), 296–318. In addition, there are two chapters (chs 5 and 6) on festivals in my *Spanish Society, 1400–1600* (London, 2001) that deal with this topic in general.

Index

administrative structures, 112–27
Afonso II of Portugal (1211–23), 17
agriculture
  before 1300, 23, 24, 26
  geography, 6, 7, 8, 9–13
  population, 29–31, 33–4, 46
al Andalus, *see* Andalusia
Albuquerque, Leonor de, 102
alcabala (sales tax), 36, 130
Alfonso, Infante of Castile (Alfonso XII), 96, 97, 98, 99
Alfonso III of Aragon (1285–91), 66
Alfonso IV of Aragon (1327–36), 61, 67–8, 133–4
Alfonso V of Aragon (1416–58; the Magnanimous), 88, 90, 91–2, 96, 102–7, 108, 113, 165, 189
Alfonso X of Castile (1252–84), 23, 25, 53, 142, 153, 166, 181
Alfonso XI of Castile (1312–50), 57–63, 78
  bureaucracies, 113–14
  coronation, 135
  legal reforms, 117
  plague, 45
  rebellions, 48
  representative assemblies, 123, 126
  royal officials, 121
  symbols of power, 135, 136
  tax base, 31, 36, 131
  violence, 39–40, 58, 60–1
  war, 44, 61–3

Alfonso XII of Castile (Infante of Castile), 96, 97, 98, 99
Andalusia
  anti-Jewish violence, 84
  before 1300, 16, 23, 24–5, 143
  geography, 11–12
  war, 44
Andorra, 8–9
Arabic literature, 166
Aragon, kingdom of
  before 1300, 3, 15, 26, 64, 65–6, 149
  geography, 8–10
  late Middle Ages: economic life, 37, 69–70, 129; political life, 68, 69, 75, 86, 101–2, 103; population, 30, 32–3, 37; representative assemblies, 122–4, 125; royal officials, 119–20; symbols of power, 133–4; taxation, 129; war, 44, 69, 74, 79–80
Aragon, Realms of, *see* Crown of Aragon
Aristotelian philosophy, 159–60
Arnau de Vilanova, Valencian, 182
Asturias, 3, 7, 8
Athens, Duchy of, 66, 69
Avila, the "farce" of, 98

Bailén, battle, 11
Balearic Islands
  before 1300, 4, 26, 64, 66
  late Middle Ages, 32–3, 68–9, 73, 74, 75

Barcelona
    before 1300, 17–18, 26, 27, 65, 149,
        151
    late Middle Ages: coinage, 37;
        culture, 170, 171, 192–3;
        famine, 43–4; plague, 47,
        69–70; political life, 68, 69, 76,
        106, 109; population, 33, 47;
        religious minorities, 156, 159;
        representative assemblies, 124,
        125, 127; royal entries, 192–3;
        violence, 39, 47, 75, 159; war,
        79–80
Basque country, 3, 7, 8, 119
Benedict XIII, 75–6, 84–5, 89, 102
Benjamin, Walter, 181
Bernáldez, Andrés, 155, 198
Bisson, Thomas, 32, 65, 66, 76–7, 104,
    108–9
Black Death (plague), 28, 42, 43,
    45–8, 69–70
Black Prince, 38, 44, 80–1
Blanca (wife of Henry IV), 95, 147, 190
Blanca (wife of John, Infante of
    Aragon), 95
Blanche of Bourbon (wife of Peter I),
    79, 80
Blanquerna, 183
Blumenthal, Debra, 160
Book of Good Love, 172–3
books, 171, 180
Boti, Bernart, 170
bourgeois culture, 19
Braudel, Fernand, 6, 9
bubonic plague, 28, 42, 43, 45–8, 69–70
Burckhardt, Jacob, 189
bureaucracies, 113–14

calendar dating methods, 2
Canary Islands, 84
cancioneros, 174–5
Cantabria, 7, 8
Cárcel de amor, 177
Castile, kingdom of
    before 1300, 3; economic life, 16,
        18–19, 23–5, 129; language, 7,
        21–2; Mediterranean possessions,

26–7; pilgrimage, 16, 18–19; the
    Reconquest, 14, 15, 23, 24–5;
    religious minorities, 146, 147,
    149, 151, 152, 153–4
    geography, 7, 8, 9–10, 12
    late Middle Ages, 29; bureaucracies,
        113–14; chronicles, 180–1;
        cities, 120, 121; conversos, 161;
        coronations, 135–6; culture,
        165–81, 183–7, 190–1; economic
        life, 34–6, 46, 87, 129, 131;
        education, 169, 170, 171; famine,
        43; language, 166, 174–5; law,
        117; plague, 45–6; poetry,
        172–9; political life, 52–63, 71,
        72, 77–85, 86–103, 108, 111–12,
        196–9; population, 30–1, 32,
        33–4, 46; rebellions, 48, 49;
        religious minorities, 141, 156,
        158, 162; religious writing,
        183–7; representative assemblies,
        122, 123, 124–6, 130–1; royal
        court, 114–15, 137; royal
        officials, 118–19, 120, 121;
        sumptuary laws, 136–8; symbols
        of power, 132–3, 135–6, 137–8;
        taxation, 128–31; violence, 38,
        39–42, 78–9, 84, 156, 162; war,
        44, 55–7, 72, 73–4, 79–84, 85
Catalina of Lancaster, 85, 87, 89
Catalonia
    before 1300, 3–4, 64, 65–6; land
        tenancy, 9, 21; language, 22–3;
        the Reconquest, 25–6
    geography, 7, 8–9
    late Middle Ages: agriculture, 30,
        34; chronicles, 181; culture,
        166–8, 170, 171, 179–80, 181,
        182–3; economic life, 37, 69–70,
        129; education, 170, 171; famine,
        43–4; law, 117; plague, 47,
        69–70; poetry, 179–80; political
        life, 68, 69, 75, 86, 101–2, 103–6,
        108–9; population, 30, 32, 33,
        34, 37, 47; rebellions, 49–50,
        106; religious minorities, 156;
        representative assemblies, 122–4,

Catalonia (*cont.*):
  126–7; royal officials, 118, 120; symbols of power, 133; taxation, 129; violence, 39, 42, 47; war, 44, 69, 79
Catholic Monarchs, *see* Ferdinand II of Aragon; Isabella of Castile
celebrations, *see* festivities
Cerda, Alfonso de la, 53, 55–6, 57, 61
ceremonials, 115, 116, 132–8
  religious minorities, 146–7
  see also festivities
charity, 19–20
Charles (Carlos) of Viana, 96, 107, 108–9
chivalry, 190, 193–5
Christian Spain
  before 1300; bourgeois values, 19–20; language–laicization relation, 22; pilgrimage, 16, 18–19; the Reconquest, 14–16, 23–7; religious minorities, 140, 144–5; repopulation, 16, 24, 26
  education, 168–9
  late Middle Ages; conversions/conversos, 149, 155, 156–8, 159–63; festivals, 188; papal schism, 76, 84–5, 102; plague, 47; rebellions, 49; religious writings, 182–7; role of ecclesiastics, 111, 134, 168, 169, 171; sumptuary laws, 136–7; symbols of power, 132–6; taxation, 128–30; violence, 38, 42, 47, 84; war, 44
  Muslim-Jew-Christian relations, 139–63, 168–9
chronicles, 180–2
cities, *see* urban communities
civil war, 38–9, 55–7, 69, 72
climate, 5–8, 9, 10, 12, 13
clothing, 136–8
Cluniac monasteries, 15, 16, 169
Compostela, 16, 18–19, 61, 193–4
Compromise of Caspe, 77
conversions/conversos, 149, 155, 156–8, 159–63

Coplas por la muerte de su padre, 177–9
Córdoba, 3
  the Reconquest, 14, 23, 24–5
  religious minorities, 143, 156, 160
coronations, 132–6
Corsica, 104
Cortes (Corts), 121–7, 128, 130–1, 150–1
Cortes of Valladolid (1295), 54
Costa Gomes, Rita, 114–15
court society, *see* royal courts
courtly romances, 193–5
crises, years of, 28–50, 199–201
Crown, authority of, *see* royal authority
Crown of Aragon
  before 1300, 3–4, 63–6; economic life, 26–7; language, 22–3; Mediterranean expansion, 4, 26–7, 64–5, 66; the Reconquest, 15, 23, 25–7; religious minorities, 148, 149, 151, 154–5; repopulation, 16, 26
  geography, 7, 8–10, 12–13
  late Middle Ages, 29; agriculture, 30, 33–4; bureaucracies, 113–14; chronicles, 180–2; conversos, 161; culture, 165, 166–8, 169, 170, 171, 174, 179–83, 190; economic life, 35, 36–7, 68, 69–70, 77, 91, 106, 129; education, 169, 170, 171; famine, 43–4; Mediterranean possessions, 67, 68–9, 72, 73, 74, 75, 102–6, 107, 108; plague, 47, 69–70; poetry, 174, 179–80; political life, 52, 63–70, 71, 72, 73–8, 86–92, 96, 100–9, 111–12, 196–9; population, 30, 32–4, 36–7, 47; rebellions, 48, 49–50, 69, 106; religious minorities, 156–8, 159; religious writing, 182–3; representative assemblies, 122–4, 125, 126–7, 130; royal court, 115; royal officials, 118–20; symbols of power, 132, 133–4; taxation, 128, 129, 130; violence, 39, 42,

47, 75, 159; war, 44, 55, 56, 69,
    70, 72, 73–4, 79–81, 109
crusade, *see* Reconquest
Cuéllar, Pedro de, 185–7
Cueva, Beltrán de la, 96, 97, 98
cultural production, 164–5
    Catholic Monarchs, 200
    chronicles, 180–2
    courtly romances, 193–5
    education, 168–72
    festivities, 188–93, 195
    language, 22–3, 166–8, 174–5, 179,
        182
    performative, 187–93
    poetry, 166, 172–80, 201
    religious minorities, 153
    symbols of power, 132, 192–3
    see also literature

dating methods, 2
death, representations, 48, 177–9, 180,
    201
demographics, 16, 29–34, 36–7, 46–7
Díaz de Games, Gutierre, 184, 194
Diputatió del General, 124
documentos rodados, 59
dressing, 136–8
Du Guesclin, Bertram, 38, 44, 80, 81

ecclesiastical income, 128–9
ecclesiastics
    education, 168, 169, 171
    guide for, 185–7
    role of, 15, 16, 111, 134
economic life
    before 1300, 17–20; after the
        conquests, 23–7; geography, 6, 7,
        8, 9–13; Granada, 5; pilgrimage,
        16, 18–19; religious minorities,
        141–2, 144, 145, 146, 148, 150–1;
        repopulation, 16, 24, 26; taxation,
        129
    late Middle Ages, 30–2, 33–7, 46;
        political life and, 68, 69–70, 77,
        87, 91, 106; religious minorities,
        160; taxation, 30–1, 33, 36, 122,
        127–31

education, 168–72
Edward, Prince of Wales, 38, 44, 80–1
Elliott, John H., 6
England
    Hundred Years War, 7, 38, 42, 44,
        80–1
    Trastámara Spain and, 82, 83

famine, 42, 43–4
Ferdinand of Antequera, *see*
    Ferdinand I of Aragon
Ferdinand I of Aragon (1412–16;
    Ferdinand of Antequera), 77–8,
    85, 86, 87, 88, 101–2
Ferdinand II of Aragon (the Catholic),
    50, 52, 86, 100–1, 106, 109,
    196–200
Ferdinand III of Castile (1217–52), 17,
    23, 25, 59
Ferdinand IV of Castile (1295–1312),
    1, 31, 40, 43–4, 52–7, 130–1
Ferrán (son of James II), 67, 69
Ferrández de Bezla, John, 40
Ferrante (son of Alfonso V), 105, 107
Ferrer, Vincent, 157–8
festivities, 187, 188–93, 195, 200
    coronations, 134
    royal courts, 115, 116, 137
    sumptuary laws, 136–8
fiscal matters, *see* taxation
food, 136, 137, 191–2
Fourth Lateran Council (1215), 140,
    141–2, 149–50
Fradrique of Benavente, 78, 79, 84
France
    before 1300, 4, 63–4, 65, 70
    Hundred Years War, 38, 42, 44,
        80–1
    Trastámara Spain and, 82, 83, 84,
        107–8
Frederick (viceroy of Sicily), 66, 101
Frederick II (German emperor), 64,
    65
Freedman, Paul, 21, 42, 49–50

Galicia, 3, 7, 166, 169
García de Cortázar, J. A., 32

García de Valdeavellano, Luis, 113
Generalitat, 124
Genoa, 69, 73, 79, 104
geography, 5–13
Gibraltar, siege of, 63
González, Julio, 17
González Mínguez, C., 53
governmental lieutenancy, 118
Granada, kingdom of, 5, 15, 26, 70
  geography, 12
  late Middle Ages, 29, 44, 70–1;
    Castilian politics, 55, 57, 60,
    61–2, 79, 85, 95, 96; literature,
    166; taxation, 129
Great Papal Schism, 76, 84–5, 102
Greece, the Duchy of Athens, 66
Guzmán, Dominic de, 169
Guzmán, Leonor de, 62, 63, 78

ha-Levi, Selomah, 159
Halorqui, Yoshua, 159, 160
head taxes, 129–30
Hebrew, 166
Henry, Infante of Aragon, 88, 89–90,
  91, 92, 93, 103
Henry, Infante of Castile (13th cent.),
  54, 57
Henry, Infante of Castile (15th cent.),
  see Henry IV of Castile
Henry II of Castile (1369–79; Henry
  of Trastámara), 44, 78, 79–80,
  81–3, 114
Henry III of Castile (1390–1406),
  84–5, 126
Henry IV of Castile (1454–74), 93,
  94–101, 108, 137–8, 191, 196,
  198
Henry IV of France, 4
Henry of Trastámara, see Henry II of
  Castile
Hermandiños, rebellion of, 7, 41
Hernández, Francisco, 117
Holy Week ceremonies, 146–7
Huizinga, Johannes, 29, 37–8
Hundred Years War, 38, 42, 44,
  80–1
hunger (famine), 42, 43–4

Imperial, Francisco, 174–5
inflation, 23, 34–5, 37
Isabella of Castile, 52, 86, 96, 97,
  98–100, 196–200
Italy, 4, 66, 67, 68, 88, 102–6, 107,
  108, 165

James I of Aragon (1213–76), 17, 26,
  64, 154, 181
James II of Aragon (1291–1327), 55,
  56, 66–7, 68
Jaume d'Urgell, 77, 101
Jewish population, 139–63
  culture, 166, 168–9, 171
  Golden Age, 143
  sumptuary laws, 136–7
  taxation, 129–30, 144, 150–1
  violence, 47, 48, 49, 75, 83, 84,
    139–42, 147–8, 152, 155–63
Joanna (daughter of Henry IV), 196,
  197
João I of Portugal, 83
John, Infante of Aragon (John II of
  Aragon; 1458–79), 88, 89–91, 92,
  93, 95, 96, 102, 105–6, 107–9,
  196, 197
John, Infante of Castile (Don Juan;
  died 1319), 54, 55, 58, 59, 60
John, Infante of Castile (son of Don
  Juan), 60–1
John of Gaunt, 82, 83
John I of Aragon (1387–96), 74–6
John I of Castile (1379–90), 83–4
John II of Aragon, see John, Infante of
  Aragon
John II of Castile (1406–54), 85, 86,
  87–94, 190, 191
John of Navarre, see John, Infante of
  Aragon
Juan Carlos, 4
Juan Manuel, Don (1282–1348), 42,
  59, 61, 62, 184
Juana, Infanta of Castile, 97, 98,
  99–100
Juana Enríquez (wife of John II of
  Aragon), 109
Juana of Portugal, 95, 97, 99, 100

king's men, *see* royal officials
knight-errantry, 187, 190, 193–5

Laberinto de fortuna, 175
Lalaigny, Jacques de, 194
land tenure, 7, 8, 9, 20–1, 24, 30–1,
    33–4
language(s), 7, 21–3, 125–6, 166–8,
    174–5, 179, 182
Lara family, 54
Las Navas de Tolosa (1212), battle, 11,
    15, 25, 70
Latin, use of, 21–2, 125, 126, 167, 182,
    185
legal code (*Siete partidas*), 20, 117,
    142, 153–4
legal measures, religious minorities,
    152–5
legal system, 21–2, 116–17
León, 3, 7, 9, 18, 122
Leonor of Castile, 67, 68
letrados, 170
libraries, 171
Libro becerro de las behetrías, 119
Libro de buen amor, 172–3
lieutenancy, governmental, 118
Linage Conde, Antonio, 185
Linehan, Peter, 53, 129, 135, 186
literature, 41, 42, 48, 164, 165, 166–8,
    171–2
    chronicles, 180–2
    festivals and, 190–1, 195
    philosophical writing, 182–3
    poetry, 41, 48, 166, 172–80, 201
    religious minorities, 140, 152, 154,
        155
    religious writing, 182–7
    romances, 187
Llull, Ramón, 157, 179, 182–3
local administration, 116–25
Lodi, treaty of, 107
López de Ayala, Pero, 173–4
Louis of Anjou, 77
Louis XI of France, 108
Luna, Alvaro de, 87, 89–94, 95, 96
Luna, María de, 76
Luna, Pedro de, *see* Benedict XIII

Machado, Antonio, 9
Majorca
    before 1300, 4, 64, 66
    late Middle Ages, 32–3, 68–9, 73,
        74, 75
Málaga, 12
Manrique, Jorge, 172, 175, 177–9
Manrique, Juana, 93
Manuel, Don Juan, *see* Juan Manuel,
    Don
March, Ausiàs, 179–80
Maria of Castile (wife of Alfonso V),
    103, 105–6, 113, 118
María of Portugal, 61, 63, 78
Martín, José Luis, 185
Martin I of Aragon (1396–1410; the
    Humane), 74, 76–7, 101
Martínez, Ferrán, 158–9
Martorell, Johanot, 195
Mediterranean expansion, 4, 26–7,
    64–5, 66
Mediterranean possessions, 67, 68–9,
    72, 73, 74, 75, 102–6, 107, 108
Mena, Juan de, 175
Mendoza, Iñigo López de, 41, 171,
    175–6
merindades (territorial units), 118–19
merinos (royal agents), 118–19
Metge, Bernat, 179
Meyerson, Mark, 49, 140, 161
migration, 16, 24, 26, 30, 31, 33
Milton, Gregory, 142, 170
Molina, 3
Molina, María de, 53–7, 58, 60, 63, 130
monarchical authority, *see* royal
    authority
monasteries, 15, 16, 30–1, 168, 169
Moreta Velayos, Salustiano, 41
Morocco, *see* North Africa
Mudejars, *see* Muslim population
Muhammad III (1302–9), 57
Muntaner, Ramón, 66, 133–4, 181–2
Murcia, 3, 12, 26, 57, 74
Muslim population, 139–63
    Alfonso XI's reign, 62
    before 1300, 5, 12–13, 14–16, 18,
        23–7, 49, 64, 70, 143–4

Muslim population (*cont.*):
  culture, 166, 168–9
  education, 168–9
  Henry IV's reign, 96
  plague, 47
  symbols of power, 136
  taxation, 129, 144
  violence, 38, 42, 47, 49, 139–42,
    147–8, 152, 155
  war, 44

Naples, 4, 88, 103, 104–6, 107, 108,
    165, 174–5, 189
Navarre, kingdom of, 4, 29, 70
  political life, 70, 82, 83, 92, 102,
    107–8
  population, 32
  religious minorities, 156
Nebrija, Antonio de, 167
Netanyahu, B., 160–1
Nieto Soria, J. M., 135
Nirenberg, David, 141, 145, 146–7
nobles
  culture, 171–2, 174, 175, 193–5
  royal authority and, 25, 110, 112;
    1300–50: 54–7, 58, 59–61, 62,
    65–7; 1350–1412: 74, 76–7, 78,
    81–2, 83, 84; 1412–69: 86–7,
    89–90, 91, 92–4, 95, 96–101,
    103–4, 106; ecclesiastics, 111;
    representative assemblies, 124–7;
    royal courts, 115–16; sumptuary
    laws, 137; symbols of power, 133;
    taxation, 128, 130
  violence, 39–42, 48
North Africa, 5, 15, 57, 61–3
novelty, taste for, 17

Ode on the Death of his Father, 177–9
Olmedo, battle, 93–4, 108

Pacheco, Juan (marquis of Villena),
    93, 94, 95, 96–8
Pact of the Toros of Guisando,
    99–100, 197
Padilla, María de, 78, 79, 80
Páez de Ribera, Ruy, 41

Palace Rhymes, 173
Palencia, Alfonso de, 168
papal schism, 76, 84–5, 102
Paul of Burgos, 159
peasant life
  before 1300, 7, 9, 21
  late Middle Ages, 30–1, 33–4,
    39–42, 46; the monarchy, 97–8;
    rebellions, 7, 41, 43, 49–50, 106
Pérez de Guzmán, Fernán, 184
performative culture, 187–93
Peter, Infante of Castile (Don Pedro),
    58, 59, 60
Peter I of Castile (1350–69; the
    Cruel), 44, 45, 63, 73, 78–81, 82,
    83, 119, 173
Peter II of Aragon (1196–1213), 25, 63
Peter III of Aragon (1276–85), 64–6,
    133
Peter IV of Aragon (1336–87; the
    Ceremonious), 33, 37, 52, 68–70,
    73–4, 82, 127, 182
Philip, Infante of Castile (Don Felipe),
    59, 60
Philip IV of France (1285–1314), 35
philosophical works, 182–3
pilgrimage, 16, 18–19, 193–4
plague, 28, 42, 43, 45–8, 69–70
Poema de Fernán González, 8, 154
poetry, 41, 48, 166, 172–80, 201
political life, 3–5, 25–7
  geographical factors, 6, 7, 13
  late Middle Ages, 110–12; 1300–50:
    51–71; 1350–1412: 72–85;
    1412–69: 86–109; 1469–74:
    196–200; administrative structures,
    112–27; culture, 166–7, 192–3;
    economic life, 36; language of
    power, 125–6; rebellions, 49–50,
    106; violence, 38–41
population, 16, 24, 26, 29–34, 36–7, 46
Portugal, 5, 44
  Castilian politics and: Alfonso XI,
    61–2; Ferdinand IV, 55, 57;
    Infantes of Aragon, 92; Peter I,
    79; Trastámaras, 82, 83, 196
poverty, 19–20

power
  administrative structures, 112–27
  cultural production and, 132, 164,
    192–3
  language of, 125–6
  symbols of, 131–8, 192–3
Primera crónica general, 8, 154, 181
Prison of Love, 177
property, bourgeois values, 19
Pulgar, Hernando del, 198
Purgatory, 19–20
Pyrenees, 7, 8

Quiñones, Suero de, 193–4, 195

Ray, Jonathan, 140, 145–6
rebellions, 7, 41, 42–3, 48–50, 69
Reconquest, the, 14–16, 23–7
religion
  bourgeois values, 19–20
  Muslim–Jew–Christian relations,
    75, 129–30, 139–63
  papal schism, 76, 84–5, 102
  the Reconquest, 14–16
  restrictions in 1200s, 17
  writings, 180, 182–7
  see also Christian Spain; Muslim
    population
remenças uprising, 49–50, 106
Renaissance culture, 165, 188
repopulation, 16, 24, 26
representative assemblies, 121–7, 128,
  130–1, 150–1
revolutions, *see* rebellions
Rimado de palacio, 173
Rioja, the, 10, 13
Riquer, Martín de, 182, 194
rituals
  of power, 132–8
  religious minorities, 146–7
roads, 7, 8–9, 11
romanceros, 175, 177
romances, 187, 193–5
Round, Nicholas, 89
royal authority, 25, 110–12
  1300–50: 54–7, 58, 59–61, 62, 65–7
  1350–1412: 74, 76–7, 78, 81–2, 83, 84

1412–69: 86–7, 89–90, 91, 92–4,
    95, 96–101, 103–4, 106
administrative structures, 112–27
Catholic Monarchs, 197–200
religious minorities, 144–5, 148,
    151–2
sumptuary laws, 136–8
symbols of power, 131–8, 192–3
taxation, 127–31
royal courts, 114–16, 137
  culture, 174–5, 180, 190–1, 193–5
  romances, 190, 193–5
royal entries, 137–8, 147, 189–90,
    191, 192–3
royal officials, 117–20, 121, 144–5,
    170
royal visits, 115–16
  see also royal entries
Rucquoi, Adeline, 168
Ruiz, Juan, 172–3
Russell, Peter, 171–2

sacred monarchies, 132–6
Salado, battle, 62
sales tax (*alcabala*), 36, 130
San Pedro, Diego de, 177
Sancho the Great (1000–35), 4
Sancho IV, 53, 56, 121, 155
Santa Fe, Jerónimo de, 159, 160
Santa María, Pablo de, 159
Sardinia, 4, 66, 67, 68, 69, 73, 75,
    104–5, 108
Sentob de Carrión, 173
serfdom
  before 1300, 9, 21
  late Middle Ages, 30, 33–4, 42,
    49–50, 106
serranillas, 175–7
Seville, 3
  before 1300, 18, 23, 24–5
  population, 33
  religious minorities, 156, 158, 160
Sicily
  before 1300, 4, 26, 64–5, 66
  late Middle Ages, 68, 69, 75, 76,
    102, 104–5, 108
Siete partidas, 20, 117, 142, 153–4

social structures
  before 1300, 16, 18–20, 24, 25, 26
  geography, 6, 7, 8, 9, 10
  late Middle Ages, 42
  see also rebellions
spaces, 192
Starr-LeBeau, Gretchen, 161
Strayer, Joseph R., 50
Strong, Sir Roy, 188
Suárez Fernández, Luis, 88, 90, 91, 99
sumptuary laws, 136–8
symbols of power, 131–8, 192–3

taxation, 25, 36, 127–31
  population, 30–1, 33
  religious minorities, 129–30, 144,
    150–1
  representative assemblies, 122
Tetzel, 8
Tirant lo Blanch, 194–5
Toledo, 3, 33, 156, 157
topography, 6–13
Toros of Guisando Pact, 99–100, 197
trade, 17–20, 23–4, 87, 129
Trastámaras, 44, 52, 63, 77–8, 81–5,
    86, 101–6
tribute money, 24–5
  see also taxation

Ubieto Arteta, A., 141
universities, 169, 170
urban communities, 36, 37, 39, 40
  administration, 120–1, 122, 124–7
  before 1300, 19–20, 25
  Isabella of Castile, 197–8
  religious minorities, 140, 144–5,
    146, 147, 149–52, 156, 160
  royal authority, 54–61, 63, 77, 92,
    106, 110, 112, 130–1
  royal entries, 137–8, 189–90, 191,
    192–3
  royal visits, 115–16
  taxation, 128, 130–1
urban spaces, 192

Valencia, kingdom of, 4, 16, 26–7, 64,
    65–6
  economic life, 37, 69–70
  education, 170
  geography, 12–13
  political life, 67, 68, 69, 75, 76, 86,
    101–2, 103
  population, 30, 32–3, 34, 36, 37
  rebellions, 48, 69
  religious minorities, 149, 151,
    156–7, 159, 160
  representative assemblies, 125
  royal officials, 120
  taxation, 129
  violence, 75, 159
  war, 44, 69, 74, 79–80
Villasandino, 174
Villena, marquis of (Juan Pacheco),
    93, 94, 95, 96–8
Villena family, 196, 197
violence, 35, 37–42, 47, 48–9
  Alfonso XI, 39–40, 58, 60–1
  John I, 75
  Peter I (the Cruel), 78–80
  religious minorities, 47, 48, 49, 75,
    83, 84, 139–42, 147–8, 151–2,
    155–63
  Trastámara Spain, 84
  see also war
Visigothic Spain, 14, 143, 154, 169

war, 38–9, 42, 44, 72
  Alfonso XI, 44, 61–3
  Ferdinand IV, 55–7
  fictitious, 190
  Peter I, 79–81
  Peter IV, 69, 70, 73–4
  Trastámara Spain, 82–4, 85,
    109
wealth, 19, 25
  sumptuary laws, 136–8
Winer, Rebecca, 168
Wolff, Philippe, 75
wool trade, 87